Lecture Notes in Artificial Intelligence 5214

Edited by R. Goebel, J. Siekma

Subseries of Lecture Notes

Jürgen Dix   Michael Fisher
Peter Novák (Eds.)

Computational Logic in Multi-Agent Systems

10th International Workshop, CLIMA X
Hamburg, Germany, September 9-10, 2009
Revised Selected and Invited Papers

 Springer

Volume Editors

Jürgen Dix
Technische Universität Clausthal, Institut für Informatik
Julius-Albert-Straße 4, 38678 Clausthal-Zellerfeld, Germany
E-mail: dix@tu-clausthal.de

Michael Fisher
University of Liverpool, Department of Computer Science
Ashton Street, Liverpool, L69 3BX, UK
E-mail: MFisher@liverpool.ac.uk

Peter Novák
Technische Universität Clausthal, Institut für Informatik
Julius-Albert-Straße 4, 38678 Clausthal-Zellerfeld, Germany
E-mail: peter.novak@tu-clausthal.de

Library of Congress Control Number: 2010938000

CR Subject Classification (1998): I.2.11, I.2, F.4.1, C.2.4, H.3, H.4

LNCS Sublibrary: SL 7 – Artificial Intelligence

ISSN   0302-9743
ISBN-10   3-642-16866-3 Springer Berlin Heidelberg New York
ISBN-13   978-3-642-16866-6 Springer Berlin Heidelberg New York

Preface

These are the proceedings of the 10th International Workshop on Computational Logic in Multi-Agent Systems (CLIMA-X), held September 9–10, 2009 in Hamburg, co-located with MATES.

The purpose of the CLIMA workshops is to provide a forum for discussing techniques, based on computational logic, for representing, in a formal way, programming and reasoning about agents and multi-agent systems.

Multi-agent systems are communities of problem-solving entities that can perceive and act upon their environment in order to achieve both their individual goals and their joint goals. The work on such systems integrates many technologies and concepts from artificial intelligence and other areas of computing as well as other disciplines. Over recent years, the agent paradigm gained popularity, due to its applicability to a full spectrum of domains, such as search engines, recommendation systems, educational support, e-procurement, simulation and routing, electronic commerce and trade, etc. Computational logic provides a well-defined, general, and rigorous framework for studying the syntax, semantics and procedures for the various tasks in individual agents, as well as the interaction between, and integration among, agents in multi-agent systems. It also provides tools, techniques and standards for implementations and environments, for linking specifications to implementations, and for the verification of properties of individual agents, multi-agent systems and their implementations.

These proceedings feature nine regular papers (from a total of 18 papers submitted), as well as one paper based on the invited talk given by Tran Cao Son.

In the invited paper by Tran Cao Son, Enrico Pontelli, and Ngoc-Hieu Nguyen, "Planning for Multi-Agents Using ASP-Prolog," the action language $\mathcal{B}$ is extended to the multi-agent case. The used technology is based on answer set programming.

The contribution by Nils Bulling and Berndt Farwer on "Expressing Properties of Resource-Bounded Systems: The Logics **RTL*** and **RTL**" investigates the problem of introducing resources to CTL-like logics. They determine the boundary between decidable and undecidable fragments.

The paper "Reasoning About Multi-Agent Domains Using Action Language $\mathcal{C}$: A Preliminary Study" by Chitta Baral, Tran Cao Son, and Enrico Pontelli extends the action language $\mathcal{C}$, originally developed for single-agent domains, to the multi-agent case. Limitations of the approach are also discussed.

In "Model Checking Normative Agent Organizations," Louise Dennis, Nick Tinnemeier, and John-Jules Meyer introduce the concept of an organization programmed in a certain language, OOPL, while the agents are implemented in different BDI languages. The authors also introduce model checking techniques based on LTL.

The paper "Operational Semantics for BDI Modules in Multi-Agent Programming," by Mehdi Dastani and Bas R. Steunebrink, presents an operational semantics for BDI modules in arbitrary multi-agent programming languages. Emphasis is put on allowing software engineering techniques like encapsulation and information hiding.

"InstQL: A Query Language for Virtual Institutions Using Answer Set Programming," by Luke Hopton, Owen Cliffe, Marina De Vos, and Julian Padget, introduces a high-level query and constraint language to formalize and describe institutions. This language is an extension of a domain-specific action language for normative frameworks. It is implemented using answer set technology from logic programming.

In "Interacting Answer Sets," Chiaki Sakama and Tran Cao Son deal with the problem of modeling agent societies. They approach this problem by using logic programs under the answer set semantics.

Wietske Visser, Koen V. Hindriks, and Catholijn M. Jonker deal with intelligent decision support systems: "Argumentation-Based Preference Modeling with Incomplete Information." Such systems need information about the preferences of the users, which is difficult to model. The paper proposes an argumentation framework, which is well-suited to deal with incomplete information.

The paper "A Characterization of Mixed-Strategy Nash Equilibria in PCTL Augmented with a Cost Quantifier," by Pedro Arturo Góngora and David A. Rosenblueth, considers the problem of characterizing Nash equilibria in suitable logics. The authors develop an extension of probabilistic CTL to achieve this.

Finally, in "On the Implementation of Speculative Constraint Processing," Jiefei Ma, Alessandra Russo, Krysia Broda, Hiroshi Hosobe, and Ken Satoh extend their approach of speculative computation by introducing a practical multi-threaded implementation.

We thank all the authors of submissions for CLIMA-X for submitting papers and for revising their contributions to be included in these proceedings. We are very grateful to the members of the CLIMA-X Program Committee and the additional reviewers. Their service ensured the high quality of the accepted papers. A special thank you goes to the local organizers in Hamburg for their help and support. We are very grateful to them for handling the registration and a very enjoyable social program.

July 2010

Jürgen Dix
Michael Fisher
Peter Novák

Conference Organization

Program Chairs

Jürgen Dix   Clausthal University of Technology, Germany
Michael Fisher   University of Liverpool, UK
Peter Novák   Czech Technical University, Czech Republic

Program Committee

Thomas Ågotnes   Bergen, Norway
Natasha Alechina   Nottingham, UK
Jose Julio Alferes   Lisbon, Portugal
Rafael Bordini   Durham, UK
Gerhard Brewka   Leipzig, Germany
Keith Clark   Imperial, UK
Stefania Costantini   L'Aquila, Italy
Mehdi Dastani   Utrecht, The Netherlands
Louise Dennis   Liverpool, UK
Chiara Ghidini   Trento, Italy
James Harland   RMIT, Australia
Hisashi Hayashi   Toshiba, Japan
Koen Hindriks   Delft, The Netherlands
Wiebe van der Hoek   Liverpool, UK
Katsumi Inoue   NII, Japan
Wojtek Jamroga   Clausthal, Germany
Viviana Mascardi   Genoa, Italy
Paola Mello   Bologna, Italy
John-Jules Meyer   Utrecht, The Netherlands
Leora Morgenstern   Stanford, USA
Naoyuki Nide   Nara, Japan
Mehmet Orgun   Macquarie, Australia
Maurice Pagnucco   NSW, Australia
Jeremy Pitt   Imperial, UK
Enrico Pontelli   New Mexico, USA
Chiaki Sakama   Wakayama, Japan
Renate Schmidt   Manchester, UK
Tran Cao Son   New Mexico, USA

Kostas Stathis   RHUL, UK
Michael Thielscher   Dresden, Germany
Marina de Vos   Bath, UK
Cees Witteveen   Delft, The Netherlands

External Reviewers

Gauvain Bourgne   Wojciech Jamroga
Carlos Iván Chesñevar   Mehrnoosh Sadrzadeh
Agostino Dovier   Christoph Sprenger
Rubén Fuentes-Fernández   Yingqian Zhang
Ullrich Hustadt

Steering Committee

Jürgen Dix   Clausthal University of Technology, Germany
Michael Fisher   University of Liverpool, UK
João Leite   New University of Lisbon, Portugal
Fariba Sadri   Imperial College London, UK
Ken Satoh   National Institute of Informatics, Japan
Francesca Toni   Imperial College London, UK
Paolo Torroni   University of Bologna, Italy

Table of Contents

Planning for Multiagent Using ASP-Prolog 1
    Tran Cao Son, Enrico Pontelli, and Ngoc-Hieu Nguyen

Expressing Properties of Resource-Bounded Systems: The Logics
RTL*and **RTL** 22
    Nils Bulling and Berndt Farwer

Reasoning about Multi-agent Domains Using Action Language $\mathcal{C}$:
A Preliminary Study 46
    Chitta Baral, Tran Cao Son, and Enrico Pontelli

Model Checking Normative Agent Organisations 64
    Louise Dennis, Nick Tinnemeier, and John-Jules Meyer

Operational Semantics for BDI Modules in Multi-agent
Programming... 83
    Mehdi Dastani and Bas R. Steunebrink

Inst*QL*: A Query Language for Virtual Institutions Using Answer Set
Programming... 102
    Luke Hopton, Owen Cliffe, Marina De Vos, and Julian Padget

Interacting Answer Sets... 122
    Chiaki Sakama and Tran Cao Son

Argumentation-Based Preference Modelling with Incomplete
Information 141
    Wietske Visser, Koen V. Hindriks, and Catholijn M. Jonker

A Characterization of Mixed-Strategy Nash Equilibria in PCTL
Augmented with a Cost Quantifier 158
    Pedro Arturo Góngora and David A. Rosenblueth

On the Implementation of Speculative Constraint Processing 178
    *Jiefei Ma, Alessandra Russo, Krysia Broda, Hiroshi Hosobe, and
    Ken Satoh*

Author Index 197

Planning for Multiagent Using ASP-Prolog

Tran Cao Son, Enrico Pontelli, and Ngoc-Hieu Nguyen

Department of Computer Science
New Mexico State University
Las Cruces, NM 88003, USA
{tson,epontell,nhieu}@cs.nmsu.edu

Abstract. This paper presents an Answer Set Programming based approach to multiagent planning. The proposed methodology extends the action language $\mathcal{B}$ in [12] to represent and reason about plans with cooperative actions of an individual agent operating in a multiagent environment. This language is used to formalize multiagent planning problems and the notion of a joint plan for multiagent in the presence of cooperative actions. Finally, the paper presents a system for computing joint plans based on the ASP-Prolog system.

1   Introduction

Cooperative actions are important for agents operating in a multiagent environment. Cooperative actions differ from individual actions in that they might affect other agents or require other agents. Cooperative actions are important not only in situations where multiple agents have to work together to accomplish a common goal, but also in situations where each agent has its own goals. The following story,[1] taken from [26], illustrates this point.

Example 1. Three individuals A, B, and C plan to decorate their rooms. Each would like to hang one of their objects on the wall: A would like to hang a mirror, B a diploma, and C a painting. A and B can use either a nail or a screw to complete their jobs, while C can only use a screw. A has neither a nail or a screw; B has both; C has only a nail. To use a nail, one needs a hammer. Among the three agents, only B has a hammer.

Can all the agents achieve their goals? In other words, do the agents have a joint-plan that allows each of them to achieve his/her own goal?

Intuitively, we can see that only B can accomplish her job independently from A and C. The three can achieve their goals if B uses the hammer and the nail to hang her diploma and then gives A the hammer and C the screw, respectively. C, on the other hand, should give A the nail and use the screw to hang her painting. A uses the nail (from C) and the hammer (from B) to hang her mirror. Of course, to avoid unpleasant moments, A should ask for the nail (from C) and the hammer (from B) and C should ask for the screw (from B).

It is also easy to see that if neither B nor C want to give out anything, then only B can achieve her goal. Furthermore, if B decides to use the screw instead of using the nail in hanging her diploma, then C will have no way of achieving her goal. ◇

---

[1] This is a modified version of the story in [21].

J. Dix, M. Fisher, and P. Novák (Eds.): CLIMA X, LNAI 6214, pp. 1–21, 2010.

In the above example, the action of giving a nail, a hammer, or a screw between the individuals can be considered as *cooperative actions*. The action of requesting something from others can also be considered as a cooperative action. It is obvious that without some cooperative actions, not all agents can achieve their own goals. Even with the cooperative actions at their disposal, the individuals might still need to coordinate in creating their corresponding plans. In the rest of this paper, we will often refer to a cooperative actions as *exchange actions* and use the two terms interchangeably.

In Example 1, agents (the individuals) maintain their own local worlds and their actions generally do not affect the world view of other agents. Observe that there are situations in which an action of an agent might affect the world of another agent. This can be seen in the following example.

Example 2. Two agents A and B enter a building through different entrances. Near each entrance there is a light switch that, when flipped, will turn on or off the light of the building, depending on the status of the light. Let us assume that A and B maintain their world representation separately. Obviously, if A flips the switch next to the entrance that she is using, then also the world of B will need to change.   ◇

In this paper, we will study multiagent planning problems in which each agent maintains its own representation about the world and its capabilities—which include individual actions and cooperative actions—and has its own goal. We will be mainly interested in the process of creating a joint plan prior to its execution. We will begin by extending the language B in [12] to allow cooperative actions for a single agent. The semantics of the new language is defined by a transition function which maps pairs of actions and states to states. We then define the multiagent planning problems and the notion of a joint plan for multiagent in presence of cooperative actions. Finally, we present an implementation for computing joint plans using the ASP-Prolog system [10].

2 An Action Language with Cooperative Actions

In this section, we present a language for representing and reasoning about plans for an agent in the multiagent environment with cooperative actions. To this end, we extend the language B in [12] to allow cooperative actions[2]. We will call the new language B^C.

In this paper, we consider two types of cooperative actions, one that requests the establishment of a condition in the world of the agent requesting the action execution, and another establishes some conditions in the world of another agent.

We will assume an arbitrary but fixed set of agent identifiers $\mathcal{AG}$. A planning problem of an agent in $\mathcal{AG}$ is defined over a set of fluents (or state variables) F, a set of *individual actions* A, and a set of *cooperative actions* C. We will assume that A always contains a special action wait which does not have any effect on the agent's world.[3] Furthermore,

---

[2] Observe that the formalization of cooperative actions can be adapted for any action languages. For example, using the action language B with concurrent actions [28] will allow us to consider other types of actions involving multiple agents such as joint actions, coordinated actions, etc.

[3] We envision a multiagent environment where agents may have to wait for other agents to finish some actions before they can go on with their course of actions.

we will require that actions in C do not appear in A. This highlights the fact that the co-operative actions are introduced specifically to address the issues of interaction among different agents.

A *fluent literal* (or *literal*) is either a fluent or its negation. Fluent formulae are propositional formulae constructed from literals and the traditional propositional connectives.

2.1 Specifying Individual Actions

A *domain specification DI* over F and A describes the individual actions of an agent and consists of laws of the following forms:

$$a \textbf{ causes } l \textbf{ if } \varphi \tag{1}$$

$$a \textbf{ executable } \varphi \tag{2}$$

$$l \textbf{ if } \varphi \tag{3}$$

where a is an individual action (from A), l is a fluent literal and φ is a set of fluent literals (viewed as a conjunction of literals). A law of the form (1), called a *dynamic law*, states that if a is executed when φ is true then l becomes true. (2) is an *executability condition* and says that a can be executed only if φ is true. (3) is a *static law* and states that l is true whenever φ is true. The semantics of a domain specification is defined by the notion of *state* and by a *transition function* Φ, that specifies the result of the execution of an action a in a state s.

A set of literals S satisfies a literal l (l holds in S), denoted by $S \models l$, if $l \in S$. For a set of literals φ, $S \models \varphi$ if $S \models l$ for every $l \in \varphi$. A set of fluent literals S satisfies a static law (l **if** φ) if $S \models \varphi$ implies $S \models l$; S satisfies set of static laws C if it satisfies every law in C. A set of fluent literals S is closed under a set of static laws C if S satisfies C. Given a set of fluent literals S, $Cn_C(S)$ denotes the minimal set of fluent literals which is closed under C and contains S.

A *state* s is a set of fluent literals that is *closed* under all static laws, *consistent*, and *complete*, i.e., for every $f \in$ F, either $f \in s$ or $\neg f \in s$ but $\{f, \neg f\} \not\subseteq s$. In the following, $\bar{l}$ denotes the negation of l, i.e., if $l = f$ and $f \in$ F, then $\bar{l} = \neg f$; if $l = \neg f$ for some $f \in$ F, then $\bar{l} = f$. For a set of literals S, $\bar{S} = \{\bar{l} \mid l \in S\}$.

An action a is *executable* in a state s if there exists an executability condition (a **executable** φ) in DI such that $s \models \varphi$.

Let $e_a(s) = \{l \mid \exists (a \textbf{ causes } l \textbf{ if } \varphi) \in DI \text{ s.t. } s \models \varphi\}$. The result of the execution of a in s is defined next.

Definition 1 (Transition function). *Let DI be a domain specification. The transition function Φ of DI, denoted by Φ_{DI}, is a mapping of pairs of actions and states to sets of states and is defined as follows. For any pair of a state s and an action a,*

- $\Phi_{DI}(a, s) = \emptyset$ *if a is not executable in s; and*
- $\Phi_{DI}(a, s) = \{s' \mid s' \text{ is a state and } s' = Cn_{C_{DI}}((s \cap s') \cup e_a(s))\}$ *if a is executable in s and C_{DI} denotes the set of all static laws in DI.*

A domain specification DI is *consistent* if $\Phi_{DI}(a, s) \neq \emptyset$ holds for every pair of action a and state s such that a is executable in s. DI is *deterministic* if $|\Phi_{DI}(a, s)| \leq 1$ for every pair of state s and action a. Φ_{DI} can be extended to reason about the effects of a sequence of actions as follows.

Definition 2 (Transition function). *Let DI be a domain specification, s be a state, and $\alpha = [a_1; \ldots ; a_n]$ be a sequence of actions.*
- $\hat{\Phi}_{DI}(\alpha, s) = \{s\}$ *if $n = 0$;*
- $\hat{\Phi}_{DI}(\alpha, s) = \bigcup_{s' \in \hat{\Phi}_{DI}([a_1; \ldots ; a_{n-1}], s)} \Phi_{DI}(a_n, s')$, *otherwise.*

An agent can use the transition function to reason about the effects of its actions and to perform planning. An action sequence α is a *plan* achieving a set of literals O from a state I iff O is true in $\hat{\Phi}_{DI}(\alpha, I)$.

Example 3. The domain specification DI_A for A in Example 1 is defined over $F_A = \{h\_nail, h\_screw, mirror\_on, h\_ham\}$ and $A_A = \{hw\_nail, hw\_screw\}$ with the set of laws:[4]

hw_nail	**causes**	$mirror\_on$	hw_screw	**causes**	$mirror\_on$
hw_nail	**causes**	$\neg h\_nail$	hw_screw	**causes**	$\neg h\_screw$
hw_nail	**executable**	h_nail, h_ham	hw_screw	**executable**	h_screw

In all of the above, the prefix "hw" stands for "hang with" and "h" stands for "has."   ◇

In the following, we often use Φ instead of Φ_{DI} whenever the domain DI is clear from the context.

2.2 Specifying Cooperative Actions

The specification of the set of cooperative actions of an agent, denoted by DC, is defined over C and F and consists of laws of the following form:

$$a \text{ \textbf{exchanges\_with} } A_i \text{ \textbf{gets} } \varphi \text{ \textbf{gives} } \psi \text{ \textbf{causes} } \gamma \qquad (4)$$

where a is an action name in C, γ, φ, and ψ are sets of literals, and A_i is an agent identifier in $\mathcal{AG}$. a is called an *exchange* of ψ for φ. We will also assume that executability conditions for actions in C are specified as usual, using laws of the form (2).

Intuitively, laws of the form (4) represent exchanges that can be made by the agent; if the agent makes the request for φ in exchange for ψ directed to agent A_i then $\gamma \cup \varphi$ will become true. This action is similar to the individual actions in A of an agent. The main difference is that they also change the worlds of other agents.

Example 4. In Example 1, it is reasonable for A to request and/or offer other agents on the literal h_nail. An action for requesting for (offering of) h_nail for A can be specified by

$get(nail, X)$ **exchanges_with** X **gets** h_nail **gives** $true$ **causes** $true$
$give(nail, X)$ **exchanges_with** X **gets** $true$ **gives** h_nail **causes** $\neg h\_nail$
$exchange\_screw\_nail(X)$ **exchanges_with** X **gets** h_nail **gives** h_screw **causes** $\neg h\_screw$

---

[4] To simplify the representation, we often write $l_1, \ldots, l_n$ instead of $\{l_1, \ldots, l_n\}$ in describing the domain.

where $X \in \{B, C\}$. $get(nail, B)$ *allows A to ask B for a nail,* $give(nail, B)$ *provides B with a nail without A's receiving anything in return, and* $exchange\_screw\_nail(B)$ *describes an exchange of a nail for a screw between A and B.*

Observe that it is realistic to assume that A can only give a nail if she has it. As a result,

$$give(nail, X) \textbf{ executable } h\_nail$$

should be included in the domain specification of A. $\diamond$

Since an agent might agree to an unconditional exchange, i.e., she might give out something without receiving anything back or she might ask for something and does not provide anything in return, we will often use the following shorthands:

$$a \textbf{ gets\_from}(\mathbf{A_i}) \; \varphi \textbf{ causes } \gamma \tag{5}$$

$$a \textbf{ gives\_to}(\mathbf{A_i}) \; \psi \textbf{ causes } \gamma \tag{6}$$

With the introduction of cooperative actions, we define planning problems with cooperative actions as follows.

Definition 3 (Planning problem with cooperative actions). *A planning problem with cooperative actions[5] $\mathcal{P}$ is a tuple $\langle DI, I, O, DC \rangle$ where DI is a domain specification, I is a state representing the initial state, O is a set of literals representing the goal, and DC is a set of laws of the form (4).*

Given a planning problem $\mathcal{P} = \langle DI, I, O, DC \rangle$, we need to specify what is a "plan" achieving O in the presence of the cooperative actions. Intuitively, we can consider these actions as the actions of the agent and use the notion of a plan mentioned in the previous subsection.

We extend the transition function Φ of the domain specification DI to consider cooperative actions. We will use $\Phi_\mathcal{P}$ to denote the transition function of $DI \cup DC$. By assuming that cooperative actions are different from the individual actions (i.e., $\mathsf{A} \cap \mathsf{C} = \emptyset$), it suffices to specify what is the result of the execution of a cooperative action in a given state.

For simplicity of the presentation, we assume that each individual agent executes only one action at a time. The method presented in this paper can be easily extended to the case where individual agents can execute parallel actions.

Assume that s is a state and a is a cooperative action of the form

$$a \textbf{ exchanges\_with } \mathbf{A_i} \textbf{ gets } \varphi \textbf{ gives } \psi \textbf{ causes } \gamma$$

then we define $e_a(s) = \varphi \cup \gamma$. The modified transition function is as in Definition 1, i.e., $\Phi_\mathcal{P}(a, s) = \{s' \mid s' = Cn_{C_{DI}}(e_a(s) \cup (s \cap s'))\}$ if a is executable in s; otherwise, $\Phi_\mathcal{P}(a, s) = \emptyset$.

The transition function can be extended to reason about plans as follows.

Definition 4 (Plan with cooperative actions). *Let $\mathcal{P}$ be a planning problem with cooperative actions $\langle DI, I, O, DC \rangle$.*

---

[5] For simplicity of presentation, we will use planning problem instead of planning problem with cooperative actions whenever no confusion is possible.

- *A sequence $s_0, a_0, s_1, \ldots, a_{n-1}, s_n$, where s_i's are states and a_j's are actions, is a* trajectory *if $s_{i+1} \in \Phi_{\mathcal{P}}(a_i, s_i)$ for $0 \leq i < n$.*
- *Given a trajectory $s_0, a_0, s_1, \ldots, a_{n-1}, s_n$, this represents a* possible plan *achieving O (or a possible solution of $\mathcal{P}$) if $s_0 = I$ and $s_n \models O$.*

Example 5. Let $\mathcal{P}_A = \langle DI_A, I_A, O_A, DC_A \rangle$ be the planning problem for A with DI_A (Example 3), with

$$I_A = \{\neg h\_nail, \neg h\_screw, \neg h\_ham, \neg mirror\_on\}$$
$$O_A = \{mirror\_on\}$$

DC_A is the set of actions $give(nail, X)$ and $get(nail, X)$, whose specifications has been given earlier (Example 4), and the two additional actions

$get(ham, X)$	**gets_from**(X)	h_ham **causes** h_ham
$give(ham, X)$	**gives_to**(X)	h_ham **causes** $\neg h\_ham$
$give(ham, X)$	**executable**	h_ham

for $X \in \{B, C\}$. We can easily check the following:
- *For $n \leq 2$, the problem has no possible plan.*
- *For $n = 3$, $\mathcal{P}_A$ has a possible plan which is the following trajectory:*

$$s_0^A, get(nail, C), s_1^A, get(ham, B), s_2^A, hw\_nail, s_3^A$$

where

$$s_0^A = \{\neg h\_nail, \neg h\_ham, \neg h\_screw, \neg mirror\_on\}$$
$$s_1^A = \{h\_nail, \neg h\_ham, \neg h\_screw, \neg mirror\_on\}$$
$$s_2^A = \{h\_nail, h\_ham, \neg h\_screw, \neg mirror\_on\}$$
$$s_3^A = \{\neg h\_nail, h\_ham, \neg h\_screw, mirror\_on\}$$

$\diamond$

3 Planning for Multiagent

In a multiagent environment, each agent needs to know her capabilities, i.e., what actions can she do and how does her actions change her world. She also needs to know whom she can ask for help and/or provide help, if she wishes to do so. Furthermore, it is also common that groups of agents need to know about their joint capabilities. It is also possible that agents might talk the same language. This can be summarized as follows.

- Each agent has her own planning problem, which is described as in the previous section.
- The agent might or might not share the same world representation. By default, the world representation of the agent is local. For example, the three agents in Example 1 can use the same set of fluents and actions; agent A has $\neg h\_nail$ in her initial state whereas B has h_nail in hers, yet this is not a contradictory statement about the world since the fluents are local. On the other hand, the two agents in Example 2 share certain features (e.g., the status of the light) and therefore the fluents encoding these features should have the same value in their representations.

- Agents can exchange the properties in their world representations with each other. For example, A might ask B to give her the nail or exchange a screw with C for a nail.
- There might be actions that a set of agents should not execute in parallel. For example, two cars—one going north-south and another east-west—cannot cross an intersection at the same time.
- There might be actions that a set of agents should execute in parallel. For example, the action of lifting a table by two agents need to be done in parallel.

The language $\mathcal{B}^C$ can be extended to represent and reason about plans/actions of agents in a multiagent environment. We define a multiagent planning problem as follows.

Definition 5 (Multiagent planning problem). *A multiagent planning problem $\mathcal{M}$ is a tuple $\langle \mathcal{AG}, \{\mathcal{P}_i\}_{i \in \mathcal{AG}}, \mathcal{F}, \mathcal{IC}, \mathcal{C} \rangle$ where*

- $\mathcal{AG}$ *is a set of agents,*
- $\mathcal{P}_i$ *is a planning problem with cooperative actions for each agent $i \in \mathcal{AG}$,*
- $\mathcal{F}$ *is a set of tuples of the form (i, j, f) where $i, j \in \mathcal{AG}$ and $f \in F_i \cap F_j$, and*
- $\mathcal{IC}$ *and $\mathcal{C}$ are sets of sets of agent/action pairs of the form (i, a_i), where i is an agent and a_i is an action in A_i.*

Intuitively, each tuple (i, j, f) in $\mathcal{F}$ indicates that f represents the same state variable in the worlds of two agents i and j and can be changed by either i or j. This mean that they should have the same value in every state of i and j. A set of agent/action pairs $\{(i_1, a_{i_1}), \ldots, (i_k, a_{i_k})\} \in \mathcal{IC}$ indicates that the agents $i_1, \ldots, i_k$ cannot execute the actions $a_{i_1}, \ldots, a_{i_k}$ at the same time. On the other hand, a set of agent/action pairs $\{(i_1, a_{i_1}), \ldots, (i_k, a_{i_k})\} \in \mathcal{C}$ indicates that the agents $i_1, \ldots, i_k$ must execute the actions $a_{i_1}, \ldots, a_{i_k}$ concurrently for their effects to be materialized. The sets $\mathcal{F}$, $\mathcal{IC}$, and $\mathcal{C}$ are called constraints of $\mathcal{M}$.

Example 6. The planning problem in Example 1 can be represented by

$$\mathcal{M}_1 = \langle \{A, B, C\}, \{\mathcal{P}_A, \mathcal{P}_B, \mathcal{P}_C\}, \emptyset, \emptyset, \emptyset \rangle$$

where

- *A, B, and C are the agents from Example 1;*
- *$\mathcal{P}_A$ is defined as in Example 5;*
- *$\mathcal{P}_B = \langle DI_B, I_B, O_B, DC_B \rangle$ where DI_B is defined over $F_B = \{h\_nail, h\_screw, diploma\_on, h\_ham\}$ and $A_B = \{hw\_nail, hw\_screw\}$ with the set of laws:*

hw_nail **causes** $diploma\_on$	hw_nail **causes** $\neg h\_nail$
hw_nail **executable** h_ham, h_nail	hw_screw **causes** $diploma\_on$
hw_screw **causes** $\neg h\_screw$	hw_screw **executable** h_screw

$I_B = \{h\_nail, h\_screw, h\_ham, \neg diploma\_on\}$ and $O_B = \{diploma\_on\}$, and DC_B contains cooperative actions similar to that in DC_A and DC_C (below).

- $\mathcal{P}_C = \langle DI_C, I_C, O_C, DC_C \rangle$ where DI_C is defined over

$$\mathbf{F}_C = \{h\_nail, h\_screw, painting\_on\} \qquad \mathbf{A}_C = \{hw\_screw\}$$

with the set of laws:

$$hw\_screw \ \textbf{causes} \ \ painting\_on$$
$$hw\_screw \ \textbf{causes} \ \ \neg h\_screw$$
$$hw\_screw \ \textbf{executable} \ \ h\_screw$$

$I_C = \{h\_nail, \neg h\_screw, \neg painting\_on\}$, $O_C = \{painting\_on\}$, and DC_C contains the following laws:

$$get(screw, X) \quad \textbf{gets\_from}(X) \ h\_screw \ \textbf{causes} \ \ h\_screw$$
$$give(screw, X) \quad \textbf{gives\_to}(X) \quad h\_screw \ \textbf{causes} \ \ \neg h\_screw$$
$$give(screw, X) \quad \textbf{executable} \qquad h\_screw$$

$\diamondsuit$

Example 7. The problem in Example 2 can be represented by $\mathcal{M}_2$ as follows. $\mathcal{M}_2 = \langle\{A, B\}, \{\mathcal{P}_A, \mathcal{P}_B\}, \mathcal{F}, \mathcal{IC}, \emptyset\rangle$ where

$$\mathcal{IC} = \{\{(A, flip_1), (B, flip_2)\}\} \qquad\qquad \mathcal{F} = \{(A, B, light\_on)\}$$

$\mathcal{P}_A$ and $\mathcal{P}_B$ are the planning problems of A and B, respectively, where
- *$\mathcal{P}_A = \langle DI_A, I_A, O_A, \emptyset \rangle$ where DI_A is defined over $\mathbf{F}_A = \{light\_on\}$ and $\mathbf{A}_A = \{flip_1\}$ with the set of laws:*

$$flip_1 \ \textbf{causes} \ \ light\_on \ \textbf{if} \ \neg light\_on \qquad flip_1 \ \textbf{causes} \ \neg light\_on \ \textbf{if} \ light\_on$$

In this case, $I_A = \{\neg light\_on\}$ and $O_A = \{light\_on\}$.
- *$\mathcal{P}_B = \langle DI_B, I_B, O_B, \emptyset \rangle$ where DI_B is defined over $\mathbf{F}_B = \{light\_on\}$ and $\mathbf{A}_B = \{flip_2\}$ with the set of laws:*

$$flip_2 \ \textbf{causes} \ \ light\_on \ \textbf{if} \ \neg light\_on \qquad flip_2 \ \textbf{causes} \ \neg light\_on \ \textbf{if} \ light\_on$$

In this case, $I_B = \{\neg light\_on\}$ and $O_B = \{light\_on\}$. $\diamondsuit$

We now define the notion of a solution for a planning problem.

Definition 6 (Joint plan for Multiagent). *Let $\mathcal{M} = \langle \mathcal{AG}, \{\mathcal{P}_i\}_{i\in\mathcal{AG}}, \mathcal{F}, \mathcal{IC}, \mathcal{C}\rangle$ be a multiagent planning problem. For each $i \in \mathcal{AG}$, let $S_i = [s_0^i a_0^i, \ldots, a_{n-1}^i s_n^i]$ be a possible plan of $\mathcal{P}_i$. We say that $\{S_i\}_{i\in\mathcal{AG}}$ is a joint plan (or solution) of length n for $\mathcal{M}$ if for every $0 \le k \le n$:*
- *For each $(i, j, f) \in \mathcal{F}$, $f \in s_k^i$ iff $f \in s_k^j$;*
- *For each $S \in \mathcal{IC}$, there exists some $(i, a) \in S$ such that $a_k^i \ne a$; and*
- *For each $S \in \mathcal{C}$, either $\{a \mid (i, a) \in S$ and $a = a_k^i\} = \{a \mid (i, a) \in S\}$ or $\{a \mid (i, a) \in S$ and $a = a_k^i\} = \emptyset$.*

- *For each pair of $i, j \in \mathcal{AG}$,*

$$a_k^i \text{ \textbf{exchanges\_with} } j \text{ \textbf{gets} } \varphi \text{ \textbf{gives} } \psi \text{ \textbf{causes} } \gamma$$

is a law in DC_i if and only if

$$a_k^j \text{ \textbf{exchanges\_with} } i \text{ \textbf{gets} } \psi \text{ \textbf{gives} } \varphi \text{ \textbf{causes} } \delta$$

is a law in DC_j.

Intuitively, a joint plan is composed of individual plans which allow the agents to achieve their own goals and satisfy the various constraints of the problem. In the process, agents can help each other in establishing certain conditions. However, if the joint plan contains a an exchange made by an agent (requestor agent) to another agent (receiver agent) then there must exist a counter exchange made by the receiver agent to the requestor agent.

The first item above states that the individual plans must agree with each other on their effects of shared fluents, i.e., it enforces the constraints in $\mathcal{F}$. The second and third items make sure that non-parallel and parallel constraints in $\mathcal{IC}$ and $\mathcal{C}$ are maintained by the joint plan.

Example 8. For the multiagent planning problem $\mathcal{M}_1$ from Example 6, we can easily check the following:

- *For $n \leq 2$, $\mathcal{M}_1$ has no solution.*
- *For $n = 3$, it has a solution consisting of the following plans*
  - *$S_A = [s_0^A, \text{ } get(nail, C), s_1^A, \text{ } get(ham, B), \text{ } s_2^A, hw\_nail, \text{ } s_3^A, \text{ \texttt{wait}}, \text{ } s_4^A]$*
  - *$S_B = [s_0^B, \text{ } hw\_nail, s_1^B, \text{ } give(ham, A), \text{ } s_2^B, \text{ } give(screw, C), s_3^B, \text{ \texttt{wait}}, \text{ } s_4^B]$*
  - *$S_C = [s_0^C, \text{ } get(nail, A), \text{ } s_1^C, \text{ \texttt{wait}}, s_2^C, \text{ } give(screw, B), \text{ } s_3^C, \text{ } hw\_screw, \text{ } s_4^C]$*
  - *where all exchanges are satisfied and the states are uniquely determined by the initial states and the executed actions, i.e., using the extended transition functions of $\mathcal{P}_A$, $\mathcal{P}_B$, and $\mathcal{P}_C$.* $\diamond$

The joint plan for the agents in Example 8 requires that each agent executes some cooperative actions. It is easy to see that any joint plan for the two agents in the problem $\mathcal{M}_2$ requires that only one agent flips the switch next to her while the other agent waits.

4   Computing Joint Plans

In this section, we will present different approaches to computing joint plans. Our approaches utilize answer set programming [18,19], a declarative programming paradigm that has recently emerged from the study of logic programming under the answer set semantics [11].

4.1   Answer Set Semantics of Logic Programs

A logic program Π is a set of rules of the form

$$a_0 \leftarrow a_1, \ldots, a_m, not\ a_{m+1}, \ldots, not\ a_n \tag{7}$$

where $0 \leq m \leq n$, each a_i is an atom of a propositional language[6] and *not* represents *negation-as-failure*. A negation as failure literal (or naf-literal) is of the form $not\ a$ where a is an atom. For a rule of the form (7), the left (right) hand side of the rule is called the *head* (*body*) of the rule. The head and the body can be empty (but not at the same time). A rule is a *constraint* if its head is empty; it is a *fact* if its body is empty.

Consider a set of ground atoms X. The body of a rule of the form (7) is *satisfied* by X if $\{a_{m+1}, \ldots, a_n\} \cap X = \emptyset$ and $\{a_1, \ldots, a_m\} \subseteq X$. A rule of the form (7) with nonempty head is satisfied by X if either its body is not satisfied by X or $a_0 \in X$. In other words, X satisfies a rule of the form (7) if its head belongs to X whenever X satisfies its body. A constraint is *satisfied* by X if its body is not satisfied by X.

For a set of ground atoms S and a program Π, the *reduct* of Π w.r.t. S, denoted by Π^S, is the program obtained from the set of all ground instances of Π by deleting

1. each rule that has a naf-literal $not\ a$ in its body with $a \in S$, and

2. all naf-literals in the bodies of the remaining rules.

S is an *answer set* of Π if it satisfies the following conditions:

1. If Π does not contain any naf-literal, i.e., $m = n$ in every rule of Π, then S is the smallest set of atoms that satisfies all the rules in Π.

2. If the program Π does contain some naf-literal ($m < n$ in some rule of Π), then S is an answer set of Π if S is the answer set of Π^S. Note that Π^S does not contain naf-literals, thus its answer set is defined in the first item.

A program Π is said to be *consistent* if it has an answer set. Otherwise, it is inconsistent. To make answer set style programming easier, Niemelä et al. [20] introduce a new type of rules, called *cardinality constraint rule* (a special form of the *weight constraint rule*) of the following form:

$$A_0 \leftarrow A_1, \ldots, A_m, not\ A_{m+1}, \ldots, not\ A_n$$

where each A_i is a *choice atom* of the form $l\{b_1, \ldots, b_k\}u$ with b_j are atoms and l and u are two integers, $l \leq u$. An atom $l\{b_1, \ldots, b_k\}u$ is said to be true w.r.t. a set of literals S iff $l \leq |S \cap \{b_1, \ldots, b_k\}| \leq u$. The satisfaction of a rule w.r.t. a set of atoms is extended in the usual way. Using rules of this type, one can greatly reduce the number of rules of programs in answer set programming. The semantics of logic programs with such rules is given in [20].

4.2   Finding a Possible Plan for One Agent

We will represent each individual problem of each agent $\mathcal{P}_i$ as a logic program. The program will consist of rules describing the effects of actions, the initial knowledge of the agent, and the goal of the agent. Answer set planning [16] refers to the use of answer set programming in planning. This method has been applied to a variety of problems [9,27]. Let $\mathcal{P} = \langle DI, I, O, DC \rangle$ be a planning problem. We will now describe the program $\Pi(\mathcal{P})$ that encodes $\mathcal{P}$. The encoding makes use of a parameter denoting the maximal length of the plan that the agent considers permissible. The key predicates of $\Pi(\mathcal{P})$ are:

---

[6] A rule with variables is a shorthand for the set of its ground instances.

- $h(l, t)$—fluent literal l holds at the time step t;
- $o(a, t)$—action a is executed (by the agent) at the time step t;
- $possible(a, t)$—action a can be executed at the time step t.

$h(l, t)$ can be extended to define $h(\phi, t)$ for an arbitrary fluent formula ϕ, which states that ϕ holds at the time moment t. In writing the program, we use $h(\{l_1, \ldots, l_k\}, T)$ as a shorthand for $h(l_1, T), \ldots, h(l_k, T)$. The rules of the program are divided into groups:

- *Group 1*: For each fluent $f \in$ F, the program contains the rule

$$fluent(f) \leftarrow \qquad (8)$$

and for each action $a \in$ A $\cup$ C, the program contains the rule

$$action(a) \leftarrow \qquad (9)$$

These facts declare the fluents and the actions of the problem. In addition, for each cooperative action

$$a \textbf{ exchanges\_with } A_j \textbf{ gets } \varphi \textbf{ gives } \psi \textbf{ causes } \gamma$$

in C of an agent j, the program $\Pi(\mathcal{P})$ contains the fact

$$exchange(a, j, A_j, \varphi, \psi)$$

- *Group 2*: rules for reasoning about effects of actions. For each action $a \in$ A $\cup$ C,
    - if DI contains the law (a **executable** ϕ) then $\Pi(\mathcal{P})$ contains the rules

$$possible(a, T) \leftarrow h(\phi, T) \qquad (10)$$
$$\leftarrow o(a, T), not\ possible(a, T) \qquad (11)$$

    - if DI contains the law (a **causes** l **if** ϕ) then $\Pi(\mathcal{P})$ contains the rule

$$h(l, T + 1) \leftarrow o(a, T), h(\phi, T) \qquad (12)$$

    - if DI contains the law (l **if** ϕ) then $\Pi(\mathcal{P})$ contains the rule

$$h(l, T + 1) \leftarrow h(\phi, T) \qquad (13)$$

    - if DC contains the law

$$a \textbf{ exchanges\_with } A_j \textbf{ gets } \varphi \textbf{ gives } \psi \textbf{ causes } \gamma$$

then $\Pi(\mathcal{P})$ contains the rules

$$h(\gamma \cup \varphi, T + 1) \leftarrow o(a, T) \qquad (14)$$

where (14) is a shorthand for the collection of rules $h(l, T + 1) \leftarrow o(a, T)$ for $l \in \gamma \cup \varphi$.

- *Group 3*: rules describing the initial state. For each literal $l \in I$, $\Pi(\mathcal{P})$ contains the fact

$$h(l, 0) \leftarrow \qquad (15)$$

- *Group 4*: rules encoding the goal state. For each literal $l \in O$, $\Pi(\mathcal{P})$ contains the rule

$$\leftarrow not\ h(l, n) \qquad (16)$$

where n is the desired length of the plan.

- *Group 5*: rules for reasoning by inertia. For each fluent $F \in \mathbf{F}$, $\Pi(\mathcal{P})$ contains

$$h(F, T+1) \leftarrow h(F, T), not\ h(\neg F, T+1) \qquad (17)$$
$$h(\neg F, T+1) \leftarrow h(\neg F, T), not\ h(F, T+1) \qquad (18)$$
$$\leftarrow h(F, T), h(\neg F, T) \qquad (19)$$

- *Group 6*: rules for generating action occurrences. $\Pi(\mathcal{P})$ contains the rule

$$1\ \{o(A, T) : action(A)\}\ 1 \leftarrow T < n \qquad (20)$$

which states that at any time step, the agent must execute one of its actions.[7]

Example 9. As an example, some of the rules encoding the problem $\mathcal{P}_A$ in Example 3 is given next

$$fluent(h\_nail) \leftarrow$$
$$h(mirror\_on, T+1) \leftarrow o(hw\_nail, T)$$
$$h(\neg h\_nail, T+1) \leftarrow o(hw\_nail, T)$$
$$possible(hw\_nail, T) \leftarrow h(h\_nail, T), h(h\_ham, T)$$
$$\leftarrow o(hw\_nail, T), not\ possible(hw\_nail, T)$$
$$h(\neg h\_nail, 0) \leftarrow$$
$$h(\neg h\_screw, 0) \leftarrow$$
$$\leftarrow not\ h(mirror\_on, n)$$

The first rule defines the fluent h_nail. The next four rules encode the executability condition of the action hw_nail and its effects. The next two rules specify a part of the initial state and the last rule encodes the goal. For the action give(nail, b), we have the following rules:

$$possible(give(nail, X), T) \leftarrow h(\neg h\_nail, T)$$
$$\leftarrow o(get(nail, b), T), not\ possible(get(nail, b), T)$$
$$h(h\_nail, T) \leftarrow o(get(nail, b), T)$$

---

[7] Since we assume that `wait` always belongs to the set of actions of an agent, this is not a strict requirement as it might sound.

and for the action $give(nail, X)$, we have the rules:

$$possible(give(nail, b), T) \leftarrow h(h\_nail, T)$$
$$\leftarrow o(give(nail, b), T), possible(give(nail, b), T)$$
$$h(\neg h\_nail, T + 1) \leftarrow o(give(nail, b), T)$$

Let $\mathcal{P} = \langle DI, I, O, DC \rangle$ be a planning problem and $\Pi(\mathcal{P}, n)$ denote the set of ground rules of $\Pi(\mathcal{P})$ in which the variable T is instantiated with integers between 0 to n. Let M be an answer set of $\Pi(\mathcal{P}, n)$. Let $s_t[M] = \{l \mid l$ is a fluent literal and $h(l, t) \in M\}$. By $\alpha[M]$ we denote the sequence $s_0[M], a_0, s_1[M], \ldots, a_{n-1}, s_n[M]$ where $o(a_i, i) \in M$. We can show the following:

Theorem 1. *Let $\mathcal{P} = \langle DI, I, O, DC \rangle$ be a planning problem. Then,*

- *For each possible plan α of $\mathcal{P}$ there exists an n and an answer set M of $\Pi(\mathcal{P}, n)$ such that $\alpha = \alpha[M]$;*
- *For each n, if $\Pi(\mathcal{P}, n)$ has an answer set M then $\alpha[M]$ is a possible solution of $\mathcal{P}$; and*
- *For each n, if $\Pi(\mathcal{P}, n)$ is inconsistent then $\mathcal{P}$ does not have a solution of length less than or equal to n.*

Proof. (Sketch) The proof of the first two items is similar to the proof of Theorem 3.2 in [23] and relies on the following properties of an answer set M of $\Pi(\mathcal{P}, n)$:

- if $o(a, i) \in M$ then a is executable in $s_i[M]$ and $s_{i+1} \in \Phi_{\mathcal{P}}(a, s_i[M])$; and
- O is satisfied by $s_n[M]$.

The last item is obvious given the first two items. $\diamond$

An important special case of Theorem 1 is that of deterministic domains. In this case, we have that each answer set of $\Pi(\mathcal{P}, n)$ corresponds to a solution of $\mathcal{P}$.

4.3   Compatible Answer Sets and Joint Plan

Individual possible plans can be computed using the program $\Pi(\mathcal{P}_i)$. We will now discuss an approach for combining them to create a plan for all the agents. Intuitively, we need to make sure that if a request is assumed to be satisfied by an agent then there exists an instance of an offer-action matching this request. This can be easily characterized by the notion of a compatible answer sets.

Definition 7 (Compatible answer sets). *Let $\mathcal{M} = \langle \mathcal{AG}, \{\mathcal{P}_i\}_{i \in \mathcal{AG}}, \mathcal{F}, \mathcal{IC}, \mathcal{C} \rangle$ be a multiagent planning problem and $M = \langle M_i \rangle_{i \in \mathcal{AG}}$ be a sequence of answer sets of $\langle \Pi(\mathcal{P}_i, n) \rangle_{i \in \mathcal{AG}}$ where the constant n is fixed. M is a set of compatible answer sets if for each $k \leq n$,*

- *For each $i \in \mathcal{AG}$, if $o(a_k^i, k) \in M_i$ and*

$$a_k^i \textbf{ exchanges\_with } j \textbf{ gets } \varphi \textbf{ gives } \psi \textbf{ causes } \gamma$$

is a law of the form (4) in DC_i then a_k^j, where $o(a_k^j, k) \in M_j$, must appear in the law

$$a_k^j \textbf{ exchanges\_with } i \textbf{ gets } \psi \textbf{ gives } \varphi \textbf{ causes } \delta$$

belonging to DC_j.

- *For each (i, j, f) in $\mathcal{F}$, $h(f, k) \in M_i$ (resp. $h(\neg f, k) \in M_i$) iff $h(f, k) \in M_j$ (resp. $h(\neg f, k) \in M_j$);*
- *For each $S \in \mathcal{IC}$ there exists some $(i, a_i) \in S$ such that $o(a_i, k) \notin M_i$; and*
- *For each $S \in \mathcal{C}$, either $\{a_i | (i, a_i) \in S$ and $o(a_i, k) \in M_i\} = \{a | (i, a) \in S\}$ or $\{a_i | (i, a_i) \in S$ and $o(a_i, k) \in M_i\} = \emptyset$.*

Intuitively, a set of compatible answer sets corresponds to a joint plan (as we will prove in the next theorem) similar to the correspondence between answer sets and plans in the case of a single agent. The first item requires that exchanges have to made in parallel, by the parties involved. The conditions imposed on a set of compatible answer sets make sure that the collection of individual plans extracted from them satisfies the constraints of the planning problem as well as the requirement that satisfied requests must be matched with offers.

Theorem 2. *Let $\mathcal{M} = \langle \mathcal{AG}, \{\mathcal{P}_i\}_{i \in \mathcal{AG}}, \mathcal{F}, \mathcal{IC} \rangle$ be a multiagent planning problem and n be an integer.*

- *A sequence of answer sets $M = \langle M_i \rangle_{i \in \mathcal{AG}}$ is compatible iff there exists a solution $S = \langle \alpha_i \rangle_{i \in \mathcal{AG}}$ such that $\alpha[M_i] = \alpha_i$ for every $i \in \mathcal{AG}$.*
- *If $\langle \Pi(\mathcal{P}_i, n) \rangle_{i \in \mathcal{AG}}$ does not have a set of compatible answer sets then $\mathcal{M}$ does not have a solution with length n.*

Proof. (Sketch) The conclusion of the first item can be derived from the definition of compatibility answer sets, Theorem 1, and the definition of a solution. The conclusion of the second item follows from the first item and Theorem 1.   □

Example 10. Let $\mathcal{M}_1$ be the multiagent planning problem from Example 6. We can easily check the following:

- *$\{\Pi(\mathcal{P}_i, n)\}_{i \in \{A,B,C\}}$ for $n \leq 3$ does not have compatible answer sets,*
- *For $n = 4$, the three answer sets M_A, M_B, and M_C of $\Pi(\mathcal{P}_A, 4)$, $\Pi(\mathcal{P}_B, 4)$, and $\Pi(\mathcal{P}_C, 4)$, satisfy the following properties:*

$$\{o(get(nail, c), 0), get(ham, b), 1), o(hw\_nail, 2), o(\texttt{wait}, 3)\} \subseteq M_A$$
$$\{o(hw\_nail, 0), o(give(ham, a), 1), o(give(screw, c), 2), o(\texttt{wait}, 3)\} \subseteq M_B$$
$$\{o(give(nail, a), 0), o(\texttt{wait}, 1), o(get(screw, b), 2), o(hw\_screw, 3)\} \subseteq M_C$$

These answer sets are compatible and correspond to the solution in Example 5. ◇

Definitions 6 and 7 provide us with a way for computing joint plans of length n for a planning problem $\mathcal{M}$. The process involves (*i*) computing a set $\{M_i\}_{i \in \mathcal{AG}}$ of answer sets, where M_i is an answer set of $\Pi(\mathcal{P}_i, n)$; and (*ii*) checking the compatibility of $\{M_i\}_{i \in \mathcal{AG}}$. In what follows, we present a system for computing joint plans.

4.4 ASP-Prolog

The **ASP-Prolog** system [10,22] has been developed to provide a tight and semantically well-defined integration of ASP in Prolog. The language of **ASP-Prolog** has been developed using the module and class capabilities of Prolog. **ASP-Prolog** allows programmers to assemble a variety of different modules to create a program; along with the traditional types of modules supported by Prolog, **ASP-Prolog** allows the presence of an arbitrary number of *ASP modules*, each being a collection of ASP rules and facts. Each Prolog module can access any ASP module (using the traditional module qualification of Prolog), read its content, access its models, and modify it (using the traditional `assert` and `retract`).

The language of **ASP-Prolog** includes a traditional logic programming signature $\langle \mathcal{F}, \mathcal{V}, \Pi \rangle$, where $\mathcal{V}$ is a denumerable set of variables, $\mathcal{F}$ is a set of function symbols, and Π is a set of predicate symbols. In particular, we assume that Π contains the distinguished predicates $\{\texttt{assert}, \texttt{retract}, \texttt{model}\}$.

The **ASP-Prolog** language redefines the notion of *atoms* and *literals*. A *qualified atom* is of the form $t : A$ where A is an atom of the language and t is a term. A literal is either an atom, a qualified atom, the negation $not\ A$ of an atom or the negation $not\ t : A$ of a qualified atom. This allows us to generalize logical rules (referred to as **ASP-Prolog** rules) by allowing the presence of qualified atoms in the body of the rules (negated or not).

An **ASP-Prolog** module M_t is a set of **ASP-Prolog** rules, together with a module interface:

$$\begin{aligned} &\leftarrow module : t \\ &\leftarrow import : t_1, \ldots, t_k \\ &\leftarrow export : q_1, \ldots, q_m \end{aligned}$$

where t is the name of the module (a ground term), $t_1, \ldots, t_k$ are names of other modules (ground terms), and $q_1, \ldots, q_m \in \Pi$.

Each module creates a local knowledge base, and possibly different semantics can be employed depending on the structure of rules present in the module. If the rules in module M_t do not contain any qualified atoms, then we denote with $NAT(M_t)$ the set of interpretations (i.e., sets of ground atoms) that describe the semantics of M_t; for example, in presence of negation as failure, $NAT(M_t)$ could correspond to the set of answer sets of M_t.

An **ASP-Prolog** program P is composed of a collection of *modules* $\{M_{t_1}, \ldots, M_{t_n}\}$. Given P, we can develop a dependency graph among modules: module t_i depends on module t_j if t_j is imported by t_i. For the sake of simplicity, we assume that the dependency graph is acyclic; furthermore, when we write the set of modules composing P, we will assume that $t_1, \ldots, t_n$ represents a topological sorting of the dependency graph of P. Finally, we assume that the semantics of P is provided by the semantics of the last module t_n—i.e., t_n represents the "entry point" to the program P.

In absence of occurrences of `assert` and `retract`, it is possible to provide a declarative static semantics for a program P. Intuitively, the semantics builds on establishing a mapping from ground terms to interpretations (i.e., a *model naming* function). We will denote with τ an arbitrary function naming interpretations. Whenever a qualified term $t : A$ is used in a rule, if t is not the name of a module, then we are intuitively testing whether the atom A is satisfied in the interpretation named t. Similarly, if $t : A$

is a qualified atom and t is the name of a module, then we would like to verify whether A is satisfied in all the possible accepted models of the module M_t. The semantics of P can be constructed iteratively:

- since M_{t_1} cannot contain any imports, then its semantics is $NAT(M_{t_1})$;
- the semantics (i.e., collection of accepted models) of any other module M_{t_i} is obtained via a reduction process, where:
  - if a rule contains a qualified atom $t : A$ (literal $not\ t : A$) in the body, t is the name of an imported module (which must precede t_i in the topological sorting), the predicate of A appears in the export list of M_t, and A is true in each accepted model of M_t in the semantics of P, then the literal (the rule) is removed, otherwise the whole rule (the literal) is discarded;
  - if a rule contains a qualified atom $t : A$ (literal $not\ t : A$) in the body, t is not the name of an imported module, there is an imported module t_j such that one of its accepted models in the semantics of P has name t (i.e., $\tau(t)$ corresponds to such model), the predicate of A is in the export list of M_{t_j}, then the qualified atom (the whole rule) is removed, otherwise the whole rule (the literal) is discarded.

The specialized predicate model is used in qualified atoms to identify components of the model naming function: $t : model(s)$ is entailed if t is the name of a module (being imported) and $\tau(s)$ is an accepted model of module t in the semantics of the given program. The collection of accepted models for M_{t_i} corresponds to the natural semantics NAT for the reduct of the module.

In presence of assert and retract, it is necessary to develop instead an operational semantics, where the semantics is expressed with respect to goal entailment and a dynamically changing program (as described in detail in [10]).

Finally, let us underline that **ASP-Prolog** allows modules to contain standard Prolog code, including extra-logical predicates; in this case, the module is going to have Prolog semantics as its natural NAT semantics.

4.5   Finding Joint Plans

The problem of finding joint plans can be encoded using **ASP-Prolog**. Let us denote the ASP encoding of the planning problem of agent $\mathcal{P}_i$ as $\Pi_i = \Pi(\mathcal{P}_i, n)$ (constructed as discussed in section 4.2). Let us also assume that $\mathcal{AG}$ contains k agents. We can generate a **ASP-Prolog** module M_i which contains:

- all the rules of Π_i;
- the module interface:

$$\leftarrow module : mod_i$$
$$\leftarrow import : \epsilon$$
$$\leftarrow export : o, exchange$$

An additional module M_{k+1} is required to provide the services of computing joint plans—i.e., verifying that the plans individually computed by the different agents can be combined into a joint plan. Effectively, M_{k+1} is in charge of implementing the notion of compatible answer sets presented earlier.

The simplest construction for M_{k+1} can be expressed by performing a brute force combination of the plans generated by the various agents. The header of M_{k+1} contains

$$\leftarrow module : lead$$
$$\leftarrow import : mod_1, \dots, mod_k$$
$$\leftarrow export : o$$

The module can collect the joint plans by selecting arbitrary answer sets produced by the other modules and validate them for compatibility. The predicate

$$collect([X_1, \dots, X_k]) \leftarrow mod[1] : model(X_1), \dots, mod[k] : model(X_k)$$

generates all possible combinations of answer sets from the different Π_i programs. mod denotes an array used to store the names of the imported modules.

The test for compatibility of a solution we can use the following code:

$$
\begin{aligned}
unmatched(List, I, J, T) \leftarrow\ & nth(I, List, P1), nth(J, List, P2),\\
& P1 : o(A1, T), P2 : o(A2, T),\\
& (P1 : exchange(A1, I, J, Prop1, Prop2),\\
& \qquad \backslash + P2 : exchange(A2, J, I, Prop2, Prop1);\\
& P2 : exchange(A2, J, I, Prop2, Prop1),\\
& \qquad \backslash + P1 : exchange(A1, I, J, Prop1, Prop2))\\
reject(List) \leftarrow\ & in(I, 1, n), in(J, 1, n), in(T, 1, length),\\
& unmatched(List, I, J, T)\\
compatible(List) \leftarrow\ & compatible(List), \backslash + reject(List)
\end{aligned}
$$

An alternative approach is to use the exchanges generated by one agent to guide the construction of the plans of the other agents. A main loop will cycle and collect the names of the answer sets that are compatible, one agent at a time:

```
 1 :  compatible(List, List, _, k).
 2 :  compatible(List, Final, Exchanges, I) ← I < k,
 3 :       mod[I] : model(New), I1 is I + 1,
 4 :       collect_exchanges(New, Ex),
 5 :       check_past_exchanges(Ex, Exchanges, I),
 6 :       add_future_exchanges(Ex, I),
 7 :       append(Ex, Exchanges, NewExchanges),
 8 :       compatible([New|List], Final, NewExchanges, I1)
 9 :  collect_exchanges(Model, List) ←
10 :       findall([A, T], (Model : o(A, T), Model : exchange(A, _, _, _, _)), List)
11 :  check_past_exchanges(New, Old, Index) ← member([A, T], New),
12 :       mod[From] : exchange(B, From, To, P1, P2), To < Index,
13 :       mod[To] : exchange(A1, To, From, P2, P1),
14 :       \ + member([B, T], Old), !, fail
15 :  add_future_exchanges([], _)
16 :  add_future_exchanges([[A, T]|Rest], Index) ←
17 :       mod[Index] : exchange(A, Index, To, P1, P2), To > Index,
18 :       mod[To] : exchange(B, To, Index, P2, P1),
19 :       mod[To] : assert(o(B, T)),
20 :       add_future_exchanges(Rest, Index)
```

Intuitively:

- The predicate *collect_exchanges* extracts from an answer set (i.e., an agent's plan), the list of exchanges required by the plan (lines 9-10);
- The predicate *check_past_exchanges* ensures that the plan for the agent does not impose additional exchanges with the agents whose plans have already been established (lines 11-14);
- The predicate *add_future_exchange* fixes the steps in the plan of the other agents requiring exchanges (lines 15-20).

It is easy to generalize the proof of correctness of this code from the results presented in the earlier sections.

5   Related Works

Our work is strongly related to the work in [26]. In fact, the proposed approach of computing joint plans in this paper is complementary to the approach of computing join plans in [26]. The main differences between this work and [26] lie in (*i*) the use of a more expressive language for representing and reasoning about actions of individual agents; (*ii*) the view of *request* and *provide* actions as *exchanges* between agents, which allows for a simpler formalization of cooperative actions; and (*iii*) the use of **ASP-Prolog**, a system for integrating of answer set programming and Prolog, in computing joint plans.

As in [26], the multiagent planning problem considered in this paper could be viewed as a special case of distributed problem solving [8]. Furthermore, our main goal is to generate a joint plan for the agents before its execution. In this regards, our work differs from many distributed continual planning systems that were discussed in the survey [6] and many papers presented in the recent AAMAS conferences which concentrate on planning and replanning or dealing with unexpected events during the plan execution. Nevertheless, the `assert` and `retract` capabilities provided by **ASP-Prolog** can be used to move the current approach towards continual planning—a topic of future exploration. Last but not least, **ASP-Prolog** provides a way to facilitate limited sharing between individual agents, a feature that might be important in various multiagent planning scenarios.

The proposed method for the generation of joint plans follows the approach presented in [5] where

Multiagent planning = Planning + Coordination

We use answer set programming [16], a method that has been used for single agent planning [9,27], in computing the individual plans. As such, our plan representation allows for the coordination to be done by using time-steps presented in individual plans. This is different from several other systems in which partial order plans are used for plan representation and refinement planning is used for coordination (e.g., [3,2] or earlier works such as the Partial Global Planning framework). Our use of the system **ASP-Prolog** is similar to the spirit of that in [7], where an attempt is made to construct joint plan using SAT-based single agent planners.

Observe that cooperative actions—as defined in this paper—are also suitable for the modeling of multiagent planning with resources. Requesting a resource and offering a resource can be modeled in a similar fashion to that of asking and offering a nail (Example 4). Since our focus is on the generation of joint plans before execution, the proposed language is different from the resource logic introduced in [4], whose focus is on the plan merging phase. The exchange actions can be seen as special case of *negotiation actions* discussed in [29].

We use the action language $\mathcal{B}$ because of its simple semantics and its close relationship to PDDL [13]. This means that other extensions or variations of $\mathcal{A}$ (e.g., $\mathcal{C}$ [12], $\mathcal{E}$ [14]) could also be extended to formalize cooperative actions. Observe that there are subtle differences between request actions and non-deterministic actions. First, a cooperative action changes the world of other agents while a non-deterministic action does not. Second, a cooperative action does not change the world of the agent executing this action, while a non-deterministic action does. In this sense, a cooperative action of an agent is like an exogenous action for other agents. Thus, modeling cooperative actions using non-deterministic actions might not be the most natural way. Finally, we would like to note that $\mathcal{B}$ allows arbitrary static laws which cannot be easily included in other languages for reasoning about actions and changes (e.g., event calculus [15]) or the planning language PDDL).

Finally, we observe that the proposed framework differs from approaches to multiagent planning based on alternating-time temporal logic (ATL) in a similar way that domain-independent planning differs from planning with domain specific knowledge. In our approach, the description of the planning problem is minimal, i.e., it contains only the initial state, the goal state, and the specification of agents' actions. A specification in ATL is richer in that it can include extra information such as the requirement that a certain action has to be executed immediately after the execution of a given action. Our approach can be extended to consider various types of domain specific knowledge as in [23].

6   Conclusions and Future Works

In this paper, we extended the action language $\mathcal{B}$ to define a language for representing and reasoning about actions and their effects in multiagent domains that considers both individual and cooperative actions. We defined the notion of a plan in presence of cooperative actions and used it in formalizing the notion of a joint plan. We also proposed a prototype system as an application of the **ASP-Prolog** system, which generates joint plans.

Our immediate goal for the future is to investigate the scalability and efficiency of the proposed system and use it in developing a system to integrate multiagent planning and negotiation, as described in [25]. Additionally, we would like to explore the use of more expressive languages (e.g., action languages with constraints and sensing actions and/or preferences [24]) in representing and reasoning about joint plans of Multiagent by addressing various questions mentioned in [1].

Acknowledgment

The research was partially supported by NSF grants IIS-0812267, CBET-0754525, and HRD-0420407.

References

1. Brenner, M.: Planning for Multiagent Environments: From Individual Perceptions to Coordinated Execution. In: Work. on Multiagent Planning & Scheduling, ICAPS, pp. 80–88 (2005)
2. Cox, J.S., Durfee, E.H.: An efficient algorithm for multiagent plan coordination. In: AAMAS 2005, pp. 828–835 (2005)
3. Cox, J.S., Durfee, E.H., Bartold, T.: A Distributed Framework for Solving the Multiagent Plan Coordination Problem. In: AAMAS, pp. 821–827. ACM Press, New York (2005)
4. de Weerdt, M., Bos, A., Tonino, H., Witteveen, C.: A resource logic for multi-agent plan merging. Ann. Math. Artif. Intell. 37(1-2), 93–130 (2003)
5. de Weerdt, M., ter Mors, A., Witteveen, C.: Multi-agent planning: An introduction to planning and coordination. In: Handouts of the Euro. Agent Summer School, pp. 1–32 (2005)
6. des Jardins, M., Durfee, E.H., Ortiz, C.L., Wolverton, M.: A survey of research in distributed, continual planning. AI Magazine 20(4), 13–22 (1999)
7. Dimopoulos, Y., Moraitis, P.: Multi-agent coordination and cooperation through classical planning. In: IEEE/WIC/ACM/IAT, pp. 398–402. IEEE Comp. Society, Los Alamitos (2006)
8. Durfee, E.: Distributed Problem Solving and Planning. In: Multiagent Systems (A Modern Approach to Distributed Artificial Intelligence), pp. 121–164. MIT Press, Cambridge (1999)
9. Eiter, T., Faber, W., Leone, N., Pfeifer, G., Polleres, A.: Answer Set Planning under Action Costs. Journal of Artificial Intelligence Research 19, 25–71 (2003)
10. El-Khatib, O., Pontelli, E., Son, T.C.: ASP-PROLOG: A System for Reasoning about Answer Set Programs in Prolog. In: Jayaraman, B. (ed.) PADL 2004. LNCS, vol. 3057, pp. 148–162. Springer, Heidelberg (2004)
11. Gelfond, M., Lifschitz, V.: The stable model semantics for logic programming. In: Int. Conf. on Logic Programming, pp. 1070–1080 (1988)
12. Gelfond, M., Lifschitz, V.: Action languages. ETAI 3(6) (1998)
13. Ghallab, M., Howe, A., Knoblock, C., McDermott, D., Ram, A., Veloso, M., Weld, D., Wilkins, D.: PDDL — the Planning Domain Definition Language. Ver. 1.2. TR1165. Yale, London (1998)
14. Kakas, A.C., Miller, R., Toni, F.: E-RES: Reasoning about Actions, Events and Observations. In: Eiter, T., Faber, W., Truszczyński, M. (eds.) LPNMR 2001. LNCS (LNAI), vol. 2173, pp. 254–266. Springer, Heidelberg (2001)
15. Kowalski, R., Sergot, M.: A logic-based calculus of events. New Generation Computing 4, 67–95 (1986)
16. Lifschitz, V.: Action languages, answer sets and planning. In: The Logic Programming Paradigm: a 25-Year Perspective, pp. 357–373. Springer, Heidelberg (1999)
17. Lifschitz, V., Turner, H.: Splitting a logic program. In: ICLP, pp. 23–38 (1994)
18. Marek, V., Truszczyński, M.: Stable models and an alternative logic programming paradigm. In: The Log. Prog. Paradigm: a 25-year Perspective, pp. 375–398 (1999)
19. Niemelä, I.: Logic programming with stable model semantics as a constraint programming paradigm. AMAI 25(3,4), 241–273 (1999)
20. Niemelä, I., Simons, P., Soininen, T.: Stable model semantics for weight constraint rules. In: Proc. Logic Programming and Non Monotonic Reasoning, pp. 315–332 (1999)
21. Parsons, S., Sierra, C., Jennings, N.R.: Agents that reason and negotiate by arguing. J. of Log. and Comp. 8(3), 261–292 (1998)
22. Pontelli, E., Son, T.C., Baral, C.: A Logic Programming Based Framework for Intelligent Web Service Composition. In: Managing Web Service Quality: Measuring Outcomes and Effectiveness. IGI Publisher (2008)
23. Son, T.C., Baral, C., Tran, N., McIlraith, S.: Domain-Dependent Knowledge in Answer Set Planning. ACM Transactions on Computational Logic 7(4) (2006)

24. Son, T.C., Pontelli, E.: Planning with Preferences using Logic Programming. Journal of Theory and Practice of Logic Programming (TPLP) 6, 559–607 (2006)
25. Son, T.C., Pontelli, E., Sakama, C.: Logic Programming for Multiagent Planning with Negotiation. In: Hill, P.M., Warren, D.S. (eds.) ICLP 2009. LNCS, vol. 5649, pp. 99–114. Springer, Heidelberg (2009)
26. Son, T.C., Sakama, C.: Reasoning and Planning with Cooperative Actions for Multiagents Using Answer Set Programming. In: Baldoni, M., Bentahar, J., van Riemsdijk, M.B., Lloyd, J. (eds.) DALT 2009. LNCS, vol. 5948, pp. 208–227. Springer, Heidelberg (2010)
27. Tu, P.H., Son, T.C., Baral, C.: Reasoning and Planning with Sensing Actions, Incomplete Information, and Static Causal Laws using Logic Programming. TPLP 7, 1–74 (2006)
28. Tu, P.H., Son, T.C., Gelfond, M., Morales, R.: Approximation of action theories and its application to conformant planning. Artificial Intelligence (2010), doi:10.1016/j.artint.2010.04.007
29. Wooldridge, M., Parsons, S.: Languages for negotiation. In: Proceedings of ECAI (2000)

Expressing Properties of Resource-Bounded Systems: The Logics **RTL*** and **RTL**

Nils Bulling[1] and Berndt Farwer[2]

[1] Department of Informatics, Clausthal University of Technology, Germany
[2] School of Engineering and Computing Sciences, Durham University, UK

Abstract. Computation systems and logics for modelling such systems have been studied to a great extent in the past decades. This paper introduces resources into the models of systems and discusses the *Resource-Bounded Tree Logics* **RTL** and **RTL***, based on the well-known *Computation Tree Logics* **CTL** and **CTL***, for reasoning about computations of such systems. We present initial results on the complexity/decidability of model checking.

1 Introduction

The basic idea of rational agents being autonomous entities perceiving changes in their environment and acting according to a set of rules or plans in the pursuit of goals does not take resources into account. However, many actions that an agent would execute in order to achieve a goal can – in real life – only be carried out in the presence of certain resources. Without sufficient resources some actions are not available, leading to plan failure. The analysis of agents and (multi-agent) systems with resources is still in its infancy and has been tackled almost exclusively in a pragmatic and experimental way. This paper takes first steps in modelling resource bounded systems (which can be considered as the single-agent case of the scenario just described). Well-known computational models are combined with a notion of resource to enable a more systematic and rigorous specification and analysis of such systems. The main motivation of this paper is to propose a fundamental formal setting. In the future we plan to focus on a more practical aspect, i.e., how this setting can be used for the verification of systems.

The proposed logic builds on *Computation Tree Logic* [6]. Essentially, the existential path quantifier $\mathsf{E}\varphi$ (there is a computation that satisfies φ) is replaced by $\langle\rho\rangle\gamma$ where ρ represents a set of available resources. The intuitive reading of the formula is that there is a computation *feasible with the given resources ρ* that satisfies γ.

Finally, we turn to the decidability of model checking the proposed logics. We show that **RTL** (*Resource-Bounded Tree Logic*), the less expressive version, has a decidable model checking problem as well as restricted variants of the full logic **RTL*** and its models.

The remainder of the paper is structured as follows. In Section 2 we recall the computation tree logic **CTL*** and define multisets used as a representation for

J. Dix, M. Fisher, and P. Novák (Eds.): CLIMA X, LNAI 6214, pp. 22–45, 2010.

resources. Section 3 forms the main part of the paper. We introduce resources into the computation tree logics and their models. Subsequently, in Section 4 we show some properties of the logics. Section 5 includes the analysis of the model checking complexity, and finally, we conclude with an outlook on future work in Section 6.

2 Preliminaries

In this section we present the computation tree logics **CTL** and **CTL*** as well as multisets which we will use to represent resources.

2.1 Computation Tree Logic and Transition Systems

A *Kripke frame* $\mathcal{T} = (Q, \rightarrow)$ consists of a finite set of states Q and a (serial) binary relation $\rightarrow \subseteq Q \times Q$ between states. We say that a state q' is *reachable* from a state q if $q \rightarrow q'$. A *Kripke model* is defined as $\mathfrak{M} = (Q, \rightarrow, \mathcal{P}rops, \pi)$ where $(Q, \rightarrow)$ is a transition system, $\mathcal{P}rops$ a non-empty set of *propositions*, and $\pi : Q \rightarrow \mathcal{P}(\mathcal{P}rops)$ a *labelling function* that indicates which propositions are true in a given state. Such models represent the temporal behaviour of systems. There are no restrictions on the number of times a transition is used.

A *path* λ of a transition system is an infinite sequence $q_0 q_1 \cdots \in Q^\omega$ of states such that $q_i \rightarrow q_{i+1}$ for all $i = 0, 1, 2, \ldots$. Given a path λ we use $\lambda[i]$ and $\lambda[i, j]$ to refer to state q_i and to the path $q_i q_{i+1} \ldots q_j$ where $j = \infty$ is permitted, respectively. A path starting in q is called q-*path*. The set of all paths in $\mathfrak{M}$ is denoted by $\Lambda_\mathfrak{M}$ and the set of all q-paths by $\Lambda_\mathfrak{M}(q)$.

Formulae of **CTL*** [8] are defined by the following grammar:

$$\varphi ::= \mathsf{p} \mid \neg\varphi \mid \varphi \wedge \varphi \mid \mathsf{E}\gamma \quad \text{where} \quad \gamma ::= \varphi \mid \neg\gamma \mid \gamma \wedge \gamma \mid \varphi \mathcal{U} \varphi \mid \bigcirc\varphi$$

and $\mathsf{p} \in \mathcal{P}rops$. Formulae φ (resp. γ) are called *state* (resp. *path*) formulae. There are two temporal operators: $\bigcirc$ (in the next moment in time) and $\mathcal{U}$ (until). The temporal operators $\Diamond$ (sometime in the future) and $\square$ (always in the future) can be defined as abbreviations.

CTL* formulae are interpreted over Kripke structures; truth is given by the satisfaction relation in the usual way: For state formulae we have

$\mathfrak{M}, q \models \mathsf{p}$ iff $\lambda[0] \in \pi(\mathsf{p})$ and $\mathsf{p} \in \mathcal{P}rops$;
$\mathfrak{M}, q \models \neg\varphi$ iff $\mathfrak{M}, q \not\models \varphi$;
$\mathfrak{M}, q \models \varphi \wedge \psi$ iff $\mathfrak{M}, q \models \varphi$ and $\mathfrak{M}, q \models \psi$;
$\mathfrak{M}, q \models \mathsf{E}\varphi$ iff there is a path $\lambda \in \Lambda_\mathfrak{M}(q)$ such that $\mathfrak{M}, \lambda \models \varphi$;

and for path formulae

$\mathfrak{M}, \lambda \models \varphi$ iff $\mathfrak{M}, \lambda[0] \models \varphi$;
$\mathfrak{M}, \lambda \models \neg\gamma$ iff $\mathfrak{M}, \lambda \not\models \gamma$;
$\mathfrak{M}, \lambda \models \gamma \wedge \delta$ iff $\mathfrak{M}, \lambda \models \gamma$ and $\mathfrak{M}, \lambda \models \delta$;
$\mathfrak{M}, \lambda \models \bigcirc\gamma$ iff $\lambda[1, \infty], \pi \models \gamma$; and

$\mathfrak{M}, \lambda \models \gamma \mathcal{U} \delta$ iff there is an $i \in \mathbb{N}_0$ such that $\mathfrak{M}, \lambda[i, \infty] \models \delta$ and $\mathfrak{M}, \lambda[j, \infty] \models \gamma$ for all $0 \le j < i$;

A less expressive fragment of **CTL*** called **CTL** [6] has become popular due to its *better computational properties*. **CTL** restricts **CTL*** such that every temporal operator must directly be preceded by a path quantifier. The formula $\mathsf{E}\Box \Diamond\; \mathsf{p}$, for instance, is a formula of the full language but not of the restricted version.

2.2　Multisets

We define some variations of multisets used in the following sections. We assume that $\mathbb{N}_0 = \{0, 1, 2, \dots\}$ and $\mathbb{Z} = \{\dots, -2, -1, 0, 1, 2, \dots\}$.

Definition 1 ($\mathbb{Z}/\mathbb{Z}^\infty$-multiset,$X_\infty^\pm$, $X^\pm$, $\mathbb{N}_0/\mathbb{N}_0^\infty$-multiset, $X_\infty^\oplus$, $X^\oplus$). *Let X be a non-empty set.*

(a) *A $\mathbb{Z}$-multiset $\mathbf{Z} : X \longrightarrow \mathbb{Z}$ over the set X is a mapping from the elements of X to the integers.*
　　A $\mathbb{Z}^\infty$-multiset $\mathbf{Z} : X \longrightarrow \mathbb{Z} \cup \{-\infty, \infty\}$ over the set X is a mapping from the elements of X to the integers extended by $-\infty$ and ∞.
　　The set of all $\mathbb{Z}$-multisets (resp. $\mathbb{Z}^\infty$-multisets) over X is denoted by $X^\pm$ (resp. $X_\infty^\pm$).
(b) *An $\mathbb{N}_0$-multiset (resp. $\mathbb{N}_0^\infty$-multiset) $\mathbf{N}$ over X is a $\mathbb{Z}$-multiset (resp. $\mathbb{Z}^\infty$-multiset) over X such that for each $x \in X$ we have $\mathbf{N}(x) \ge 0$. The set of all $\mathbb{N}_0$-multisets (resp. $\mathbb{N}_0^\infty$-multisets) over X is denoted by $X^\oplus$ (resp. $X_\infty^\oplus$).*

Whenever we speak of a 'multiset' without further specification, the argument is supposed to hold for any variant from Def. 1. In general, we overload the standard set notation and use it also for multisets, i.e., $\subseteq$ denotes multiset inclusion, $\emptyset$ is the empty multiset, etc. We assume a global set of resource types $\mathcal{R}$. The resources of an individual agent form a multiset over this set. $\mathbb{Z}$-multiset operations are straightforward extensions of $\mathbb{N}_0$-multiset operations.

Multisets are frequently written as formal sums, i.e., a multiset $\mathbf{M} : X \longrightarrow \mathbb{N}_0$ is written as $\sum_{x \in X} \mathbf{M}(x)$. Given two multisets $\mathbf{M} : X \longrightarrow \mathbb{N}_0$ and $\mathbf{M}' : X \longrightarrow \mathbb{N}_0$ over the same set X, multiset union is denoted by $+$, and is defied as $(\mathbf{M} + \mathbf{M}')(x) := \mathbf{M}(x) + \mathbf{M}'(x)$ for all $x \in X$. Multiset difference is defined only if $\mathbf{M}$ has at least as many copies of each element as $\mathbf{M}'$. Then, $(\mathbf{M} - \mathbf{M}')(x) := \mathbf{M}(x) - \mathbf{M}'(x)$ for all $x \in X$. For $\mathbb{Z}$-multisets, $+$ is defined exactly as for multisets, but the condition is dropped for multiset difference, since for $\mathbb{Z}$-multisets negative multiplicities are possible. Finally, for $\mathbb{Z}^\infty$-multisets we assume the standard arithmetic rules for $-\infty$ and ∞ (for example, $x + \infty = \infty$, $x - \infty = -\infty$, etc.).

We define multisets with a bound on the number of elements of each type.

Definition 2 (Bounded multisets). *Let $k, l \in \mathbb{Z}$. We say that a multiset $\mathbf{M}$ over a set X is k-bounded iff $\forall x \in X\ (\mathbf{M}(x) \le k)$. We use $^k X_\infty^\pm$ to denote the set of all k-bounded $\mathbb{Z}^\infty$-multisets over X; and analogously for the other types of multisets.*

Finally, we define the (positive) restriction of a multiset with respect to another multiset, allowing us to focus on elements with a positive multiplicity.

Definition 3 ((Positive) restriction, M $\upharpoonright_{\mathbf{N}}$). *Let* **M** *be a multiset over* X *and let* **N** *be a multiset over* Y. *The* (positive) *restriction of* **M** *regarding* **N**, **M** $\upharpoonright_{\mathbf{N}}$, *is the multiset* **M** $\upharpoonright_{\mathbf{N}}$ *over* $X \cup Y$ *defined as follows:*

$$\mathbf{M} \upharpoonright_{\mathbf{N}} (x) := \begin{cases} \mathbf{M}(x) & \text{if } \mathbf{N}(x) \geq 0 \text{ and } x \in Y \\ 0 & \text{otherwise.} \end{cases}$$

So, the multiset **M** $\upharpoonright_{\mathbf{N}}$ equals **M** for all elements contained in **N** which have a non-negative quantity, and 0 for all others elements.

3   Modelling Resource-Bounded Systems

In this section we introduce *resource-bounded models* (RBMs) for modelling system with limited resources. Then, we propose the logics **RTL*** and **RTL** (resource-bounded tree logics), for the verification of such systems. Subsequently, we introduce cover models and graphs and consider several properties and special cases of RBMs.

3.1   Resource-Bounded Systems

A resource-bounded agent has at its disposal a (limited) repository of resources. Performing actions reduces some resources and may produce others; thus, an agent might not always be able to perform all of its available actions. In the single agent case that we consider here this corresponds to the activation or deactivation of transitions.

Definition 4 (Resources $\mathcal{R}$, resource quantity (set), feasible)
An element of the non-empty and finite set $\mathcal{R}$ is called resource. *A tuple* $(r, c) \in \mathcal{R} \times \mathbb{Z}^\infty$ *is called* resource quantity *and we refer to c as the* quantity *of r. A* resource-quantity set *is a $\mathbb{Z}^\infty$-multiset $\rho \in \mathcal{R}_\infty^\pm$. Note that ρ specifies a resource quantity for each $r \in \mathcal{R}$.*

Finally, a resource-quantity set ρ is called feasible *iff $\rho \in \mathcal{R}_\infty^\oplus$; that is, if all resources have a non-negative quantity.*

We model resource-bounded systems by an extension of Kripke frames, allowing each transition to *consume* and *produce* resources. We assign pairs $(\mathbf{c}, \mathbf{p})$ of resource-quantity sets to each transition, denoting that a transition labelled $(\mathbf{c}, \mathbf{p})$ *produces* **p** and *consumes* **c**.

Definition 5 (Resource-bounded model). *A resource-bounded model (RBM) is given by* $\mathfrak{M} = (Q, \rightarrow, \mathcal{P}rops, \pi, \mathcal{R}, t)$ *where*

- Q, $\mathcal{R}$, *and $\mathcal{P}rops$ are finite sets of states, resources, and propositions, respectively;*

- $(Q, \rightarrow, \mathcal{P}rops, \pi)$ is a Kripke model; and
- $t : Q \times Q \rightarrow \mathcal{R}^{\oplus} \times \mathcal{R}^{\oplus}$ is a (partial) resource function, assigning to each transition (i.e., tuple $(q, q') \in \rightarrow$) a tuple of feasible resource-quantity sets. Instead of $t(q, q')$ we sometimes write $t_{q,q'}$ and for $t_{q,q'} = (\mathbf{c}, \mathbf{p})$ we use ${}^{\bullet}t_{q,q'}$ (resp. $t_{q,q'}^{\bullet}$) to refer to $\mathbf{c}$ (resp. $\mathbf{p}$).

Hence, in order to make a transition from q to q', where $q \rightarrow q'$, the resources given in ${}^{\bullet}t_{q,q'}$ are *required*; and in turn, $t_{q,q'}{}^{\bullet}$ are *produced* after executing the transition. Note, that we only allow finite productions and consumptions.

A *path* of an RBM is a path of the underlying Kripke structure. We also use the other notions for paths introduced above.

The consumption and production of resources of a path can now be defined in terms of the consumptions and productions of the transitions it comprises. Intuitively, not every path of an RBM is feasible; consider, for instance, a system consisting of a single state q only where $q \rightarrow q$ and $t_{q,q}^{\bullet} = {}^{\bullet}t_{q,q}$. It seems that the transition "comes for free" as it produces the resources it consumes; however, this is not the case. The path $qqq \ldots$ is not feasible as the initial transition is not enabled due to the lack of initial resources. Hence, in order to enable it, at least the resources given in ${}^{\bullet}t_{q,q}$ are necessary. Intuitively, a path is said to be ρ-*feasible* if each transition in the sequence can be executed with the resources available at the time of execution.

Definition 6 (ρ-feasible path, resource-extended path). *A path $\lambda = q_1 q_2 q_3 \cdots \in \Lambda_{\mathfrak{M}}(q)$ where $q = q_1$ is called ρ-feasible if for all $i \in \mathbb{N}$ the resource-quantity set*

$$\left(\rho + \Sigma_{j=1}^{i-1}(t_{q_j q_{j+1}}^{\bullet} - {}^{\bullet}t_{q_j q_{j+1}})\right) \restriction {}^{\bullet}t_{q_i q_{i+1}} - {}^{\bullet}t_{q_i q_{i+1}} \text{ is feasible.}$$

A resource-extended path is given by $\lambda \in (Q \times \mathcal{R}_\infty^{\pm})^{\omega}$ such that the restriction of λ to states, denoted $\lambda|_Q$, is a path in the model and the second component keeps track of the currently available resources; we use $\lambda|_{\mathcal{R}}$ to refer to the projection to the second component.

3.2 Resource-Bounded Tree Logic

We present a logic based on **CTL*** which can be used to verify systems with limited resources. In the logic we replace the **CTL*** path quantifier E by $\langle \rho \rangle$ where ρ is a resource-quantity set. The intuitive reading of a formula $\langle \rho \rangle \gamma$ is that there is a(n) (infinite) ρ-feasible path λ on which γ holds. Note that E (there is a path in the system) can be defined as $\langle \rho^{\infty} \rangle$ where ρ^{∞} is the resource set assigning ∞ to each resource type. Formally, the language is defined as follows.

Definition 7 ($\mathcal{L}_{RTL^{\star}}$). *Let $\mathcal{R}$ be a set of resources and let $\mathcal{P}rops$ a set of propositions. The language $\mathcal{L}_{RTL^{\star}}$ is defined by the following grammar:*

$$\varphi ::= \mathsf{p} \mid \neg\varphi \mid \varphi \wedge \varphi \mid \langle \rho \rangle \gamma \text{ where } \gamma ::= \varphi \mid \neg\gamma \mid \gamma \wedge \gamma \mid \varphi \mathcal{U} \varphi \mid \bigcirc\varphi$$

and $\mathsf{p} \in \mathcal{P}rops$ and $\rho \in \mathcal{R}_\infty^{\pm}$. Formulae φ (resp. γ) are called state (resp. path) formulae.

Moreover, we define fragments of $\mathcal{L}_{RTL^\star}$ *in which the domain of* ρ *is restricted. Let* X *be any set of multisets over* $\mathcal{R}$. *Then* $\mathcal{L}_{RTL^\star_X}$ *restricts* $\mathcal{L}_{RTL^\star}$ *in such a way that* $\rho \in X$. *Finally, we define* $[\rho]$, *the dual of* $\langle \rho \rangle$, *as* $\neg \langle \rho \rangle \neg$.

Analogously to the language of **CTL** we define $\mathcal{L}_{RTL}$ as the fragment of $\mathcal{L}_{RTL^\star}$ in which each temporal operator is immediately preceded by a path quantifier.

Definition 8 ($\mathcal{L}_{RTL}$). *Let* $\mathcal{R}$ *be a set of resources and let* $\mathcal{P}rops$ *a set of propositions. The language* $\mathcal{L}_{RTL}$ *is defined by the following grammar:*

$$\varphi ::= \mathsf{p} \mid \neg \varphi \mid \varphi \wedge \varphi \mid \langle \rho \rangle \bigcirc \varphi \mid \langle \rho \rangle \square\, \varphi \mid \langle \rho \rangle \varphi \mathcal{U} \varphi$$

where $\mathsf{p} \in \mathcal{P}rops$, $\rho \in \mathcal{R}^\pm_\infty$. *Fragments* **RTL**$_X$ *are defined in analogy to Def. 7.*

As in the language of **CTL** we define $\lozenge\, \varphi$ as $\top \mathcal{U} \varphi$ and we use the following abbreviations for the universal quantifiers (they are not definable as duals in $\mathcal{L}_{RTL}$ as, for example, $\neg \langle \rho \rangle \neg \square\, \varphi$ is not an admissible $\mathcal{L}_{RTL}$-formula):

$[\rho] \bigcirc \varphi \equiv \neg \langle \rho \rangle \bigcirc \neg \varphi,$
$[\rho] \square\, \varphi \equiv \neg \langle \rho \rangle \lozenge \neg \varphi,$
$[\rho] \varphi \mathcal{U} \psi \equiv \neg \langle \rho \rangle ((\neg \psi) \mathcal{U} (\neg \varphi \wedge \neg \psi)) \wedge \neg \langle \rho \rangle \square\, \neg \psi,$

Next, we give the semantics for both languages.

Definition 9 (Semantics, RTL*). *Let* $\mathfrak{M}$ *be an RBM, let* q *be a state in* $\mathfrak{M}$, *and let* $\lambda \in \Lambda_{\mathfrak{M}}$. *The semantics of* $\mathcal{L}_{RTL^\star}$-*formulae is given by the satisfaction relation* $\models$ *which is defined as follows:*

$\mathfrak{M}, q \models \mathsf{p}$ *iff* $\lambda[0] \in \pi(\mathsf{p})$ *and* $\mathsf{p} \in \mathcal{P}rops$;
$\mathfrak{M}, q \models \varphi \wedge \psi$ *iff* $\mathfrak{M}, q \models \varphi$ *and* $\mathfrak{M}, q \models \psi$
$\mathfrak{M}, q \models \langle \rho \rangle \varphi$ *iff there is a* ρ-*feasible path* $\lambda \in \Lambda(q)$ *such that* $\mathfrak{M}, \lambda \models \varphi$
$\mathfrak{M}, \lambda \models \varphi$ *iff* $\mathfrak{M}, \lambda[0] \models \varphi$;

and for path formulae:

$\mathfrak{M}, \lambda \models \neg \gamma$ *iff not* $\mathfrak{M}, \lambda \models \gamma$
$\mathfrak{M}, \lambda \models \gamma \wedge \psi$ *iff* $\mathfrak{M}, \lambda \models \gamma$ *and* $\mathfrak{M}, \lambda \models \psi$
$\mathfrak{M}, \lambda \models \square\, \varphi$ *iff for all* $i \in \mathbb{N}$ *we have that* $\lambda[i, \infty] \models \varphi$;
$\mathfrak{M}, \lambda \models \bigcirc \varphi$ *iff* $\lambda[1, \infty] \models \varphi$; *and*
$\mathfrak{M}, \lambda \models \varphi \mathcal{U} \psi$ *iff there is an* $i \geq 0$ *such that* $\mathfrak{M}, \lambda[i, \infty] \models \psi$ *and* $\mathfrak{M}, \lambda[j, \infty] \models \varphi$ *for all* $0 \leq j < i$;

We consider the logic **RTL*** *as the tuple* $(\mathcal{L}_{RTL^\star}, \models)$ *over all RBMs and analogously for all other fragments. These clauses are also used to define the semantics for* $\mathcal{L}_{RTL}$ *(therefore, we also stated the clause for* $\square\, \varphi$).

Thus the meaning of $[\rho] \square\, \mathsf{p}$ is that proposition p holds in every state on any ρ-feasible path.

We now discuss some interpretations of the formula $\langle \rho \rangle \gamma$ considering various resource-quantity sets. For $\rho \in \mathcal{R}^\oplus$ it is assumed that ρ consists of an initial (positive) amount of resources which can be used to achieve γ where the quantity of each resource is finite. $\rho \in \mathcal{R}^\oplus_\infty$ allows to *ignore* some resources (i.e., it is assumed that there is an infinite quantity of them). Initial debts of resources can be modelled by $\rho \in \mathcal{R}^\pm_\infty$.

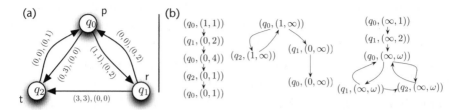

Fig. 1. In Figure (a) a simple RBM $\mathfrak{M}$ is shown and (b) presents some corresponding cover graphs

Example 1. Consider the RBM $\mathfrak{M}$ in Figure 1(a). Each transition is labeled by $(c_1, c_2), (p_1, p_2)$ with the interpretation: The transition consumes c_i and produces p_i quantities of resource r_i for $i = 1, 2$. We encode the resource-quantity set by (a_1, a_2) to express that there are a_i quantities of resoure r_i for $i = 1, 2$.

- If there are infinitely many resources available proposition t can become true infinitely often: $\mathfrak{M}, q_0 \models \langle\langle(\infty, \infty)\rangle\rangle\square \Diamond$ t
- We have $\mathfrak{M}, q_0 \not\models \langle\langle(1, 1)\rangle\rangle\square \top$ as there is no $(1, 1)$-feasible path. The formula $\langle\langle(1, \infty)\rangle\rangle\square$ (p $\vee$ t) holds in q_0.
- Is there a way that the system runs forever given specific resources? Yes, if we assume, for instance, that there are infinitely many resources of r_1 and at least one resource of r_2: $\mathfrak{M}, q_0 \models \langle\langle(\infty, 1)\rangle\rangle\top$

These simple examples show, that it is not always immediate whether a formula is satisfied, sometimes a rather tedious calculation might be required.

3.3 Cover Graphs and Cover Models

In this section we introduce a transformation of RBMs into Kripke models. This allows us, in general, to translate truth in **RTL** to truth in **CTL** as shown in Section 4.1.

We say that a resource-quantity set *covers* another, if it has at least as many resources of each type with at least one amount actually exceeding that of the other resource-quantity set. We are interested in cycles of transition systems that produce more resources than they consume, thereby giving rise to unbounded resources of some type(s). This is captured by a *cover graph* for RBMs, extending ideas from [11] and requiring an ordering on resource quantities.

Definition 10 (Resource ordering $<$). *Let ρ and ρ' be resource sets in $\mathcal{R}_\infty^\pm$. We say $\rho < \rho'$ iff $(\forall r \in \mathcal{R} \ (\rho(r) \leq \rho'(r))) \wedge (\exists r \in \mathcal{R} \ (\rho(r) < \rho'(r)))$. We say ρ has strictly less resources than ρ' or ρ' covers ρ.*

The ordering is extended to allow values of ω by defining for $x \in \mathbb{N}$ that $\infty + \omega = \infty$, $\infty - \omega = \infty$, $\omega - \infty = -\infty$, $\omega + x = \omega$, $\omega - x = \omega$, and $\omega < \infty$.

Definition 11 (ρ-feasible transition, $\xrightarrow{\rho}$). *We say that a transition $q \to q'$ is ρ-feasible and write $q \xrightarrow{\rho} q'$ if for all $r \in \mathcal{R}$ we have that $0 < {}^{\bullet}t_{q,q'}(r)$ implies ${}^{\bullet}t_{q,q'}(r) \leq \rho(r)$.*

So, given a specific amount of resources ρ a transition is said to be ρ-feasible if it can be traversed given ρ. A node of the cover graph consists of tuples $(q, (x_i)_{i=1,\ldots,|\mathcal{R}|})$ where q is a state of the RBM and $(x_i)_i$ is a vector representing the currently available resources. The variable x_i denotes that there are x_i units of resource r_i.

Definition 12 ((ρ, q)-cover graph of an RBM, path, $\lambda|_Q$). *Let $\mathfrak{M} = (Q, \to, \mathcal{P}rops, \pi, \mathcal{R}, t)$, let q be a state in Q, and let $\rho \in \mathcal{R}_\infty^{\pm}$. Without loss of generality, assume $\mathcal{R} = \{r_1, \ldots, r_n\}$ and consider $(x_i)_i$ as an abbreviation for the sequence $(x_i)_{i=1,\ldots,n}$. The (ρ, q)-cover graph $\mathcal{C}\mathcal{G}(\mathfrak{M}, \rho, q)$ for $\mathfrak{M}$ with initial state $q \in Q$ and an initial resource-quantity set ρ is the graph (V, E) defined as the least fixed-point of the following specification:*

1. $(q, (\rho(r_i))_i) \in V$ *(the root vertex).*

2. *For $(q', (x_i)_i) \in V$ and $q'' \in Q$ with $q' \xrightarrow{(x_i)_i} q''$ then either:*
   (a) if there is a vertex $(q'', (\hat{x}_i)_i)$ on the path from the root to $(q', (x_i)_i)$ in V, with $(\hat{x}_i)_i < (x_i - {}^{\bullet}t_{q',q''}(r_i) + t_{q',q''}{}^{\bullet}(r_i))_i$ then $(q'', (\tilde{x}_i)_i) \in V$ and $((q', (x_i)_i), (q'', (\tilde{x}_i)_i)) \in E$ where we define

$$\tilde{x}_i := \begin{cases} \max\{\omega, x_i - {}^{\bullet}t_{q',q''}(r_i) + t_{q',q''}{}^{\bullet}(r_i)\} & \text{if } \hat{x}_i < x_i, \\ x_i - {}^{\bullet}t_{q',q''}(r_i) + t_{q',q''}{}^{\bullet}(r_i) & \text{otherwise;} \end{cases}$$

   (b) or else $(q'', (x_i - {}^{\bullet}t_{q',q''}(r_i) + t_{q',q''}{}^{\bullet}(r_i))_i) \in V$ and $((q', (x_i)_i), (q'', (x_i - {}^{\bullet}t_{q',q''}(r_i) + t_{q',q''}{}^{\bullet}(r_i))_i)) \in E$.

A path in $\mathcal{C}\mathcal{G}(\mathfrak{M}, \rho, q)$ is an infinite sequence of pairwise adjacent states. Given a path $\lambda = (q_1, (x_{1_i})_i)(q_2, (x_{2_i})_i) \ldots$ we use $\lambda|_Q$ to denote the path $q_1 q_2 \ldots$, i.e., the states of $\mathfrak{M}$ are extracted from the states in V.

Cover graphs can be viewed as Kripke frames. It is obvious how they can be extended to models given an RBM.

Definition 13 ((ρ, q)-cover model of an RBM). *Let $G = (V, E)$ be the (ρ, q)-cover graph of an RBM $\mathfrak{M} = (Q, \to, \mathcal{P}rops, \pi, \mathcal{R}, t)$. The (ρ, q)-cover model of $\mathfrak{M}$, $\mathcal{C}\mathcal{M}(\mathfrak{M}, \rho, q)$, is given by $(V, E, \mathcal{P}rops, \pi')$ with $\pi'((q, (x_i)_i)) := \pi(q)$ for all $(q, (x_i)_i) \in V$.*

Figure 2 shows the RBM $\mathfrak{M}$ in (a) and its cover model $\mathcal{C}\mathcal{M}(\mathfrak{M}, 0, q_0)$ at the very top of (b). In the cover model, ω denotes the reachability of unbounded resources.

In Section 4.1 we analyse the relation between cover models and truth in **RTL**. Unfortunately, as illustrated in the next example, "simple" cover models in their current form are not yet suitable for that.

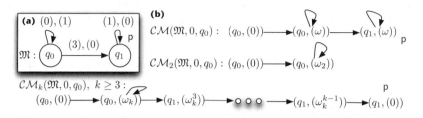

Fig. 2. An RBM $\mathfrak{M}$ (Fig. (a)), its cover model, 2-cover model, and κ-cover model (Fig. (b))

Example 2. Let λ be the path of $\mathcal{CM}(\mathfrak{M}, 0, q_0)$ from Figure 2(b) with $\lambda|_Q = q_0 q_0 (q_1)^\omega$. Obviously, this path is not 0-feasible in the model $\mathfrak{M}$ from Fig. 2(a). The problem is, that subsequent selections of the transition $q_0 \rightarrow q_0$ allows to generate any *finite* amount of resources, thus is covered by ω, but any finite amount is not enough for the subpath $(q_1)^\omega$. This implies, that we cannot directly use cover models as alternative models.

Note, however, that the following result is obvious by the definition of a cover model: Every ρ-feasible path in the model is also a path in the corresponding cover model. The other direction is the one that causes trouble.

Proposition 1. *If λ is a ρ-feasible q-path in $\mathfrak{M}$ then there is a (q, ρ)-path λ' in $\mathcal{CM}(\mathfrak{M}, \rho, q)$ such that $\lambda = \lambda'|_Q$.*

Proof. Let λ be a ρ-feasible q-path and η_i be the resources available at $\lambda[i]$ after $\lambda[0, i]$, for $i = 1, 2, \ldots$; particularly, we have that $\eta_0 = \rho$. By induction on the number of transitions we show that there is a (q, ρ)-path λ' in $\mathcal{CM}(\mathfrak{M}, \rho, q)$ where (V, E) denotes the underlying graph such that $\lambda = \lambda'|_Q$. By definition is $(\lambda[0], \rho(r_i)_i) \in V$. For every state q' with a ρ-feasible transition from $\lambda[0]$ to q' we have that $(q', \ldots) \in V$ and an edge $((\lambda[0], \rho), (q', \ldots)) \in E$ (according to the construction of the cover model). In particular, we have that $(\lambda[1], \zeta) \in V$ with $\zeta \geq_\omega \eta_1$.

Now suppose the claim is proven up to position k. Let $(\lambda[k], \zeta) \in V$ with $\zeta \geq_\omega \eta_k$ be the $k + 1$st state on λ'. Following the same reasoning as above there is a transition $((\lambda[k], \zeta), (\lambda[k + 1], \zeta')) \in E$ with $\zeta' \geq_\omega \eta_{k+1}$. □

In order to avoid the problem discussed in Example 2 we modify the cover graph construction as follows. The construction changes for those transitions that consume from the ω quantified resource type. Instead of using the rule "$\omega - k = \omega$", we (try to) expand the nodes for a fixed number of times ensuring that other loop's resource requirements can be met. But we abstain of introducing ω's as done in the cover graphs.

For the construction, we replace ω by κ new symbols ω_κ^l for $l = 0, \ldots \kappa - 1$ and $\kappa \in \mathbb{N}_0$. For $i \in \mathbb{N}_0$ we define: $\omega_\kappa^l - i = 0$ for $l + i \geq \kappa$, $\omega_\kappa^l - i = \omega_\kappa^{l+i}$ for $l + i < \kappa$, $\omega_\kappa^l + i = \omega_\kappa^{\min\{l-i, 0\}}$, and we set $\omega_\kappa = \omega_\kappa^0$. The symbol ω_κ is used to represent that at least κ units of some resource type are produced, and ω_κ^l indicates that there are $\kappa - l$ resources left.

Identifying the symbol ω_κ^l with the number $\kappa - l$ allows to extend the resource ordering from Definition 10 in a natural way; e.g. we have $i \leq \omega_\kappa^l$ iff $i \leq \kappa - l$. Moreover, this does also make it possible to lift the notation of ρ-feasible transition etc. to this extended case. Finally, we define a class of cover models.

Definition 14 ($\mathcal{CM}_\kappa(\mathfrak{M}, \rho, q)$). *The construction of the (ρ, q, κ)-cover graph is defined as in Definition 12 but ω in 2. is replaced by ω_κ; that is,*

$$\tilde{x}_i := \begin{cases} \max\{\omega_\kappa, x_i - {}^\bullet t_{q',q''}(r_i) + t_{q',q''}{}^\bullet(r_i)\} & \text{if } \hat{x}_i < x_i, \\ x_i - {}^\bullet t_{q',q''}(r_i) + t_{q',q''}{}^\bullet(r_i) & \text{otherwise;} \end{cases}$$

The (ρ, q, κ)-cover model, $\mathcal{CM}_\kappa(\mathfrak{M}, \rho, q)$, is defined analogously to Definition 13.

In Figure 2(b) we have also drawn the 2- and κ-cover model of the model $\mathfrak{M}$. In the next example we show that this generalised cover models overcome the problem discussed in Example 2.

Example 3. The "bad" path λ of Example 2 is neither possible in $\mathcal{CM}_2(\mathfrak{M}, 0, q_0)$ nor in $\mathcal{CM}_\kappa(\mathfrak{M}, 0, q_0)$ for any $\kappa \geq 0$. This is, because for any fixed κ the path $(q_1)^\omega$ will eventually have consumed all resources from ω_κ.

However, another problem arises. If the κ is chosen too small then we might abort the construction too early. The cover model $\mathcal{CM}_2(\mathfrak{M}, 0, q_0)$ illustrates the problem: Principally, it is possible to reach state q_1 if the loop $q_0 \to q_0$ is traversed at least three times. However, as ω_2 does not allow to "remember" more than two units of resources state q_1 is never visited.

In order to avoid this problem we need to find an appropriate κ such that a theorem similar to Proposition 1 with respect to κ-cover models holds. Indeed, such a κ is constructible but it is very complex (cf. the proof of Theorem 3).

We end the section with two results.

Proposition 2. *Let $\rho \in \mathcal{R}_\infty^\pm$, let $\mathfrak{M}$ be an RBM, let q be a state in $\mathfrak{M}$, and let G denote the (ρ, q)- or (ρ, q, κ) cover graph of $\mathfrak{M}$. Then, for each node $(q, (x_i)_i)$ of G the property $x_i \geq \min\{\rho(r_i), 0\}$ holds.*

Proof. Suppose there is a node $(q, (x_i)_i)$ in the cover graph G and an index i such that $x_i < \min\{\rho(r_i), 0\}$. We first consider the case in which the minimum is equal to 0. Then, there must be a transition in G which causes a non-negative quantity of r_i to become negative. But such a transition is not feasible due to the construction of G! The case in which the minimum is equal to $\rho(r_i) < 0$ yields the same contradiction as a negative quantity of r_i reduces even further which is not allowed in the construction of G. □

The proposition states that non-positive resource quantities cannot decrease further. Theorem 1 states that cover models are finite; its proof is similar to the corresponding proof for Karp-Miller graphs [11].

Theorem 1 (Finiteness of the (κ-)cover graph). *Let $\rho \in \mathcal{R}_\infty^\pm$ and $\kappa \in \mathbb{N}$. The (ρ, q)- and (ρ, q, κ)-cover graphs of the RBM $\mathfrak{M}$, $q \in Q_\mathfrak{M}$, are finite.*

Proof. Let G denote the (ρ, q)-cover graph of $\mathfrak{M}$ and let Q be the set of states in $\mathfrak{M}$. Assume G is infinite (i.e., G has infinitely many nodes). Then, there is an infinite path $l = v_1 v_2 \ldots$ in G that contains infinitely many different states. Since Q is finite there is some state, say $q' \in Q$, of $\mathfrak{M}$ and an infinite subsequence of distinct states $l' = v_{i_1} v_{i_2} \ldots$ on l with $v_{i_j} = (q', (x_k^j)_k)$ and $i_j < i_{j+1}$ for all $j = 1, 2, \ldots$. Due to the construction of the cover graph, it cannot be the case that $(x_k^j)_k \leq (x_k^{j'})_k$ for any $1 \leq j < j'$; otherwise, an ω-node would have been introduced and the infinite sequence would have collapsed. So, there must be two distinct indices, o and p, with $1 \leq o, p \leq |\mathcal{R}|$ such that, without loss of generality, $x_o^j < x_o^{j'}$ and $x_p^j > x_p^{j'}$. But by Prop. 2 we know that each $x_k^j \geq \min\{\rho(r_k), 0\}$; hence, the previous property cannot hold for all indices o, p, j, j' but for the case in which $\rho(r) = -\infty$ for some resource r. However, this would also yield a contradiction as any non-negative resource quantity is bounded by 0. This proves that such an infinite path cannot exist and that the cover graph therefore has to be finite. □

3.4   Resource-Bounded Models

In Section 5 we show that the model-checking problem is decidable for **RTL**. Decidability of model checking for (full) **RTL*** over arbitrary RBMs is still open. However, we identify interesting subclasses in which the problem is decidable. Below we consider some restrictions which may be imposed on RBMs.

Definition 15 (Production free, zero (loop) free, k-bounded)
Let $\mathfrak{M} = (Q, \rightarrow, \mathcal{P}rops, \pi, \mathcal{R}, t)$ be an RBM.

(a) *We say that $\mathfrak{M}$ is production free if for all $q, q' \in Q$ we have that $t_{q,q'} = (\mathbf{c}, \emptyset)$. That is, actions cannot produce resources they only consume them.*

(b) *We say that $\mathfrak{M}$ is zero free if there are no states $q, q' \in Q$ with $q \neq q'$ and $t_{q,q'} = (\emptyset, \mathbf{p})$. That is, there are no transitions between distinct states which do not consume any resources.*

(c) *We say that $\mathfrak{M}$ is zero-loop free if there are no states $q, q' \in Q$ with $t_{q,q'} = (\emptyset, \mathbf{p})$. That is, in addition to zero free models, loops without consumption of resources are also not allowed.*

(d) *We say that $\mathfrak{M}$ is (structurally) k-bounded for $\rho \in {}^k\mathcal{R}_\infty^\pm$ iff the available resources after any finite prefix of a ρ-feasible path are bounded by k, i.e., there is no reachable state in which the agent can have more than k resources of any resource type.*

In the following we summarise some results which are important for the model checking results presented in Section 5.

Proposition 3. *Let $\mathfrak{M}$ be an RBM and let $\rho \in \mathcal{R}_\infty^\pm$ be a resource-quantity set. Then, there is an RBM $\mathfrak{M}'$ and a $\rho' \in \mathcal{R}^\pm$, both effectively constructible from $\mathfrak{M}$ and ρ, such that the following holds: A path is ρ-feasible in $\mathfrak{M}$ if, and only if, it is ρ'-feasible in $\mathfrak{M}'$.*

Proof. Let ρ' be equal to ρ but the quantity of each resource r with $\rho(r) \in \{-\infty, \infty\}$ is 0 in ρ' and let $\mathfrak{M}'$ equal $\mathfrak{M}$ apart from the following exceptions. For each transition (q, q') with $t_{qq'} = (\mathbf{c}, \mathbf{p})$ in $\mathfrak{M}$ do the following: Set $\mathbf{c}(r) = 0$ in $\mathfrak{M}'$ for each r with $\rho(r) = \infty$; or remove the transition (q, q') completely in $\mathfrak{M}'$ if $\mathbf{c}(r) > 0$ (in $\mathfrak{M}$) and $\rho(r) = -\infty$ for some resource r. Obviously, $\rho \in \mathcal{R}^{\pm}$.

Now, the left-to-right direction of the result is straightforward as only transitions were omitted in $\mathfrak{M}'$ which can not occur on any ρ-feasible path in $\mathfrak{M}$. The right-to-left direction is also obvious as only resource quantities in $\mathfrak{M}'$ were set to 0 from which an infinite amount is available in ρ and only those transitions were removed which can never occur due to an infinite debt of resources.   □

The next proposition presents some properties of special classes of RBMs introduced above. In general there may be infinitely many ρ-feasible paths. We study some restrictions of RBMs that reduce the number of paths:

Proposition 4. *Let $\mathfrak{M} = (Q, \to, \mathcal{P}rops, \pi, \mathcal{R}, t)$ be an RBM.*

(a) *Let $\rho \in \mathcal{R}^{\pm}$ and let $\mathfrak{M}$ be production and zero-loop free; then, there are no ρ-feasible paths.*
(b) *Let $\rho \in \mathcal{R}^{\pm}$ and let $\mathfrak{M}$ be production and zero free. Then, for each ρ-feasible path λ there is an (finite) initial segment λ' of λ and a state $q \in Q$ such that $\lambda = \lambda' \circ qqq \ldots$.*
(c) *Let $\rho \in \mathcal{R}^{\pm}$ and let $\mathfrak{M}$ be production free. Then, each ρ-feasible path λ has the form $\lambda = \lambda_1 \circ \lambda_2$ where λ_1 is a finite sequence of states and λ_2 is a path such that no transition in λ_2 consumes any resource.*
(d) *Let $\rho \in \mathcal{R}^{\pm}$ and let $\mathfrak{M}$ be k-bounded for ρ. Then there are only finitely many state/resource combinations (i.e., elements of $Q \times \mathcal{R}^{\pm}$) possible on any ρ-feasible path.*

Proof (Sketch).

(a) As there are no resources with an infinite amount and each transition is production free and consumes resources some required resources must be exhausted after finitely many steps.

(b) Apart from (a) loops may come for free and this is the only way how ρ-feasible paths can result.

(c) Assume the contrary. Then, in any infinite suffix of a path there is a resource-consuming transition that occurs infinitely often (as there are only finitely many transitions). But then, as the model is production free, the path cannot be ρ-feasible.

(d) We show that there cannot be infinitely many state/resource combinations reachable on any ρ-feasible path. Since the condition of ρ-feasibility requires the consumed resources to be present, there is no possibility of infinite decreasing sequences of resource-quantity sets.This gives a lower bound for the initially available resources ρ. The k-boundedness also gives an upper bound.   □

We show that k-boundedness is decidable for RBMs.

Proposition 5 (Decidability of k-boundedness). *Given a model $\mathfrak{M}$ and an initial resource-quantity set ρ, the question whether $\mathfrak{M}$ is k-bounded for ρ is decidable.*

Proof. First, we check that $\rho \in {}^k\mathcal{R}_\infty^\oplus$. If this is not the case, then $\mathfrak{M}$ is not k-bounded for ρ. Then we construct the cover graph of $\mathfrak{M}$ and check whether there is a state $(q, (x_i)_i)$ in it so that $x_i > k$ for some i. If this is the case $\mathfrak{M}$ is not k-bounded; otherwise it is.   □

We end this section with an easy result showing a sufficient condition for a model to be k-bounded.

Proposition 6. *Let $\rho \in \mathcal{R}^\pm$. Each production-free RBM is k-bounded for ρ where $k := \max\{i \mid \exists r \in \mathcal{R} \ (\rho(r) = i)\}$.*

4   Properties of Resource-Bounded Tree Logics

Before discussing specific properties of **RTL** and **RTL*** and showing the decidability of the model-checking problem for **RTL** and for special cases of **RTL*** and its models, we note that our logics conservatively extend **CTL*** and **CTL**. This is easily seen by defining the path quantifier E as $\langle \rho^\infty \rangle$ and by setting $t_{qq'} = (\emptyset, \emptyset)$ for all states q and q' where ρ^∞ denotes the resource set assigning ∞ to each resource type. Hence, every Kripke model has a canonical representation as an RBM. Moreover, given an RBM we can express the existence of a path (neglecting resources) by E $:= \langle \rho^\infty \rangle$. This allows to directly interpret **CTL** and **CTL*** formulae over RBMs.

Proposition 7 (Expressiveness). **CTL*** *(resp. **CTL**) can be embedded in* **RTL*** *(resp. **RTL**) over Kripke models and RBMs.*

Proof. Given a **CTL*** formula φ and a Kripke model $\mathfrak{M}$ we replace every existential path quantifier in φ by $\langle \rho^\infty \rangle$ and denote the result by φ'. Then, we extend $\mathfrak{M}$ to the canonical RBM $\mathfrak{M}'$ if it is not already an RBM and have that $\mathfrak{M}, q \models \varphi$ iff $\mathfrak{M}', q \models \varphi'$.   □

4.1   RTL and Cover Models

We show that if there is a satisfying path in any κ-cover model; then, there also is a path in the corresponding RBM. Note however, this result does only hold for *positive* formulae of the kind $\langle \rho \rangle \gamma$.

Let λ be a finite sequence of states. Then, we recursively define λ^n for $n \in \mathbb{N}_0$ as follows: $\lambda^0 := \epsilon$ and $\lambda^i := \lambda^{i-1}\lambda$ for $i \geq 1$. That is, λ^n is the path which results from putting λ n-times in sequence.

The following lemma states that for flat $\mathcal{L}_{RTL}$-path formulae[1] it does not matter whether a cycle is traversed just once or many times. It can be proved by a simple induction on the path formula γ.

---

[1] A formula is said to be *flat* if it does not contain any path quantifier.

Lemma 1. *Let γ be an $\mathcal{L}_{RTL}$-path formula containing no more path quantifiers, let $\mathfrak{M}$ be an RBM and let λ be a path in $\mathfrak{M}$. Now, if $\tilde{\lambda} = q_1 \ldots q_n$ is a finite subsequence of λ with $q_1 = q_n$ (note, that a single state is permitted as well), then, λ can be written as $\lambda_1 \tilde{\lambda} \lambda_2$ where λ_1, λ_2 are subsequences of λ and we have that : $\mathfrak{M}, \lambda \models \gamma$ if, and only if, $\mathfrak{M}, \lambda_1 \tilde{\lambda}^n \lambda_2 \models \gamma$ for all $n \in \{1, 2, \ldots\}$.*

The second lemma states that one can always extend a path in the κ-cover model to a feasible path in the RBM by duplicating loops.

Lemma 2. *Let λ be a path in $\mathcal{CM}_\kappa(\mathfrak{M}, \rho, q), (q, \rho)$ and $\lambda' = \lambda|_Q$; then, there are tuples $(a_i, b_i, c_i) \in \mathbb{N}_0^2 \times \mathbb{N}$ for $i = 1, 2, \ldots$ such that for all $j = 1, 2, \ldots$ we have that $a_j \leq b_j < a_{j+1}$ and $\lambda'[a_j] = \lambda'[b_j]$ and the path*

$$(\lambda'[a_i, b_i]^{c_i})_{i=1,2,\ldots} \text{ is } \rho\text{-feasible in } \mathfrak{M}.$$

Proof. Let a $(q, (\rho(r_i))_i)$-path $\lambda = l_1 l_2 \ldots$ in $G := \mathcal{CM}_\kappa(\mathfrak{M}, \rho, q) = (V, E)$ be given. We extend λ to a path λ' (having the structure as stated in the lemma) such that $\lambda'|_Q$ is ρ-feasible in $\mathfrak{M}$.

If $\lambda|_Q$ is ρ-feasible we just take λ' as λ. So, suppose $\lambda|_Q = q_{i_1} q_{i_2} \ldots$ is not ρ-feasible. Then, there is a transition in λ that is not feasible in $\mathfrak{M}$. Let $l_1 \ldots l_{k+1}$ be the *minimal* length initial subpath of λ such that $(l_1 \ldots l_{k+1})|_Q$ is not feasible in $\mathfrak{M}$ and let $l_k = (q, (x_i)_i)$. According to the construction of cover graphs this can only be caused by a resource r_l such that $x_l = \omega_\kappa^t$ for $0 \leq t \leq \kappa$. Let $l_o = (q', (x_i')_i)$ with $1 \leq o \leq k$ and o maximal be the state on λ at which x_l' was set to ω_κ most recently. Then, there must be another state $l_p = (q', (x_i'')_i)$, $1 \leq p < o$ and p maximal, with $(x_i'')_i < (x_i')_i$ and $x_l'' < x_l'$. The setting is depicted in Figure 3.

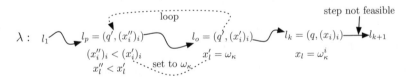

Fig. 3. Proof of Lemma 2

So, we extend λ to λ' by duplicating the subsequence $l_p l_{p+1} \ldots l_o$ in l and adjusting the resources of the states preceding l_p accordingly. Thus, we have that $\lambda'|_Q = q_{i_1} \ldots q_{i_p} q_{i_{p+1}} \ldots q_{i_o} q_{i_p} \ldots q_{i_o} q_{i_{o+1}} \ldots$. We subsequently continue this procedure (now applied to λ') and do only duplicate transitions that are also present in λ (i.e. not the new ones). It remains to show that this procedure does not force some c_i to become infinite.

Suppose that there is some c_i that becomes infinite following this construction. Then, there is a set of resources that requires the resources produced by $\lambda[a_i, b_i]$; and there is no other loop (or set of loops) that starts after $\lambda[b_i]$ that would also provide the needed resources (otherwise these loops would be duplicated as the construction looks for the latest possibility). In a κ-cover model, however, one can only "remember" κ units of a resource; hence, one can have at most κ transitions consuming of a specific resource until some other transition has to produce this very resource again. Thus, in order to ensure that λ is a path in G there must be a producing transition after $\lambda[b_i]$, in particular, a cycle introducing another ω_κ-node following the same line of argumentation as above, which contradicts our supposition. Hence, we will actually obtain a path λ' such that $\lambda'|_Q$ is ρ-feasible and has the structure $(\lambda|_Q[a_i, b_i]^{c_i})_{i=1,2,\ldots}$. $\square$

Theorem 2. *Let* $\rho \in \mathcal{R}_\infty^\pm$, *let* $\mathfrak{M}$ *be an RBM, let* q *be a state in* $\mathfrak{M}$. *Then, for any* κ *and any flat* $\mathcal{L}_{RTL}$-*formula* $\langle\rho\rangle\gamma$ *we have that:*

$$If\ \mathcal{CM}_\kappa(\mathfrak{M}, \rho, q), (q, \rho) \models \mathsf{E}\gamma \ then\ \mathfrak{M}, q \models \langle\rho\rangle\gamma.$$

Proof. The result follows from Lemma 1 and 2. Firstly, the path λ is extended to a path λ' such that $\lambda'|_Q$ is ρ-feasible according to Lemma 2; then, Lemma 1 shows that the truth of the flat path formula according to λ' does not change.

$\square$

Remark 1. Note, that the proof of Theorem 3 gives an algorithm that particularly allows to construct a fixed index κ from an RBM and $\langle\rho\rangle\gamma$ such that the "reverse" of Theorem 2 holds: If $\mathcal{CM}_\kappa(\mathfrak{M}, \rho, q), (q, \rho) \models \mathsf{E}\gamma$ then $\mathfrak{M}, q \models \langle\rho\rangle\gamma$. This construction of κ however does already "solve" the model checking problem and is computationally very expensive.

4.2   RTL* and Bounded Models

The case for **RTL*** is more sophisticated as the language is able to characterise more complex temporal patterns. It is still open whether the general case is decidable. In the following, we discuss the effects of various properties of RBMs with respect to **RTL***. For a given resource quantity it is possible to transform a structurally k-bounded RBM into a production-free RBM such that satisfaction of specific path formulae is preserved.

Proposition 8. *Let* $\rho \in \mathcal{R}^\pm$, *let* $\mathfrak{M}$ *be a structurally* k-*bounded RBM for* ρ, *and let* q *be a state in* $\mathfrak{M}$. *Then, we can construct a finite, production-free RBM* $\mathfrak{M}'$ *such that for every* $\mathcal{L}_{RTL^*}$-*path formula* γ *containing no more path quantifiers the following holds:*

$$\mathfrak{M}, q \models \langle\rho\rangle\gamma \quad if,\ and\ only\ if, \quad \mathfrak{M}', q' \models \langle\emptyset\rangle\gamma.$$

Proof (Sketch). We essentially take $\mathfrak{M}'$ as the reachability graph of $\mathfrak{M}$. This graph is build similar to the cover graph but no ω-nodes are introduced. Because there are only finitely many distinct state/resource combinations in $\mathfrak{M}$ (Prop. 4) the model is finite and obviously also production free.

Let $\mathfrak{M}, q \models \langle\rho\rangle\gamma$ and let λ be a ρ-feasible path satisfying γ. Then, the path obtained from λ by coupling each state with its available resources is a path in $\mathfrak{M}'$ satisfying γ. Conversely, let λ be a path in $\mathfrak{M}'$ satisfying γ. Then, $\lambda|_Q$ is a γ satisfying ρ-feasible path in $\mathfrak{M}$ due to the construction of $\mathfrak{M}'$. $\square$

The following corollary is needed for the model-checking results in Section 5.

Corollary 1. *Let $\rho \in \mathcal{R}^{\pm}$, let $\mathfrak{M}$ be a structurally k-bounded RBM for ρ, and let q be a state in $\mathfrak{M}$. Then, we can construct a finite Kripke model such that for every $\mathcal{L}_{RTL^*}$-path formula γ containing no more path quantifiers the following holds:*

$$\mathfrak{M}, q \models \langle \rho \rangle \gamma \quad \text{if, and only if,} \quad \mathfrak{M}', q' \models \mathsf{E}\gamma.$$

Lemma 3 states that loops that do not consume resources can be reduced to a fixed number of recurrences. For a path λ, we use $\lambda^{[n]}$ to denote the path which is equal to λ but each subsequence of states $q_1 q_2 \ldots q_k q$ occurring in λ with $q' := q_1 = q_2 = \cdots = q_k \neq q$ and $k > n$ where the transition $q' \rightarrow q'$ does not consume any resource (i.e. the first k states represent a consumption-free loop that is traversed k times) is replaced by $q_1 q_2 \ldots q_n q$. That is, states $q_{n+1} q_{n+2} \ldots q_k$ are omitted. Note, that $\lambda^{[n]}$ is also well-defined for pure Kripke models.

Lemma 3. *(a) Let $\mathfrak{M}$ be a Kripke model and γ be a path formula of **CTL*** containing no path quantifiers and length $|\gamma| = n$. For every path λ in $\Lambda_{\mathfrak{M}}$ we have that $\mathfrak{M}, \lambda \models \gamma$ if, and only if, $\mathfrak{M}, \lambda^{[n]} \models \gamma$.*

(b) Let $\mathfrak{M}$ be a production- and zero-free RBM and γ be an $\mathcal{L}_{RTL^*}$-path formula containing no path quantifiers and length $|\gamma| = n$. Then, for each path λ in $\Lambda_{\mathfrak{M}}$ the following holds true: $\mathfrak{M}, \lambda \models \gamma$ if, and only if, $\mathfrak{M}, \lambda^{[n]} \models \gamma$.

Note that we might want to allow to re-enter loops n-times for cases in which the formula has the form $\bigcirc\bigcirc\ldots\bigcirc\Diamond \varphi$.

5   Model Checking Resource-Bounded Tree Logic

We are mainly interested in the verification of systems. *Model checking* refers to the problem whether a formula φ is true in an RBM $\mathfrak{M}$ and a state q in $\mathfrak{M}$. For **CTL*** this problem is **PSPACE**-complete and for **CTL**, the fragment of **CTL*** in which every temporal operator is directly preceded by a path quantifier, it is **P**-complete [7]. So, we cannot hope for our problem to be computationally any better than **PSPACE** in the general setting; actually, it is still open whether it is decidable at all.

The following result shows that model checking **RTL** is decidable.

Theorem 3 (Model Checking RTL: Decidability). *The model-checking problem for **RTL** over RBMs is decidable.*

Proof (Idea). A more elaborated proof sketch can be found in Appendix A. The main idea is to encode an RBM as a Petri net and then use decision procedures for Petri nets, more precisely a variant of the reachability problem.   □

In the following, we consider the decidability of fragments of the full logic over special classes of RBMs (which of course, implies decidability of the restricted version over the same class of models).

Proposition 9 (Decidability: Production -, zero free). *The model-checking problem for* **RTL***$^\star_{\mathcal{R}\pm}$ over production- and zero-free* RBMs *is decidable.*

Proof (Sketch). According to Prop. 4 and Lemma 3 there are only finitely many ρ-feasible paths of interest for $\rho \in \mathcal{R}^{\pm}$. This set can be computed step by step. Then, for $\mathfrak{M}, q \models \langle\rho\rangle\gamma$ where γ is a path formula one has to check whether γ holds on one of these finitely many ρ-feasible paths starting in q. The model checking algorithm proceeds bottom-up.   □

From Corollary 1 we know that we can use a **CTL**** model checker over k-bounded models.

Proposition 10 (Decidability: k-bounded). *The model-checking problem for* **RTL***$^\star_{\mathcal{R}\pm}$ over k-bounded* RBMs *is decidable and* **PSPACE***-hard.*

By Prop. 6 and the observation that resources with an infinite quantity can be neglected in a production-free RBM we can show the following theorem.

Theorem 4 (Decidability: production free). *The model-checking problem for* **RTL**** over production-free* RBMs *is decidable and* **PSPACE***-hard.*

6   Conclusions, Related and Future Work

In this paper we have introduced resources into **CTL**** [6], which is arguably among the most important logics for computer science. The paper showed decidability results in the presence of some limiting constraints on the resource allocation for transitions in Kripke models.

While most agent models do not come with an explicit notion of resources, there is some recent work that take resources into account. [12] considers resources in conjunction with reasoning about an agent's goal-plan tree. Time, memory, and communication bounds are studied as resources in [2]. In [1] the abilities of agents under bounded memory are considered. Instead of asking for an arbitrary winning strategy a winning strategy in their setting has to obey given memory limitations.

A detailed analysis of the model checking complexity and the decidability question for the general case is left for future research. We are particularly interested in finding constraints that would make the extended logic's model-checking problem *efficiently* decidable for a relevant class of MAS.

Moreover, we are interested in the reasoning about and modelling of abilities of *multiple* agents having limited resources at their disposal. In [5] we consider an extension of the resource-bounded setting introduced here in the context of multi-agent systems (influenced by **ATL** [4] a logic for reasoning about strategic abilities of agents). In that paper we show that the problem is undecidable in general. On the other hand, if productions of resources are not allowed (as in [2]) it was recently shown that the model checking problem is decidable [3]. The authors of [3] do also propose a sound and complete axiomatisation of their resource-based extension of **ATL** (the logic is called *resource-bounded alternating-time temporal logic*).

Another direction is offered by Linear Logic. Although Girard's linear logic [9] is not directly suitable for model checking, we will be looking into possible combinations of linear logic fragments with our approach. One idea is to formalise resources and their production/consumption by means of linear logic formulae and hope to come up with an axiomatisation for our logic.

References

1. Ågotnes, T., Walther, D.: A logic of strategic ability under bounded memory. J. of Logic, Lang. and Inf. 18(1), 55–77 (2009)
2. Alechina, N., Logan, B., Nga, N.H., Rakib, A.: Verifying time, memory and communication bounds in systems of reasoning agents. In: AAMAS 2008: Proceedings of the 7th International Joint Conference on Autonomous Agents and Multiagent Systems, pp. 736–743 (2008)
3. Alechina, N., Logan, B., Nga, N.H., Rakib, A.: Resource-bounded alternating-time temporal logic. In: van der Hoek, W., Kaminka, G., Lespérance, Y., Luck, M., Sen, S. (eds.) Proceedings of the Ninth International Conference on Autonomous Agents and Multiagent Systems (AAMAS 2010), Toronto, Canada, IFAAMAS (to appear, May 2010)
4. Alur, R., Henzinger, T.A., Kupferman, O.: Alternating-time temporal logic. Journal of the ACM 49, 672–713 (2002)
5. Bulling, N., Farwer, B.: On the (Un-)Decidability of Model-Checking Resource-Bounded Agents. In: Coelho, H., Wooldridge, M. (eds.) Proceedings of the 19th European Conference on Artificial Intelligence (ECAI 2010), Porto, Portugal, August 16-20 (to appear, 2010)
6. Clarke, E.M., Emerson, E.A.: Design and synthesis of synchronization skeletons using branching time temporal logic. In: Kozen, D. (ed.) Logic of Programs 1981. LNCS, vol. 131, pp. 52–71. Springer, Heidelberg (1982)
7. Clarke, E.M., Emerson, E.A., Sistla, A.P.: Automatic verification of finite-state concurrent systems using temporal logic specifications. ACM Transactions on Programming Languages and Systems 8(2), 244–263 (1986)
8. Emerson, E.A., Halpern, J.Y.: Sometimes and not never revisited: On branching versus linear time temporal logic. In: Proceedings of the Annual ACM Symposium on Principles of Programming Languages, pp. 151–178 (1982)
9. Girard, J.-Y.: Linear logic. Theoretical Computer Science 50, 1–102 (1987)
10. Jančar, P.: Decidability of a temporal logic problem for petri nets. Theor. Comput. Sci. 74(1), 71–93 (1990)
11. Karp, R.M., Miller, R.E.: Parallel program schemata. Journal of Computer and System Sciences 3(2), 147–195 (1969)
12. Shaw, P., Farwer, B., Bordini, R.: Theoretical and experimental results on the goal-plan tree problem (short paper). In: Proceedings of AAMAS 2008, pp. 1379–1382 (2008)

A   Proof of the **RTL** Model Checking Result

Theorem 5. *The model-checking problem for* **RTL**$_{\mathcal{R}_\infty^\oplus}$ *over* RBMs *is decidable.*

Proof (Sketch). Firstly, we present the proof for feasible resource sets only. Proposition 3 allows to focus on resource-quantity sets from $\mathcal{R}^\oplus$. The main idea is to encode an RBM as a Petri net and then use decision procedures for Petri nets to solve the model checking problem. A Petri net is a tuple $N = (S, T, W, m^I)$ where S and T are non-empty and disjoint sets of places and transitions, $W : (S \times T) \cup (T \times S) \to \mathbb{N}_0$ represents arc weights that determine how many tokens are needed by and how many tokens are produced by each transition. Finally, $m^I : P \to \mathbb{N}_0$ is the initial marking, i.e., a distribution of tokens on the places of the net. A transition t is said to be enabled in a marking $m : P \to \mathbb{N}_0$) if $m(s) \geq W(s, t)$ for all $s \in S$. In this case, we also say, that t is m-enabled. Now, an m-enabled marking t may *fire* resulting in a new marking $m' := m - W(\cdot, t) + W(t, \cdot)$. Recursively, one defines the change that occurs given a sequence σ of subsequently fired transitions; thus, a *run* is an infinite sequence of subsequently enabled and firing transitions.

Now, we can encode an RBM $\mathfrak{M}$ with respect to a given set $Q' \subseteq Q_{\mathfrak{M}}$, and a feasible resource set ρ as a Petri net $N_{Q',\rho}(\mathfrak{M}) = (S, T, W, m^I)$. The main idea of encoding transitions is sketched in Figure 4. States q are encoded as places p_q and transitions between states as transitions between places. For each resource type a new place is created. For the initial marking function m^I we have that $m^I(p_q) = 1$ for all $q \in Q'$, $m^I(r) = \rho(r)$ for $r \in \mathcal{R}$, and 0 otherwise. A complete encoding of an RBM is shown in Figure 5. We denote (the unique) transition between place p_{q_i} and p_{q_j} by $t_{q_i q_j}$. (Note, that we are economical with our notation and reuse t already known from RBMs.)

Lemma 4. *Let ρ be a feasible resource set, $\mathfrak{M}$ an RBM, and $q \in Q_{\mathfrak{M}}$. Then, the following holds:*

$$q_0 q_1 \ldots \text{ is a } \rho\text{-feasible path in } (\mathfrak{M}, q) \text{ iff } \sigma = t_{q_0 q_1} t_{q_1 q_2} \ldots \text{ a run in } N_{\{q_0\},\rho}(\mathfrak{M}).$$

In order to model check specific formulae, we need to extend our encoding. For example, consider the formula $\langle \rho \rangle \lozenge \; \varphi$ where φ is a propositional formula and ρ

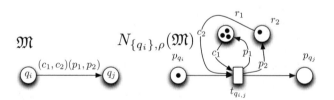

Fig. 4. Petri-net encoding $N_{\{q_i\},\rho}(\mathfrak{M})$ of an RBM $\mathfrak{M}$. Tokens inside the places r_k represent the amount of that resource (i.e., $\rho(r_1) = 3$ and $\rho(r_2) = 1$). Outgoing paths consume tokens and incoming paths produce tokens, labeled edges produce/consume the amount the edge is annotated with. E.g., if there is a token in place p_{q_i} and c_k tokens in place r_k then the token can be moved to p_{q_j} and p_k tokens can be moved to r_k for $k = 1, 2$.

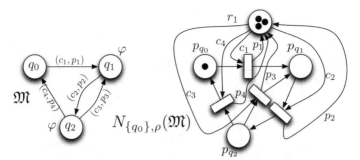

Fig. 5. Example of a complete encoding of an RBM $\mathfrak{M}$ where $\rho(r_1) = 3$

a feasible resource set. We can decompose the model checking problem into two parts:

1. Find a (finite) sequence of states feasible given ρ to a state in which φ holds; and
2. then arbitrarily extend this (finite) sequence to an infinite ρ-feasible path.

To achieve this, we introduce a new place that tells us (by marking it with a token) that φ has been made true. This place remains marked throughout the subsequent executions of the net and hence serves as an indicator of item 1 having been satisfied. To achieve this, given a propositional formula φ we extend the encoding $N_{\{q_0\},\rho}(\mathfrak{M})$ of $\mathfrak{M}$ to an encoding $N_{\{q_0\},\rho}(\mathfrak{M}, Q', \varphi)$ where $Q' \subseteq Q$ as explained in the following. The new Petri net is equal to $N_{\{q_0\},\rho}(\mathfrak{M})$ apart from the following modifications (Figure 6 illustrates the construction):

1. N' has two new places p_S and p_φ.
2. For each transition t in $N(\mathfrak{M})$ that corresponds to a transition $q \to q'$ in $\mathfrak{M}$ such that $q \in Q'$ and $q' \models^{\mathrm{prop}} \varphi$ we construct a duplicate with the fresh name $\hat{t}$ and include the following arcs: p_S is connected to t; t and $\hat{t}$ are connected to p_φ; and p_φ is also connected to $\hat{t}$; i.e. $W(p_S, t) = W(t, p_\varphi) = W(p_\varphi, \hat{t}) = W(\hat{t}, p_\varphi) = 1$.
3. p_S is initially marked.

The constructed Petri net $N_{\{q_0\},\rho}(\mathfrak{M}, \{q_0\}, \varphi)$ has the following properties.

Proposition 11

1. *A transition t can only be enabled if there is a token in p_S.*
2. *Once such a transition t has fired it can never be enabled again and there is a token in p_φ*
3. *A transitions $\hat{t}$ can only be enabled if there is a token in p_φ.*
4. *Once there is a token in p_φ it remains there forever.*
5. *p_S and p_φ contain at most one token and there is a token in p_S iff there is no token in p_φ.*

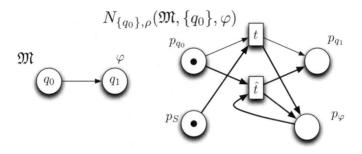

Fig. 6. The encoding $N_{\{q_0\},\rho}(\mathfrak{M}, \{q_0\}, \varphi)$ of an RBM $\mathfrak{M}$. The resource requirements are left out here.

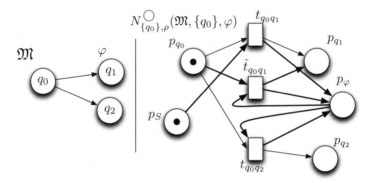

Fig. 7. The encoding $N^{\bigcirc}_{\{q_0\},\rho}(\mathfrak{M}, \{q_0\}, \varphi)$ of an RBM $\mathfrak{M}$. The resource requirements are left out here.

Additionally, for the next-operator we extend the construction and disable, in the first step, transition that do not result in a state satisfying φ. These transition are only enabled if there is a token in p_φ. The net is shown in Figure 7.

The next lemma provides the essential step to use decision procedures for Petri nets in order to solve the model checking problem.

Lemma 5

(a) $\mathfrak{M}, q_0 \models \langle \rho \rangle \Diamond \; \varphi$ iff there is a run in $N^\Diamond$ on which there is a token in p_φ at some moment where $N^\Diamond$ is the Petri net that equals $N_{\{q_0\},\rho}(\mathfrak{M}, Q_\mathfrak{M}, \varphi)$ with the exception that the initial token in p_S is in p_φ instead iff $q_0 \models^{prop} \varphi$.

(b) $\mathfrak{M}, q_0 \models \langle \rho \rangle \bigcirc \varphi$ iff there is a run in $N^{\bigcirc}_{\{q_0\},\rho}(\mathfrak{M}, \{q_0\}, \varphi)$ on which there is a token in p_φ at some moment.

(c) $\mathfrak{M}, q_0 \models \langle \rho \rangle \Box \; \varphi$ iff there is a run in $N^\Box$ on which there never is a token in $p_{\neg\varphi}$ where $N^\Box$ is the Petri net that equals $N_{\{q_0\},\rho}(\mathfrak{M}, Q_\mathfrak{M}, \neg\varphi)$ with the exception that the initial token in p_S is in $p_{\neg\varphi}$ instead iff $q_0 \not\models^{prop} \varphi$.

It remains to link the "until" case to Petri nets. For this, we consider the problem whether $\mathfrak{M}, q_0 \models \langle \rho \rangle \varphi \, \mathcal{U} \, \psi$. Let $\mathfrak{M}^\varphi$ be the restriction of $\mathfrak{M}$ to states in which φ holds. Now, $\mathfrak{M}^\mathcal{U}$ is the model that glues together $\mathfrak{M}^\varphi$ with $\mathfrak{M}$ as follows: Every state q in $\mathfrak{M}^\varphi$ is connected to a state $q' \in \mathfrak{M}$ if $q \rightarrow_{\mathfrak{M}} q'$ and q' satisfies ψ. The construction is illustrated in Figure 8.

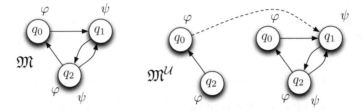

Fig. 8. Extending the RBM $\mathfrak{M}$ to $\mathfrak{M}^\mathcal{U}$ for $\varphi \, \mathcal{U} \, \psi$

Lemma 6. *Suppose $q_0 \models^{prop} \varphi$ (the other cases are trivially decidable). $\mathfrak{M}, q_0 \models \langle \rho \rangle \varphi \, \mathcal{U} \, \psi$ iff there is a run in $N^\mathcal{U}$ on which there is a token in p_ψ at some moment where $N^\mathcal{U}$ is the Petri net that equals $N_{\{q_0\},\rho}(\mathfrak{M}^\mathcal{U}, Q_{\mathfrak{M}^\mathcal{U}}, \psi)$ with the exception that the initial token in p_S is in p_ψ instead iff $q_0 \models^{prop} \psi$.*

Proof (of Lemma). The construction ensures that only states satisfying φ are visited until a state ψ is visited. The rest follows from Lemma 5(a). □

Finally, we show that the Petri net part in the previous two lemmata can be decided. Let a Petri net N and a pair (A, f) such that $A \subseteq S$ and $f : A \rightarrow \mathbb{N}_0$ be given. In [10] the following problem, here denoted by *ExtReach*, was shown to be decidable:

> Is there a run $\sigma = t_1 t_2 \ldots$ where t_1 is enabled by the initial marking $m_0 = m^I$ and firing t_1 leads to the successor marking m_1 and m_j enables t_{j+1} whose fireing leads to m_{j+1} for all $j > 1$, such that there are infinitely many indices i such that the marking m_i that occurs after t_i restricted to the states in A equals f (i.e., $m_i|_A = f$ for infinitely many i)?

We have the following reductions.

Lemma 7. *Assume the same notation as in Lemma 5 and 6.*

(a) There is a run in $N^\bigcirc$ on which there is a token in p_φ at some moment iff $(N^\bigcirc, (\{p_\varphi\}, f_1))$ is in ExtReach where f_1 is the constant function 1.

(b) There is a run in $N^\Diamond$ on which there is a token in p_φ at some moment iff $(N^\Diamond, (\{p_\varphi\}, f_1))$ is in ExtReach where f_1 is the constant function 1.

(c) There is a run in $N^\square$ on which there never is a token in $p_{\neg\varphi}$ iff $(N^\square, (\{p_{\neg\varphi}\}, f_0))$ is in ExtReach where f_0 is the constant function 0.

(d) There is a run in $N^\mathcal{U}$ on which there is a token in p_ψ at some moment iff $(N^\mathcal{U}, (\{p_\psi\}, f_1))$ is in ExtReach where f_1 is the constant function 1.

Proof (of Lemma). (a) The following follows from Proposition 11. There is a run on which there is a token in p_φ at some moment iff there is a run on which there is a token in p_φ infinitely often iff there is a run on which there is exactly one token in p_φ infinitely often iff $(N^\bigcirc, (\{p_\varphi\}, f_1))$ is in *ExtReach*.

(b-d) These cases are handled analogously. $\square$

The *ExtReach* problem is solved by applying the reachability problem for Petri nets. If a marking is reachable an appropriate sequence of transitions is constructed. This sequence can also be used to construct κ: One simply takes the maximum of all markings of all resource types along this sequence. If the state is not reachable, κ is chosen arbitrarily. $\square$

Finally, we also include non-feasible resource sets and get the main result.

Theorem 6 (Model CheckingRTL: Decidability). *The model-checking problem for* **RTL** *over* RBMs *is decidable.*

Proof (Sketch). We extend the previous construction to be able to deal with non-feasible resource sets.

For non-feasible initial resource sets, we can still have a feasible path, in case no resources with negative amount are ever required in the run (note that such resources can still be produced!).

We encode a non-feasible resource set by splitting each resource place r of the Petri net into a place for a positive number of resources, r, and a place for a negative number of resources, r^-.

Further, we need to ensure in our net, that whenever resources are produced a positive number of tokens is placed on the positive resource place (only if no tokens are present in the negative resource place) or a number of tokens is removed from the negative resource place. Combinations are possible, if the number of resources produced is larger than the negative number of resources currently available. In the latter case all resources are removed from the negative resource place and the remaining difference is placed into the positive place. Therefore, we introduce a special resource control state, r^{ctrl}, that "deactivates" the new part of the construction once a non-negative amount of resources is available.

In the following we will describe the construction in detail. Consider the transition of an RBM at the left-hand side of Figure 9. For simplicity, we only consider a single resource-type r. The transition consumes zero units of r and produces u units (note, that if the transition does also consume of this resource type we take the standard construction from Theorem 5). Suppose, we would like to model check a formula $\langle\rho\rangle\gamma$ with $\rho(r) = -d$, that is, there is an initial debt of d units of resource r. Firstly, we add a transition $t_{q_i q_j}$ from p_{q_i} to q_{q_j} which is only enabled if there are d units in the resource control state r^{ctrl} and a token on p_{q_i}. We add u transitions $t^1, \ldots, t^u$; $u - 1$ places $p^1, \ldots, p^{u-1}$; and $u - 1$ intermediate transitions $t^{p^1}, \ldots, t^{p^{u-1}}$. Their connections are shown in the right-hand part of Figure 9. Each transition t^i can only be enabled if there is a debt of resources (i.e. tokens in r^-). Such a transition takes one token from r^-

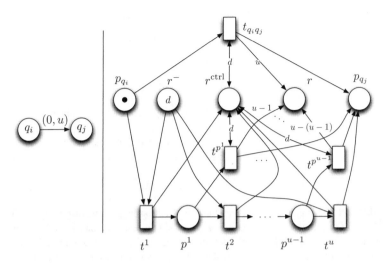

Fig. 9. Example of a PN construction for non-feasible resource sets: The left-hand RBM with a single resource r with $\rho(r) = -d$ is converted to the right-hand PN

and moves it to the control state r^{ctrl}. Once, there are d tokens in the control state the transitions t^{p^i} can be enabled (while t^i can no longer be enabled) and the remaining produced resources are added to the resource place r. The net has the following properties.

Proposition 12

1. *There are x tokens in r^- iff there are $d - x$ token in r^{ctrl} for $x \in \{0, \ldots, d\}$. (That is, r^- and r^{ctrl} are complementary places.)*
2. *Transitions $t_{q_i q_j}$ and $t^{p^1}, \ldots, t^{p^{u-1}}$ can only fire if there are d tokens in r^{ctrl}.*
3. *The number of tokens in r^{ctrl} is bounded by d and it is monotonically increasing.*
4. *The number of tokens in r^- is monotonically decreasing.*
5. *If there is a token in place p_{q_i} and there are d tokens in r^{ctrl} only the transition $t_{q_i q_j}$ is enabled.*
6. *There can only be tokens in r if there are no tokens in r^-.*

The next lemma shows that the net works as intended. The result follows from the previous proposition.

Lemma 8. *Let there be a token in p_{q_i}, $d' \leq d$ tokens in r^-, $d - d'$ tokens in r^{ctrl}, and no tokens in r. Let σ be the minimal length firing sequence such that there is a token in p_{q_j}. Then, after executing σ there are $\max\{0, d' - u\}$ tokens in r^-, $\min\{d, d - d' + u\}$ tokens in r^{ctrl}, and $\max\{0, u - d'\}$ tokens in r.*

On the other hand, if there is a token in p_{q_i}, d tokens in r^{ctrl}, zero tokens in r^- and k tokens in r then, after executing σ there are $k + u$ tokens in r, d tokens in r^{ctrl}, and zero tokens in r^-.   □

Reasoning about Multi-agent Domains Using Action Language $\mathcal{C}$: A Preliminary Study

Chitta Baral[1], Tran Cao Son[2], and Enrico Pontelli[2]

[1] Dept. Computer Science & Engineering, Arizona State University
chitta@asu.edu
[2] Dept. Computer Science, New Mexico State University
{tson,epontell}@cs.nmsu.edu

Abstract. This paper investigates the use of action languages, originally developed for representing and reasoning about single-agent domains, in modeling multi-agent domains. We use the action language $\mathcal{C}$ and show that minimal extensions are sufficient to capture several multi-agent domains from the literature. The paper also exposes some limitations of action languages in modeling a specific set of features in multi-agent domains.

1 Introduction and Motivation

Representing and reasoning in multi-agent domains are two of the most active research areas in *multi-agent system (MAS)* research. The literature in this area is extensive, and it provides a plethora of logics for representing and reasoning about various aspects of MAS domains. For example, the authors of [24] combine an action logic and a cooperation logic to represent and reason about the capabilities and the forms of cooperation between agents. The work in [16] generalizes this framework to consider domains where an agent may control only parts of propositions and to reason about strategies of agents. In [31], an extension of Alternating-time Temporal Logic is developed to facilitate strategic reasoning in multi-agent domains. The work in [30] suggests that decentralized partially observable Markov decision processes could be used to represent multi-agent domains, and discusses the usefulness of agent communication in multi-agent planning. In [18], an extension of Alternating-time Temporal Epistemic Logic is proposed for reasoning about choices. Several other works (e.g., [12,32]) discuss the problem of reasoning about knowledge in MAS.

Even though a large number of logics have been proposed in the literature for formalizing MAS, several of them have been designed to specifically focus on particular aspects of the problem of modeling MAS, often justified by a specific application scenario. This makes them suitable to address specific subsets of the general features required to model real-world MAS domains. Several of these logics are quite complex and require modelers that are transitioning from work on single agents to adopt a very different modeling perspective.

The task of generalizing some of these existing proposals to create a uniform and comprehensive framework for modeling different aspects of MAS domains is, to the best of our knowledge, still an open problem. Although we do not dispute the possibility

J. Dix, M. Fisher, and P. Novák (Eds.): CLIMA X, LNAI 6214, pp. 46–63, 2010.

of extending these existing proposals in various directions, the task does not seem easy. On the other hand, the need for a general language for MAS domains, with a formal and simple semantics that allows the verification of plan correctness, has been extensively motivated (e.g., [8]).

The state of affairs in formalizing multi-agent systems reflects the same trend that occurred in the early nineties, regarding the formalization of *single agent* domains. Since the discovery of the frame problem [22], several formalisms for representing and reasoning about dynamic domains have been proposed. Often, the new formalisms responded to the need to address shortcomings of the previously proposed formalisms within specific sample domains. For example, the well-known Yale Shooting problem [17] was invented to show that the earlier solutions to the frame problem were not satisfactory. A simple solution to the Yale Shooting problem, proposed by [2], was then shown not to work well with the Stolen Car example [20], etc. Action languages [15] have been one of the outcomes of this development, and they have been proved to be very useful ever since.

Action description languages, first introduced in [14] and further refined in [15], are formal models used to describe dynamic domains, by focusing on the representation of effects of actions. Traditional action languages (e.g., $\mathcal{A}$, $\mathcal{B}$, $\mathcal{C}$) have mostly focused on domains involving a single agent. In spite of different features and several differences between these action languages (e.g., concurrent actions, sensing actions, nondeterministic behavior), there is a general consensus on what are the essential components of an action description language in single agent domains. In particular, an action specification focuses on the *direct effects* of each action on the state of the world; the semantics of the language takes care of all the other aspects concerning the evolution of the world (e.g., the ramification problem).

The analogy between the development of several formalisms for single agent domains and the development of several logics for formalizing multi-agent systems indicates the need for, and the usefulness of, a formalism capable of dealing with multiple desired features in multi-agent systems. A natural question that arises is whether single agent action languages can be adapted to describe MAS. *This is the main question that we explore in this paper.*

In this paper, we attempt to answer the above question by investigating whether an action language developed for single agent domains can be used, with minimal modifications, to model interesting MAS domains. Our starting point is a well-studied and well-understood single agent action language—the language $\mathcal{C}$ [15]. We chose this language because it already provides a number of features that are necessary to handle multi-agent domains, such as concurrent interacting actions. The language is used to formalize a number of examples drawn from the multi-agent literature, describing different types of problems that can arise when dealing with multiple agents. Whenever necessary, we identify weaknesses of $\mathcal{C}$ and introduce simple extensions that are adequate to model these domains. The resulting action language provides a unifying framework for modeling several features of multi-agent domains. The language can be used as a foundation for different forms of reasoning in multi-agent domains (e.g., projection, validation of plans), which are formalized in the form of a query language. We expect that further development in this language will be needed to capture additional aspects such as agents' knowledge about other agents' knowledge. We will discuss them in the future.

We would like to note that, in the past, there have been other attempts to use action description languages to formalize multi-agent domains, e.g., [6]. On the other hand, the existing proposals address only some of the properties of the multi-agent scenarios that we deem to be relevant (e.g., focus only on concurrency).

Before we continue, let us discuss the desired features and the assumptions that we place on the target multi-agent systems. In this paper, we consider MAS domains as environments in which multiple agents can execute actions to modify the overall state of the world. We assume that

- Agents can execute actions concurrently;
- Each agent knows its own capabilities—but they may be unaware of the global effect of their actions;
- Actions executed by different agents can interact;
- Agents can communicate to exchange knowledge; and
- Knowledge can be private to an agent or shared among groups of agents.

The questions that we are interested in answering in a MAS domain involve

- *hypothetical reasoning*, e.g., what happens if agent A executes the action a; what happens if agent A executes a_1 while B executes b_1 at the same time; etc.
- *planning/capability*, e.g., can a specified group of agents achieve a certain goal from a given state of the world.

Variations of the above types of questions will also be considered. For example, what happens if the agents do not have complete information, if the agents do not cooperate, if the agents have preferences, etc.

To the best of our knowledge, this is the first investigation of how to adapt a single agent action language to meet the needs of MAS domains. It is also important to stress that the goal of this work is to create a framework for *modeling* MAS domains, with a query language that enables plan validation and various forms of reasoning. In this work, we do not deal with the issues of distributed plan generation—an aspect extensively explored in the literature. This is certainly an important research topic and worth pursuing but it is outside of the scope of this paper. We consider the work presented in this paper a necessary precondition to the exploration of distributed MAS solutions.

The paper is organized as follows. Section 2 reviews the basics of the action language $\mathcal{C}$. Section 3 describes a straightforward adaptation of $\mathcal{C}$ for MAS. The following sections (Sects. 4–5) show how minor additions to $\mathcal{C}$ can address several necessary features in representation and reasoning about MAS domains. Sect. 6 presents a query language that can be used with the extended $\mathcal{C}$. Sect. 7 discusses further aspects of MAS that the proposed extension of $\mathcal{C}$ cannot easily deal with. Sect. 8 presents the discussion and some conclusions.

2   Action Language $\mathcal{C}$

The starting point of our investigation is the action language $\mathcal{C}$ [15]—an action description language originally developed to describe single agent domains, where the agent is capable of performing non-deterministic and concurrent actions. Let us review a slight adaptation of the language $\mathcal{C}$.

A domain description in $\mathcal{C}$ builds on a language signature $\langle \mathcal{F}, \mathcal{A} \rangle$, where $\mathcal{F} \cap \mathcal{A} = \emptyset$ and $\mathcal{F}$ (resp. $\mathcal{A}$) is a finite collection of fluent (resp. action) names. Both the elements of $\mathcal{F}$ and $\mathcal{A}$ are viewed as propositional variables, and they can be used in formulae constructed using the traditional propositional operators. A propositional formula over $\mathcal{F} \cup \mathcal{A}$ is referred to simply as a *formula*, while a propositional formula over $\mathcal{F}$ is referred to as a *state formula*. A fluent literal is of the form f or $\neg f$ for any $f \in \mathcal{F}$.

A domain description D in $\mathcal{C}$ is a finite collection of axioms of the following forms:

$$\textbf{caused } \ell \textbf{ if } F \qquad\qquad\qquad \textit{(static causal law)}$$
$$\textbf{caused } \ell \textbf{ if } F \textbf{ after } G \qquad\qquad \textit{(dynamic causa laws)}$$

where ℓ is a fluent literal, F is a state formula, while G is a formula. The language also allows the ability to declare properties of fluents; in particular **non-inertial** ℓ declares that the fluent literal ℓ is to be treated as a non-inertial literal, i.e., the frame axiom is not applicable to ℓ.

A problem specification is obtained by adding an initial state description $\mathcal{I}$ to a domain D, composed of axioms of the form **initially** ℓ, where ℓ is a fluent literal.

The semantics of the language can be summarized using the following concepts. An *interpretation* I is a set of fluent literals, such that $\{f, \neg f\} \not\subseteq I$ for every $f \in \mathcal{F}$. Given an interpretation I and a fluent literal ℓ, we say that I satisfies ℓ, denoted by $I \models \ell$, if $\ell \in I$. The entailment relation $\models$ is extended to define the entailment $I \models F$ where F is a state formula in the usual way. An interpretation I is *complete* if, for each $f \in \mathcal{F}$, we have that $f \in I$ or $\neg f \in I$. An interpretation I is *closed* w.r.t. a set of static causal laws $\mathcal{SC}$ if, for each static causal law **caused** ℓ **if** F, if $I \models F$ then $\ell \in I$. Given an interpretation I and a set of static causal laws $\mathcal{SC}$, we denote with $Cl_{\mathcal{SC}}(I)$ the smallest set of literals that contains I and that is closed w.r.t. $\mathcal{SC}$. Given a domain description D, a *state* s in D is a complete interpretation which is closed w.r.t. the set of static causal laws in D.

The notions of interpretation and entailment over the language of $\mathcal{F} \cup \mathcal{A}$ are defined in a similar way.

Given a state s, a set of actions $A \subseteq \mathcal{A}$, and a collection of dynamic causal laws $\mathcal{DC}$, we define

$$Eff_{\mathcal{DC}}(s, A) = \left\{ \ell \mid (\textbf{ caused } \ell \textbf{ if } F \textbf{ after } G) \in \mathcal{DC}, s \,\dot\cup\, A \models G, s \models F \right\}$$

where $s \,\dot\cup\, A$ stands for $s \cup A \cup \{\neg a \mid a \in \mathcal{A} \setminus A\}$.

Let $D = \langle \mathcal{SC}, \mathcal{DC}, \mathcal{IN} \rangle$ be a domain, where $\mathcal{SC}$ are the static causal laws, $\mathcal{DC}$ are the dynamic causal laws and $\mathcal{IN}$ are the non-inertial axioms. The semantics of D is given by a transition system $(State_D, E_D)$, where $State_D$ is the set of all states and the transitions in E_D are of the form $\langle s, A, s' \rangle$, where s, s' are states, $A \subseteq \mathcal{A}$, and s' satisfies the property

$$s' = Cl_{\mathcal{SC}}(Eff_{\mathcal{DC}}(s, A) \cup ((s \setminus IFL) \cap s') \cup (\mathcal{IN} \cap s'))$$

where $IFL = \{f, \neg f \mid f \in \mathcal{IN} \text{ or } \neg f \in \mathcal{IN}\}$.

The original $\mathcal{C}$ language supports a query language (called $\mathcal{P}$ in [15]). This language allows queries of the form **necessarily** F **after** $A_1, \ldots, A_k$, where F is a state formula and $A_1, \ldots, A_k$ is a sequence of sets of actions (called a *plan*). Intuitively, the query asks whether each state s reached after executing $A_1, \ldots, A_k$ from the initial state has the property $s \models F$.

Formally, an initial state s_0 w.r.t. an initial state description $\mathcal{I}$ and a domain D is an element of $State_D$ such that $\{\ell \mid$ **initially** $\ell \in \mathcal{I}\} \subseteq s_0$. The transition function $\Phi_D : 2^{\mathcal{A}} \times State_D \rightarrow 2^{State_D}$ is defined as $\Phi_D(A, s) = \{s' \mid \langle s, A, s' \rangle \in E_D\}$, where $(State_D, E_D)$ is the transition system describing the semantics of D. This function can be extended to define Φ_D^*, which considers plans, where $\Phi_D^*([\,], s) = \{s\}$ and

$$\Phi_D^*([A_1, \ldots, A_n], s) = \begin{cases} \emptyset & \text{if } \Phi_D^*([A_1, \ldots, A_{n-1}], s) = \emptyset \vee \\ & \quad \exists s' \in \Phi_D^*([A_1, \ldots, A_{n-1}], s).[\Phi_D(A_n, s') = \emptyset] \\ \bigcup_{s' \in \Phi_D^*([A_1, \ldots, A_{n-1}], s)} \Phi_D(A_n, s') & \text{otherwise} \end{cases}$$

Let us consider an action domain D and an initial state description $\mathcal{I}$. A query **necessarily** F **after** $A_1, \ldots, A_k$ is *entailed* by $(D, \mathcal{I})$, denoted by

$$(D, \mathcal{I}) \models \textbf{necessarily } F \textbf{ after } A_1, \ldots, A_k$$

if for every s_0 initial state w.r.t. $\mathcal{I}$, we have that $\Phi_D^*([A_1, \ldots, A_k], s_0) \neq \emptyset$, and for each $s \in \Phi_D^*([A_1, \ldots, A_k], s_0)$ we have that $s \models F$.

3 $\mathcal{C}$ for Multi-agent Domains

In this section, we explore how far one of the most popular action languages developed for single agent domains, $\mathcal{C}$, can be used and adapted for multi-agent domains. We will discuss a number of incremental small modifications of $\mathcal{C}$ necessary to enable modeling MAS domains. We expect that similar modifications can be applied to other single-agent action languages with similar basic characteristics. We will describe each domain from the perspective of someone (the modeler) who has knowledge of everything, including the capabilities and knowledge of each agent. Note that this is *only a modeling perspective*—it does not mean that we expect individual agents to have knowledge of everything, we only expect the *modeler* to have such knowledge.

We associate to each agent an element of a set of *agent identifiers*, $\mathcal{AG}$. We will describe a MAS domain over a set of signatures $\langle \mathcal{F}_i, \mathcal{A}_i \rangle$ for each $i \in \mathcal{AG}$, with the assumption that $\mathcal{A}_i \cap \mathcal{A}_j = \emptyset$ for $i \neq j$. Observe that $\bigcap_{i \in S} \mathcal{F}_i$ may be not empty for some $S \subseteq \mathcal{AG}$. This represents the fact that fluents in $\bigcap_{i \in S} \mathcal{F}_i$ are relevant to all the agents in S.

The result is a $\mathcal{C}$ domain over the signature $\langle \bigcup_{i=1}^n \mathcal{F}_i, \bigcup_{i=1}^n \mathcal{A}_i \rangle$. We will require the following condition to be met: if **caused** ℓ **if** F **after** G is a dynamic law and $a \in \mathcal{A}_i$ appears in G, then the literal ℓ belongs to $\mathcal{F}_i$. This condition summarizes the fact that agents are aware of the direct effects of their actions. Observe that on the other hand, an agent might not know all the consequences of his own actions. For example, a deaf agent bumping into a wall might not be aware of the fact that his action causes noise observable by other agents. These global effects are captured by the modeler, through the use of static causal laws.

The next two sub-sections illustrate applications of the language in modeling co-operative multi-agent systems. In particular, we demonstrate how the language is already sufficiently expressive to model simple forms of cooperation between agents even though these application scenarios were not part of the original design of $\mathcal{C}$.

3.1 The Prison Domain

This domain has been originally presented in [24]. In this example, we have two prison guards, 1 and 2, who control two gates, the inner gate and the outer gate, by operating four buttons a_1, b_1, a_2, and b_2. Agent 1 controls a_1 and b_1, while agent 2 controls a_2 and b_2. If either a_1 or a_2 is pressed, then the state of the inner gate is toggled. The outer gate, on the other hand, toggles only if both b_1 and b_2 are pressed.

The problem is introduced to motivate the design of a logic for reasoning about the ability of agents to cooperate. Observe that neither of the agents can individually change the state of the outer gate. On the other hand, individual agents' actions can affect the state of the inner gate.

In $\mathcal{C}$, this domain can be represented as follows. The set of agents is $\mathcal{AG} = \{1, 2\}$. For agent 1, we have:

$$\mathcal{F}_1 = \{in\_open, out\_open, pressed(a_1), pressed(b_1)\}.$$

Here, in_open and out_open represent the fact that the inner gate and outer gate are open respectively. $pressed(X)$ says that the button X is pressed where $X \in \{a_1, b_1\}$. We have $\mathcal{A}_1 = \{push(a_1), push(b_1)\}$. This indicates that guard 1 can push buttons a_1 and b_1. Similarly, for agent 2, we have that

$$\mathcal{F}_2 = \{in\_open, out\_open, pressed(a_2), pressed(b_2)\} \quad \mathcal{A}_2 = \{push(a_2), push(b_2)\}$$

We assume that the buttons do not stay pressed—thus, $pressed(X)$, for $X \in \{a_1, b_1, a_2, b_2\}$, is a non-inertial fluent with the default value *false*. The domain specification (D_{prison}) contains:

> **non_inertial** $\neg pressed(X)$
> **caused** $pressed(X)$ **after** $push(X)$
> **caused** in_open **if** $pressed(a_1), \neg in\_open$
> **caused** in_open **if** $pressed(a_2), \neg in\_open$
> **caused** $\neg in\_open$ **if** $pressed(a_1), in\_open$
> **caused** $\neg in\_open$ **if** $pressed(a_2), in\_open$
> **caused** out_open **if** $pressed(b_1), pressed(b_2), \neg out\_open$
> **caused** $\neg out\_open$ **if** $pressed(b_1), pressed(b_2), out\_open$

where $X \in \{a_1, b_1, a_2, b_2\}$. The first statement declares that $pressed(X)$ is non-inertial and has *false* as its default value. The second statement describes the effect of the action $push(X)$. The remaining laws are static causal laws describing relationships between properties of the environment.

The dynamic causal laws are "local" to each agent, i.e., they involve fluents that are local to that particular agent; in particular, one can observe that each agent can achieve certain effects (e.g., opening/closing the inner gate) disregarding what the other agent is doing (just as if it was operating as a single agent in the environment). On the other hand, if we focus on a single agent in the domain (e.g., agent 1), then such agent will possibly see exogenous events (e.g., the value of the fluent in_open being changed by the other agent). On the other hand, the collective effects of actions performed by different agents are captured through "global" static causal laws. These are laws that the modeler introduces and they do not "belong" to any specific agent.

Let us now consider the queries that were asked in [24] and see how they can be answered by using the domain specification D_{prison}. In the first situation, both gates are closed, 1 presses a_1 and b_1, and 2 presses b_2. The question is whether the gates are open or not after the execution of these actions.

The initial situation is specified by the initial state description $\mathcal{I}_1$ containing

$$\mathcal{I}_1 = \{\ \textbf{initially}\ \neg in\_open,\quad \textbf{initially}\ \neg out\_open\ \}$$

In this situation, there is only one initial state $s_0 = \{\neg \ell \mid \ell \in \mathcal{F}_1 \cup \mathcal{F}_2\}$. We can show that

$$(D_{prison}, \mathcal{I}_1) \models \textbf{necessarily}\ out\_open \wedge in\_open\ \textbf{after}\ \{push(a_1), push(b_1), push(b_2)\}$$

If the outer gate is initially closed, i.e., $\mathcal{I}_2 = \{\ \textbf{initially}\ \neg out\_open\}$, then the set of actions $A = \{push(b_1), push(b_2)\}$ is both necessary and sufficient to open it:

$$(D_{prison}, \mathcal{I}_2) \models \textbf{necessarily}\ out\_open\ \textbf{after}\ X$$
$$(D_{prison}, \mathcal{I}_2) \models \textbf{necessarily}\ \neg out\_open\ \textbf{after}\ Y$$

where $A \subseteq X$ and $A \backslash Y \neq \emptyset$. Observe that the above entailment correspond to the environment logic entailment in [24].

3.2 The Credit Rating Domain

We will next consider an example from [16]; in this example, we have a property of the world that cannot be changed by a single agent. The example has been designed to motivate the use of logic of propositional control to model situations where different agents have different levels of control over fluents.

We have two agents, $\mathcal{AG} = \{w, t\}$, denoting the website and the telephone operator, respectively. Both agents can set/reset the credit rating of a customer. The credit rating can only be set to be ok (i.e., the fluent $credit\_ok$ set to *true*) if both agents agree. Whether the customer is a web customer (is_web fluent) or not can be set only by the website agent w. The signatures of the two agents are as follows:

$$\mathcal{F}_w = \{is\_web, credit\_ok\} \qquad \mathcal{A}_w = \left\{ \begin{array}{l} set\_web, reset\_web, \\ set\_credit(w), reset\_credit(w) \end{array} \right\}$$
$$\mathcal{F}_t = \{credit\_ok\} \qquad\qquad\ \mathcal{A}_t = \{set\_credit(t), reset\_credit(t)\}$$

The domain specification D_{bank} consists of:

> **caused** is_web **after** set_web
> **caused** $\neg is\_web$ **after** $reset\_web$
> **caused** $\neg credit\_ok$ **after** $reset\_credit(w)$
> **caused** $\neg credit\_ok$ **after** $reset\_credit(t)$
> **caused** $credit\_ok$ **after** $set\_credit(w) \wedge set\_credit(t)$

We can show that

$$(D_{bank}, \mathcal{I}_3) \models \textbf{necessarily } credit\_ok \textbf{ after } \{set\_credit(w), set\_credit(t)\}$$

where $\mathcal{I}_3 = \{ \textbf{initially } \neg\ell \mid \ell \in \mathcal{F}_w \cup \mathcal{F}_t\}$. This entailment also holds if $\mathcal{I}_3 = \emptyset$.

4   Adding Priority between Actions

The previous examples show that $\mathcal{C}$ is sufficiently expressive to model the basic aspects of agents executing cooperative actions within a MAS, focusing on capabilities of the agents and action interactions. This is not a big surprise, as discussed in [6]. We will now present a small extension of $\mathcal{C}$ that allows for the encodings of competitive behavior between agents, i.e., situations where actions of some agents can defeat the effects of other agents.

To make this possible, for each domain specification D, we assume the presence of a function $Pr_D : 2^{\mathcal{A}} \to 2^{\mathcal{A}}$. Intuitively, $Pr_D(A)$ denotes the actions whose effects will be accounted for when A is executed. This function allows, for example, to prioritize certain sets of actions. The new transition function $\Phi_{D,P}$ will be modified as follows:

$$\Phi_{D,P}(A, s) = \Phi_D(Pr_D(A), s)$$

where Φ_D is defined as in the previous section. Observe that if there is no competition among agents in D then Pr_D is simply the identity function.

4.1   The Rocket Domain

This domain was originally proposed in [31]. It was invented to motivate the development of a logic for reasoning about strategies of agents. This aspect will not be addressed by our formalization of this example as $\mathcal{C}$ lacks this capability. Nevertheless, the encoding is sufficient for determining the state of the world after the execution of actions by the agents.

We have a rocket, a cargo, and the agents $1, 2$, and 3. The rocket or the cargo are either in *london* or *paris*. The rocket can be moved by 1 and 2 between the two locations. The cargo can be loaded (unloaded) into the rocket by 1 and 3 (2 and 3). Agent 3 can refill the rocket if the tank is not full.

There are some constraints that limit the effects of the actions. They are:

- If 1 or 2 moves the rocket, the cargo cannot be loaded or unloaded;
- If two agents load/unload the cargo at the same time, the effect is the same as if it were loaded/unloaded by one agent.
- If one agent loads the cargo and another one unloads the cargo at the same time, the effect is that the cargo is loaded.

We will use the fluents $rocket(london)$ and $rocket(paris)$ to denote the location of the rocket. Likewise, $cargo(london)$ and $cargo(paris)$ denote the location of the cargo. in_rocket says that the cargo is inside the rocket and $tank\_full$ states that the tank is full. The signatures for the agents can be defined as follows.

$$\mathcal{F}_1 = \left\{ \begin{array}{l} in\_rocket, rocket(london), rocket(paris), \\ cargo(london), cargo(paris) \end{array} \right\}$$

$$\mathcal{A}_1 = \{ load(1), unload(1), move(1) \}$$

$$\mathcal{F}_2 = \left\{ \begin{array}{l} in\_rocket, rocket(london), rocket(paris), \\ cargo(london), cargo(paris) \end{array} \right\}$$

$$\mathcal{A}_2 = \{ unload(2), move(2) \}$$

$$\mathcal{F}_3 = \left\{ \begin{array}{l} in\_rocket, rocket(london), rocket(paris), \\ cargo(london), cargo(paris), tank\_full \end{array} \right\}$$

$$\mathcal{A}_3 = \{ load(3), refill \}$$

The constraints on the effects of actions induce priorities among the actions. The action *load* or *unload* will have no effect if *move* is executed. The effects of two *load* actions is the same as that of a single *load* action. Likewise, two *unload* actions have the same result as one *unload* action. Finally, *load* has a higher priority than *unload*.

To account for action priorities and the voting mechanism, we define $Pr_{D_{rocket}}$:

- $Pr_{D_{rocket}}(X) = \{move(a)\}$ if $\exists a. move(a) \in X$.
- $Pr_{D_{rocket}}(X) = \{load(a)\}$ if $move(x) \notin X$ for every $x \in \{1, 2, 3\}$ and $load(a) \in X$.
- $Pr_{D_{rocket}}(X) = \{unload(a)\}$ if $move(x) \notin X$ and $load(x) \notin X$ for every $x \in \{1, 2, 3\}$ and $unload(a) \in X$.
- $Pr_{D_{rocket}}(X) = X$ otherwise.

It is easy to see that $Pr_{D_{rocket}}$ defines priorities among the actions: if the rocket is moving then load/unload are ignored; load has higher priority than unload; etc. The domain specification consists of the following laws:

caused in_rocket **after** $load(i)$	$(i \in \{1, 3\})$
caused $\neg in\_rocket$ **after** $unload(i)$	$(i \in \{1, 2\})$
caused $tank\_full$ **if** $\neg tank\_full$ **after** $refill$	
caused $\neg tank\_full$ **if** $tank\_full$ **after** $move(i)$	$(i \in \{1, 2\})$
caused $rocket(london)$ **if** $rocket(paris), tank\_full$ **after** $move(i)$	$(i \in \{1, 2\})$
caused $rocket(paris)$ **if** $rocket(london), tank\_full$ **after** $move(i)$	$(i \in \{1, 2\})$
caused $cargo(paris)$ **if** $rocket(paris), in\_rocket$	
caused $cargo(london)$ **if** $rocket(london), in\_rocket$	

Let $\mathcal{I}_4$ consist of the following facts:

initially $tank\_full$	**initially** $rocket(paris)$
initially $cargo(london)$	**initially** $\neg in\_rocket$

We can show the following

$$(D_{rocket}, \mathcal{I}_4) \models \textbf{necessarily } cargo(paris)$$
$$\textbf{after } \{move(1)\}, \{load(3)\}, \{refill\}, \{move(3)\}.$$

Observe that without the priority function $Pr_{D_{rocket}}$, for every state s,

$$\Phi_{D_{rocket}}(\{load(1), unload(2)\}, s) = \emptyset,$$

i.e., the concurrent execution of the *load* and *unload* actions is unsuccessful.

5 Adding Reward Strategies

The next example illustrates the need to handle numbers and optimization to represent reward mechanisms. The extension of $\mathcal{C}$ is simply the introduction of *numerical fluents*—i.e., fluents that, instead of being simply true or false, have a numerical value. For this purpose, we introduce a new variant of the necessity query

$$\textbf{necessarily max } F \textbf{ for } \varphi \textbf{ after } A_1, \ldots, A_n$$

where F is a numerical expressions involving only numerical fluents, φ is a state formula, and $A_1, \ldots, A_n$ is a plan. Given a domain specification D and an initial state description $\mathcal{I}$, we can define for each fluent numerical expression F and plan α:

$$value(F, \alpha) = \max \{s(F) \mid s \in \Phi^*(\alpha, s_0), s_0 \text{ is an initial state w.r.t. } \mathcal{I}, D\}$$

where $s(F)$ denotes the value of the expression F in state s. This allows us to define the following notion of entailment of a query:

$$(D, \mathcal{I}) \models \textbf{necessarily max } F \textbf{ for } \varphi \textbf{ after } A_1, \ldots, A_n$$

if:

- $(D, \mathcal{I}) \models$ **necessarily** φ **after** $A_1, \ldots, A_n$
- for every other plan $B_1, \ldots, B_m$ such that $(D, \mathcal{I}) \models$ **necessarily** φ **after** $B_1, \ldots, B_m$ we have that $value(F, [A_1, \ldots, A_n]) \geq value(F, [B_1, \ldots, B_m])$.

The following example has been derived from [5] where it is used to illustrate the co-ordination among agents to obtain the highest possible payoff. There are three agents. Agent 0 is a normative system that can play one of two strategies—either st_0 or $\neg st_0$. Agent 1 plays a strategy st_1, while agent 2 plays the strategy st_2. The reward system is described in the following tables (the first is for st_0 and the second one is for $\neg st_0$).

st_0	st_1	$\neg st_1$
st_2	$1,1$	$0,0$
$\neg st_2$	$0,0$	$-1,-1$

$\neg st_0$	st_1	$\neg st_1$
st_2	$1,1$	$0,0$
$\neg st_2$	$0,0$	$1,1$

The signatures used by the agents are

$\mathcal{F}_0 = \{st_0, reward\}$ $\mathcal{F}_1 = \{st_1, reward_1\}$ $\mathcal{F}_2 = \{st_2, reward_2\}$
$\mathcal{A}_0 = \{play\_0, play\_not\_0\}$ $\mathcal{A}_1 \quad \{play\_1, play\_not\_1\}$ $\mathcal{A}_2 = \{play\_2, play\_not\_2\}$

The domain specification D_{gam} consists of:

> **caused** st_0 **after** $play\_0$ **caused** $\neg st_0$ **after** $play\_not\_0$
> **caused** st_1 **after** $play\_1$ **caused** $\neg st_1$ **after** $play\_not\_1$
> **caused** st_2 **after** $play\_2$ **caused** $\neg st_2$ **after** $play\_not\_2$
> **caused** $reward\_1 = 1$ **if** $\neg st_0 \land st_1 \land st_2$
> **caused** $reward\_2 = 1$ **if** $\neg st_0 \land st_1 \land st_2$
> **caused** $reward\_1 = 0$ **if** $\neg st_0 \land st_1 \land \neg st_2$
> **caused** $reward\_2 = 0$ **if** $\neg st_0 \land st_1 \land \neg st_2$
> $\ldots$
>
> **caused** $reward = a + b$ **if** $reward_1 = a \land reward_2 = b$

Assuming that $\mathcal{I} = \{$ **initially** $st_0\}$ we can show that

$$(D_{game}, \mathcal{I}) \models \text{ \textbf{necessarily max} } reward \textbf{ after } \{play_1, play_2\}.$$

6   Reasoning and Properties

In this section we discuss various types of reasoning that are directly enabled by the semantics of $\mathcal{C}$ that can be useful in reasoning about MAS. Recall that we assume that the action theories are developed from the perspective of a modeler who has the view of the complete MAS.

6.1   Capability Queries

Let us explore another range of queries, that are aimed at capturing the capabilities of agents. We will use the generic form **can** X **do** φ, where φ is a state formula and $X \subseteq \mathcal{AG}$ where $\mathcal{AG}$ is the set of agent identifiers of the domain. The intuition is to validate whether the group of agents X can guarantee that φ is achieved.

If $X = \mathcal{AG}$ then the semantics of the capability query is simply expressed as $(D, \mathcal{I}) \models$ **can** X **do** φ iff $\exists k. \exists A_1, \dots, A_k$ such that

$$(D, \mathcal{I}) \models \text{ \textbf{necessarily} } \varphi \textbf{ after } A_1, \dots, A_k.$$

If $X \neq \{1, \dots, n\}$, then we can envision different variants of this query.

Capability query with non-interference and complete knowledge: Intuitively, the goal is to verify whether the agents X can achieve φ when operating in an environment that includes *all* the agents, but the agents $\mathcal{AG} \setminus X$ are simply providing their knowledge and not performing actions or interfering. We will denote this type of queries as $\textbf{can}_k^n X$ **do** φ (n: not interference, k: availability of all knowledge).

The semantics of this type of queries can be formalized as follows: $(D, \mathcal{I}) \models \textbf{can}_k^n X$ **do** φ if there is a sequence of sets of actions $A_1, \dots, A_m$ with the following properties:

○ for each $1 \leq i \leq m$ we have that $A_i \subseteq \bigcup_{j \in X} \mathcal{A}_j$ (we perform only actions of agents in X)
○ $(D, \mathcal{I}) \models$ **necessarily** φ **after** $A_1, \dots, A_m$

Capability query with non-interference and projected knowledge: Intuitively, the query with projected knowledge assumes that not only the other agents ($\mathcal{AG} \setminus X$) are passive, but they also are not willing to provide knowledge to the active agents. We will denote this type of queries as $\textbf{can}_{\neg k}^n X$ **do** φ.

Let us refer to the *projection* of $\mathcal{I}$ w.r.t. X (denoted by $proj(\mathcal{I}, X)$) as the set of all the **initially** declarations that build on fluents of $\bigcup_{j \in X} \mathcal{F}_j$. The semantics of $\textbf{can}_{\neg k}^n$ type of queries can be formalized as follows: $(D, \mathcal{I}) \models \textbf{can}_{\neg k}^n X$ **do** φ if there is a sequence of sets of actions $A_1, \dots, A_m$ such that:

• for each $1 \leq i \leq m$ we have that $A_i \subseteq \bigcup_{j \in X} \mathcal{A}_j$
• $(D, proj(\mathcal{I}, X)) \models$ **necessarily** φ **after** $A_1, \dots, A_m$ (i.e., the objective will be reached irrespective of the initial configuration of the other agents)

Capability query with interference: The final version of capability query takes into account the possible interference from other agents in the system. Intuitively, the query with interference, denoted by **can**^{i} X **do** φ, implies that the agents X will be able to accomplish X in spite of other actions performed by the other agents.

The semantics is as follows: $(D, \mathcal{I}) \models$ **can**^{i} X **do** φ if there is a sequence of sets of actions $A_1, \ldots, A_m$ such that:

- for each $1 \leq i \leq m$ we have that $A_i \subseteq \bigcup_{j \in X} \mathcal{A}_j$
- for each sequence of sets of actions $B_1, \ldots, B_m$, where $\bigcup_{j=1}^{m} B_j \subseteq \bigcup_{j \notin X} \mathcal{A}_j$, we have that $(D, \mathcal{I}) \models$ **necessarily** φ **after** $(A_1 \cup B_1), \ldots, (A_m \cup B_m)$.

6.2 Inferring Properties of the Theory

The form of queries explored above allows us to investigate some basic properties of a multi-agent action domain.

Agent Redundancy: agent redundancy is a property of $(D, \mathcal{I})$ which indicates the ability to remove an agent to accomplish a goal. Formally, agent i is redundant w.r.t. a state formula φ and an initial state $\mathcal{I}$ if $(D, \mathcal{I}) \models$ **can** $X \setminus \{i\}$ **do** φ. The "level" of necessity can be refined, by adopting different levels of **can** (e.g., **can**$^n_{\neg k}$ implies that the knowledge of agent i is not required); it is also possible to strengthen it by enabling the condition to be satisfied for *any* $\mathcal{I}$.

Agent Necessity: agent necessity is symmetrical to redundancy—it denotes the inability to accomplish a property φ if an agent is excluded. Agent i is necessary w.r.t. φ and $(D, \mathcal{I})$ if for all sequences of sets of actions $A_1, \ldots, A_m$, such that for all $1 \leq j \leq m$ $A_j \cap \mathcal{A}_i = \emptyset$, we have that it is not the case that

$$(D, \mathcal{I}) \models \textbf{necessarily } \varphi \textbf{ after } A_1, \ldots, A_m.$$

We can also define different degrees of necessity, depending on whether the knowledge of i is available (or it should be removed from I) and whether i can interfere.

6.3 Compositionality

The formalization of multi-agent systems in $\mathcal{C}$ enables exploring the effects of composing domains; this is an important property, that allows us to model dynamic MAS systems (e.g., where new agents can join an existing coalition).

Let D_1, D_2 be two domains and let us indicate with $\langle \mathcal{F}_i^1, \mathcal{A}_i^1 \rangle_{i \in AG_1}$ and $\langle \mathcal{F}_i^2, \mathcal{A}_i^2 \rangle_{i \in AG_2}$ the agent signatures of D_1 and D_2. We assume that all actions sets are disjoint, while we allow $(\bigcup_{i \in AG_1} \mathcal{F}_i^1) \cap (\bigcup_{i \in AG_2} \mathcal{F}_i^2) \neq \emptyset$.

We define the two instances $(D_1, \mathcal{I}_1)$ and $(D_2, \mathcal{I}_2)$ to be *composable* w.r.t. a state formula φ if $(D_1, \mathcal{I}_1) \models$ **can** AG_1 **do** φ or $(D_2, \mathcal{I}_2) \models$ **can** AG_2 **do** φ implies

$$(D_1 \cup D_2, \mathcal{I}_1 \cup \mathcal{I}_2) \models \textbf{can } AG_1 \cup AG_2 \textbf{ do } \varphi$$

Two instances are composable if they are composable w.r.t. all formulae φ. Domains D_1, D_2 are composable if all the instances $(D_1, \mathcal{I}_1)$ and $(D_2, \mathcal{I}_2)$ are composable.

7   Reasoning with Agent Knowledge

In this section, we will consider some examples from [12,30,18] which address another aspect of modeling MAS, i.e., the exchange of knowledge between agents and the reasoning in presence of incomplete knowledge. The examples illustrate the limitation of $\mathcal{C}$ as a language for multi-agent domains and the inadequacy of modeling MAS from the perspective of an omniscient modeler.

7.1   Heaven and Hell Domain: The Modeler's Perspective

This example has been drawn from [30], where it is used to motivate the introduction of decentralized POMDP and its use in multi-agent planning. The following formalization does not consider the rewards obtained by the agents after the execution of a particular plan.

In this domain, there are two agents 1 and 2, a priest p, and three rooms r_1, r_2, r_3. Each of the two rooms r_2 and r_3 is either heaven or hell. If r_2 is heaven then r_3 is hell and vice versa. The priest has the information where heaven/hell is located. The agents 1 and 2 do not know where heaven/hell is; but, by visiting the priest, they can receive the information that tells them where heaven is. 1 and 2 can also exchange their knowledge about the location of $heaven$. 1 and 2 want to meet in heaven.

The signatures for the three agents are as follows ($k, h \in \{1, 2, 3\}$):

$$\mathcal{F}_1 = \{heaven_1^2, heaven_1^3, at_1^k\} \qquad \mathcal{A}_1 = \{m_1(k, h), ask_1^2, ask_1^p\}$$
$$\mathcal{F}_2 = \{heaven_2^2, heaven_2^3, at_2^k\} \qquad \mathcal{A}_2 = \{m_2(k, h), ask_2^1, ask_2^p\}$$
$$\mathcal{F}_p = \{heaven_p^2, heaven_p^3\} \qquad \mathcal{A}_p = \emptyset$$

Intuitively, $heaven_i^j$ denotes that i knows that $heaven$ is in the room j and at_i^j denotes that i is at the room j. ask_i^j is an action whose execution will allow i to know where $heaven$ is if j knows where $heaven$ is. On the other hand, $m_i(k, h)$ encodes the action of moving i from the room k to the room h.

Observe that the fact that i does not know the location of $heaven$ is encoded by the formula $\neg heaven_i^2 \wedge \neg heaven_i^3$.

The domain specification D_{hh} contains the following laws:

caused $heaven_1^j$ **if** $heaven_x^j$ **after** ask_1^x	$(j \in \{2, 3\}, x \in \{2, p\})$
caused $heaven_2^j$ **if** $heaven_x^j$ **after** ask_2^x	$(j \in \{2, 3\}, x \in \{1, p\})$
caused at_i^j **if** at_i^k **after** $m_i(k, j)$	$(i \in \{1, 2, p\}, j, k \in \{1, 2, 3\})$
caused $\neg at_i^j$ **if** at_i^k	$(i \in \{1, 2, p\}, j, k \in \{1, 2, 3\}, j \neq k)$
caused $\neg heaven_i^2$ **if** $heaven_i^3$	$(i \in \{1, 2, p\}, j \in \{2, 3\})$
caused $\neg heaven_i^3$ **if** $heaven_i^2$	$(i \in \{1, 2, p\}, j \in \{2, 3\})$

The first two laws indicate that if 1 (or 2) asks 2 or p (or 1 or p) for the location of $heaven$, then 1 (or 2) will know where $heaven$ is if $2/p$ (or $1/p$) has this information. The third law encodes the effect of moving between rooms by the agents. The fourth law represents the static law indicating that one person can be at one place at a time.

Let us consider an instance that has initial state described by $\mathcal{I}_5$ ($j \in \{2, 3\}$):

initially at_1^1	**initially** at_2^2	**initially** $heaven_p^2$
initially $\neg heaven_1^j$	**initially** $\neg heaven_2^j$	

We can show that

$$(D_{hh}, \mathcal{I}_5) \models \textbf{necessarily } at_1^2 \wedge at_2^2 \textbf{ after } \{ask_1^p\}, \{m_1(1, 2)\}$$

7.2 Heaven and Hell: The Agent's Perspective

The previous encoding of the domain has been developed considering the perspective of a domain modeler, who has complete knowledge about the world and all the agents. This perspective is reasonable in the domains encountered in the previous sections. Nevertheless, this perspective makes a difference when the behavior of one agent depends on knowledge that is not immediately available, e.g., agent 1 does not know where $heaven$ is and needs to acquire this information through knowledge exchanges with other agents. The model developed in the previous subsection is adequate for certain reasoning tasks (e.g., plan validation) but it is weak when it comes to tasks like planning.

An alternative model can be devised by looking at the problem from the perspective of each individual agent (not from a central modeler). This can be captured through an adaptation of the notion of sensing actions discussed in [25,26]. Intuitively, a sensing action allows for an agent to establish the truth value of unknown fluents. A sensing action a can be specified by laws of the form

$$\textbf{determines } l_1, \ldots, l_k \textbf{ if } F \textbf{ after } a$$

where $l_1, \ldots, l_k$ are fluent literals, F is a state formula, and a is a sensing action. Intuitively, a can be executed only when F is true and after its execution, one of $l_1, \ldots, l_k$ is set to true and all the others are set to false. The semantics of $\mathcal{C}$ extended with sensing actions can be defined in a similar fashion as in [26] and is omitted here for lack of space. It suffices to say that the semantics of the language should now account for different possibilities of the multi-agent systems due to incomplete information of the individual agents.

The signatures for the three agents are as follows ($k, h \in \{1, 2, 3\}$):

$$\mathcal{F}_1 = \{heaven_1^2, heaven_1^3, ok_1^2, ok_1^p, at_1^k\} \quad \mathcal{A}_1 = \{m_1(k, h), ask_1^2, ask_1^p, know?_1^2, know?_1^p\}$$
$$\mathcal{F}_2 = \{heaven_2^2, heaven_2^3, ok_2^1, ok_2^p, at_2^k\} \quad \mathcal{A}_2 = \{m_2(k, h), ask_2^1, ask_2^p, know?_2^1, know?_2^p\}$$
$$\mathcal{F}_p = \{heaven_p^2, heaven_p^3\} \quad \mathcal{A}_p = \emptyset$$

Intuitively, the fluent ok_y^x denotes the fact that agent y knows that agent x knows the location of heaven. The initial state for 1 is given by $I_5^1 = \{$ **initially** $at_1^1,$ **initially** $ok_1^p \}$. Similarly, the initial state for 2 is $I_5^2 = \{$ **initially** $at_2^2,$ **initially** $ok_2^p \}$, and for p is $I_5^p = \{$ **initially** $heaven_p^2 \}$. The domain specification D_1 for 1 include the last four statements of D_{hh} and the following sensing action specifications:

determines $heaven_1^2, heaven_1^3$ **if** ok_1^x **after** ask_1^x	$(x \in \{2, p\})$
determines $ok_1^x, \neg ok_1^x$ **after** $know?_1^x$	$(x \in \{2, p\})$

The domain specification D_2 for 2 is similar. The domain specification D_p consists of only the last two static laws of D_{hh}. Let $D'_{hh} = D_1 \cup D_2 \cup D_p$ and $I'_5 = I_5^1 \cup I_5^2 \cup I_5^p$, we can show that

$$(D'_{hh}, I'_5) \models \textbf{necessarily } heaven_1^2 \wedge heaven_2^2 \textbf{ after } \{ask_1^p\}, \{know?_2^1\}, \{ask_2^1\}.$$

7.3   Beyond $\mathcal{C}$ with Sensing Actions

This subsection discusses an aspect of modeling MAS that cannot be easily dealt with in $\mathcal{C}$, even with sensing actions, i.e., representing and reasoning about knowledge of agents. In Section 7.1, we use two different fluents to model the knowledge of an agent about properties of the world, similar to the approach in [26]. This approach is adequate for several situations. Nevertheless, the same approach could become quite cumbersome if complex reasoning about knowledge of other agents is involved.

Let us consider the well known *Muddy Children* problem [12]. Two children are playing outside the house. Their father comes and tells them that at least one of them has mud on his/her forehead. He then repeatedly asks "do you know whether your forehead is muddy or not?". The first time, both answer "no" and the second time, both say 'yes'. It is known that the father and the children can see and hear each other.

The representation of this domain in $\mathcal{C}$ is possible, but it would require a large number of fluents (that describe the knowledge of each child, the knowledge of each child about the other child, etc.) as well as a formalization of the axioms necessary to express how knowledge should be manipulated, similar to the fluents ok_i^j in the previous example.

A more effective approach is to introduce explicit knowledge operators (with manipulation axioms implicit in their semantics—e.g., as operators in a S5 modal logic) and use them to describe agents state. Let us consider a set of modal operators $\mathbf{K}_i$, one for each agent. A formula such as $\mathbf{K}_i \varphi$ denotes that agent i knows property φ. Knowledge operators can be nested; in particular, $\mathbf{K}^*_G \psi$ denotes all formulae with arbitrary nesting of $\mathbf{K}_G$ operators (G being a set of agents).

In our example, let us denote the children with 1 and 2, m_i as a fluent to denote whether i is muddy or not. The initial state of the world can then be described as follows:

$$\textbf{initially } m_1 \wedge m_2 \tag{1}$$

$$\textbf{initially } \neg \mathbf{K}_i m_i \wedge \neg \mathbf{K}_i \neg m_i \tag{2}$$

$$\textbf{initially } \mathbf{K}^*(m_1 \vee m_2) \tag{3}$$

$$\textbf{initially } \mathbf{K}^*_{\{1,2\} \setminus \{i\}} m_i \tag{4}$$

$$\textbf{initially } \mathbf{K}^*(\mathbf{K}^*_{\{1,2\} \setminus \{i\}} m_i \vee \mathbf{K}^*_{\{1,2\} \setminus \{i\}} \neg m_i) \tag{5}$$

where $i \in \{1, 2\}$. (1) states that all the children are muddy. (2) says that i does not know whether he/she is muddy. (3) encodes the fact that the children share the common knowledge that at least one of them is muddy. (4) captures the fact that each child can see the other child. Finally, (5) represents the common knowledge that each child knows the muddy status of the other one.

The actions used in this domain would enable agents to gain knowledge; e.g., the 'no' answer of child 1 allows child 2 to learn $\mathbf{K}_1(\neg \mathbf{K}_1 m_1 \wedge \neg \mathbf{K}_1 \neg m_1)$. This, together with the initial knowledge, would be sufficient for 2 to conclude $\mathbf{K}_2 m_2$. A discussion of how these inferences occur can be found, for example, in [12].

8   Discussion and Conclusion

In this paper, we presented an investigation of the use of the $\mathcal{C}$ action language to model MAS domains. $\mathcal{C}$, as several other action languages, is interesting as it provides well studied foundations for knowledge representation and for performing several types of reasoning tasks. Furthermore, the literature provides a rich infrastructure for the implementation of action languages (e.g., through translational techniques [27]). The results presented in this paper identify several interesting features that are necessary for modeling MAS, and they show how many of these features can be encoded in $\mathcal{C}$—either directly or with simple extensions of the action language. We also report challenging domains for $\mathcal{C}$.

There have been many agent programming languages such as the BDI agent programming AgentSpeak [23], (as implemented in Jason [4]), JADE [3] (and its extension Jadex [7]), ConGolog [10], IMPACT [1], 3APL [9], GOAL [19]. A good comparison of many of these languages can be found in [21].

We would like to stress that the paper does not introduce a new agent "programming language", in the style of languages mentioned above. Rather, we bring an action language perspective, where the concern is on succinctly and naturally specifying the transition between worlds due to actions. Thus our focus is how to extend actions languages to the multi-agent domain in a way to capture various aspects of multi-agent reasoning. The issues of implementation and integration in a distributed environment are interesting, but outside of the scope of this paper. To draw an analogy, what we propose in this paper is analogous to the role of situation calculus or PDDL in the description of single-agent domains, which describe the domains without providing implementation constructs for composing programs, as in Golog/ConGolog or GOAL. As such, our proposal could provide the underlying representation formalism for the development of an agent programming language; on the other hand, it could be directly used as input to a reasoning system, e.g., a planner [8]. Our emphasis in the representation is exclusively on the description of effects of actions; this distinguishes our approach from other logic-based formalisms, such as those built on MetateM [13].

Although our proposal is not an agent programming language, it is still interesting to analyze it according to the twelve dimensions discussed in [11] and used in [21];

1. *Purpose of use:* the language is designed for formalization and verification of MAS.
2. *Time:* the language does not have explicit references to time.
3. *Sensing:* the language supports sensing actions.
4. *Concurrency:* our proposed language enables the description of concurrent and interacting actions.
5. *Nondeterminism:* the language naturally supports nondeterminism.
6. *Agent knowledge:* our language allows for the description of agents with incomplete knowledge and can be extended to handle uncertainty.
7. *Communication:* this criteria is not applicable to our language.

8. *Team working:* the language could be used for describing interaction between agents including coordination [28] and negotiation [29].
9. *Heterogeneity and knowledge sharing:* the language does not force the agents to use the same ontology.
10. *Programming style:* this criteria is not applicable to our language since it is not an agent programming language.
11. *Modularity:* our language does not provide any explicit mechanism for modularizing the knowledge bases.
12. *Semantics:* our proposal has a clear defined semantics, which is based on the transition system between states.

The natural next steps in this line of work consist of *(1)* exploring the necessary extensions required for a more natural representation and reasoning about knowledge of agents in MAS domains (see Sect. 7); *(2)* adapting the more advanced forms of reasoning and implementation proposed for C to the case of MAS domains; *(3)* investigating the use of the proposed extension of C in formalizing distributed systems.

Acknowledgement. The last two authors are partially supported by the NSF grants IIS-0812267, CBET-0754525, CNS-0220590, and CREST-0420407.

References

1. Subrahmanian, V.S., Bonatti, P., Dix, J., Eiter, T., Kraus, S., Ozcan, F., Ross, R.: Heterogeneous Agent Systems: Theory and Implementation. MIT Press, Cambridge (2000)
2. Baker, A.: A simple solution to the Yale Shooting Problem. In: KRR, pp. 11–20 (1989)
3. Bellifemine, F.L., Caire, G., Greenwood, D.: Developing Multi-Agent Systems with JADE. J. Wiley & Sons, Chichester (2007)
4. Bordini, R.H., Hübner, J.F., Wooldridge, M.: Programming Multi-agent Systems in AgentSpeak using Jason. J. Wiley and Sons, Chichester (2007)
5. Boella, G., van der Torre, L.: Enforceable social laws. In: AAMAS 2005, pp. 682–689. ACM, New York (2005)
6. Boutilier, C., Brafman, R.I.: Partial-order planning with concurrent interacting actions. J. Artif. Intell. Res (JAIR) 14, 105–136 (2001)
7. Braubach, L., Pokahr, A., Lamersdorf, W.: Jadex: a BDI-Agent System Combining Middleware and Reasoning. In: Software Agent-based Applications, Platforms and Development Kits. Springer, Heidelberg (2005)
8. Brenner, M.: Planning for Multi-agent Environments: From Individual Perceptions to Coordinated Execution. In: Work. on Multi-agent Planning and Scheduling, ICAPS, pp. 80–88 (2005)
9. Dastani, M., Dignum, F., Meyer, J.J.: 3APL: A Programming Language for Cognitive Agents. ERCIM News, European Research Consortium for Informatics and Mathematics, Special issue on Cognitive Systems (53) (2003)
10. De Giacomo, G., Lespèrance, Y., Levesque, H.J.: ConGolog, a concurrent programming language based on the situation calculus. Artificial Intelligence 121(1–2), 109–169 (2000)
11. Jennings, N., Sycara, K., Wooldridge, M.: A roadmap of agent research and development. Autonomous Agents and Multi-Agent Systems 1, 7–38 (1998)
12. Fagin, R., Halpern, J., Moses, Y., Vardi, M.: Reasoning about Knowledge. MIT Press, Cambridge (1995)

13. Fisher, M.: A survey of Concurrent METATEM – the language and its applications. In: Gabbay, D.M., Ohlbach, H.J. (eds.) ICTL 1994. LNCS (LNAI), vol. 827, pp. 480–505. Springer, Heidelberg (1994)
14. Gelfond, M., Lifschitz, V.: Representing actions and change by logic programs. Journal of Logic Programming 17(2,3,4), 301–323 (1993)
15. Gelfond, M., Lifschitz, V.: Action languages. ETAI 3(6) (1998)
16. Gerbrandy, J.: Logics of propositional control. In: AAMAS 2006, pp. 193–200. ACM, New York (2006)
17. Hanks, S., McDermott, D.: Nonmonotonic logic and temporal projection. Artificial Intelligence 33(3), 379–412 (1987)
18. Herzig, A., Troquard, N.: Knowing how to play: uniform choices in logics of agency. In: AAMAS 2006, pp. 209–216 (2006)
19. de Boer, F.S., Hindriks, K.V., van der Hoek, W., Ch, J.-J.: Meyer. A verification framework for agent programming with declarative goals. Journal of Applied Logic 5, 277–302 (2005)
20. Kautz, H.: The logic of persistence. In: Proceedings of AAAI 1986, pp. 401–405. AAAI Press, Menlo Park (1986)
21. Mascardi, V., Martelli, M., Sterling, L.: Logic-Based Specification Languages for Intelligent Software Agents. Theory and Practice of Logic Programming 4(4), 495–537
22. McCarthy, J., Hayes, P.: Some philosophical problems from the standpoint of artificial intelligence. Machine Intelligence 4, 463–502 (1969)
23. Rao, A.S.: AgentSpeak(L): BDI Agents Speak Out in a Logical Computable Language. In: Perram, J., Van de Velde, W. (eds.) MAAMAW 1996. LNCS, vol. 1038, pp. 42–55. Springer, Heidelberg (1996)
24. Sauro, L., Gerbrandy, J., van der Hoek, W., Wooldridge, M.: Reasoning about action and cooperation. In: AAMAS 2006, pp. 185–192. ACM Press, New York (2006)
25. Scherl, R., Levesque, H.: Knowledge, action, and the frame problem. Artificial Intelligence 144(1-2) (2003)
26. Son, T.C., Baral, C.: Formalizing sensing actions - a transition function based approach. Artificial Intelligence 125(1-2), 19–91 (2001)
27. Son, T.C., Baral, C., Tran, N., McIlraith, S.: Domain-dependent knowledge in answer set planning. ACM Trans. Comput. Logic 7(4), 613–657 (2006)
28. Son, T.C., Sakama, C.: Reasoning and Planning with Cooperative Actions for Multiagents Using Answer Set Programming. In: Baldoni, M., Bentahar, J., van Riemsdijk, M.B., Lloyd, J. (eds.) DALT 2009. LNCS, vol. 5948, pp. 208–227. Springer, Heidelberg (2010)
29. Son, T.C., Pontelli, E., Sakama, C.: Logic Programming for Multiagent Planning with Negotiation. In: Hill, P.M., Warren, D.S. (eds.) Logic Programming. LNCS, vol. 5649, pp. 99–114. Springer, Heidelberg (2009)
30. Spaan, M., Gordon, G.J., Vlassis, N.A.: Decentralized planning under uncertainty for teams of communicating agents. In: AAMAS 2006, pp. 249–256 (2006)
31. van der Hoek, W., Jamroga, W., Wooldridge, M.: A logic for strategic reasoning, pp. 157–164. ACM, New York (2005)
32. van Ditmarsch, H.P., van der Hoek, W., Kooi, B.P.: Concurrent Dynamic Epistemic Logic for MAS. In: AAMAS (2003)

Model Checking Normative Agent Organisations[*]

Louise Dennis[1], Nick Tinnemeier[2], and John-Jules Meyer[2]

[1] Department of Computer Science, University of Liverpool, Liverpool, U.K.
L.A.Dennis@csc.liv.ac.uk
[2] Department of Information and Computing Sciences,
Utrecht University, Utrecht, The Netherlands
{nick,jj}@cs.uu.nl

Abstract. We present the integration of a normative programming language in the MCAPL framework for model checking multi-agent systems. The result is a framework facilitating the implementation and verification of multi-agent systems coordinated via a normative organisation. The organisation can be programmed in the normative language while the constituent agents may be implemented in a number of (BDI) agent programming languages.

We demonstrate how this framework can be used to check properties of the organisation and of the individual agents in an LTL based property specification language. We show that different properties may be checked depending on the information available to the model checker about the internal state of the agents. We discuss, in particular, an error we detected in the organisation code of our case study which was only highlighted by attempting a verification with "white box" agents.

1   Introduction

Since Yoav Shoham coined the term "agent-oriented programming" [19], many dedicated languages, interpreters and platforms to facilitate the construction of multi-agent systems have been proposed. Examples of such agent programming languages are Jason [6], GOAL [13] and 2APL [8]. An interesting feature of the agent paradigm is the possibility for building heterogeneous agent systems. That is to say, a system in which multiple agents, implemented in different agent programming languages and possibly by different parties, interact. Recently, the area of agent programming is shifting attention from constructs for implementing single agents, such as goals, beliefs and plans, to social constructs for programming multi-agent systems, such as roles and norms. In this view a multi-agent system is seen as a computational organisation that is constructed separately from the agents that will interact with it. Typically, little can be assumed about the internals of these agents and the behaviour they will exhibit. When little can be assumed about the agents that will interact with the organisation, a norm enforcement mechanism – a process that is responsible for detecting when norms are violated and responding to these violations by imposing sanctions – becomes crucial

---

[*] Work partially supported by EPSRC under grant EP/D052548 and by the CoCoMAS project funded through the Dutch Organization for Scientific Research (NWO).

J. Dix, M. Fisher, and P. Novák (Eds.): CLIMA X, LNAI 6214, pp. 64–82, 2010.

to regulate their behaviour and to achieve and maintain the system's global design objectives [20].

One of the challenges in constructing multi-agent systems is to verify that the system meets its overall design objectives and satisfies some desirable properties. For example, that a set of norms actually enforces the intended behaviour and whether the agents that will reside in the system will be able to achieve their goals. In this paper we report on the extension of earlier work [11] of one of the authors on the automatic verification of heterogeneous agent systems to include organisational (mostly normative) aspects also, by incorporating the normative programming language as presented in [9]. The resulting framework allows us to use automated verification techniques for multi-agent systems consisting of a heterogeneous set of agents that interact with a norm governed organisation. The framework in [11] is primarily targeted at a rapid implementation of agent programming languages that are endowed with an *operational semantics* [16]. The choice for the integration of the normative programming language proposed in [9] is mainly motivated by the presence of an operational semantics which facilitates the integration with [11].

It should be noted that we are not the first to investigate the automatic verification of multi-agent systems and computational organisations. There are already some notable achievements in this direction. Examples of work on model checking techniques for multi-agent systems are [4,5,15]. In contrast to [11] the work on model checking agent systems is targeted at homogeneous systems pertaining to the less realistic case in which all agents are built in the same language. Most importantly, these works (including [11]) do not consider the verification of organisational concepts. Work related to the verification of organisational aspects has appeared, for example, in [14,7,21,1], but in these frameworks the internals of the agents are (intentionally) viewed as unknown. This is explained by the observation that in a *deployed* system little can be assumed about the agents that will interact with it. Still, we believe that for verification purposes at *design time* it would be useful to also take the agents' architecture into account. Doing so allows us, for example, to assert the correctness of a (prototype) agent implementation in the sense that it will achieve its goals without violating a norm. In designing a normative organisation a programmer puts norms into place to enforce desirable behaviour of the participating agents. Implementing prototypical agents and employing them in the organisation allows us to verify whether the actual behaviour accords with the intended behaviour of the system as a whole. A proven prototypical implementation of a norm-abiding agent might then be published to serve as a guideline for external agent developers.

The rest of the paper is structured as follows: In section 2 we give an overview of the language for programming normative organisations (which we will name ORWELL from now on) and discuss the general properties of the agent variant of the dining philosophers problem we use as a running example throughout the paper. Section 3 describes the MCAPL framework for model checking multi-agent systems programmed in a variety of BDI-style agent programming languages. Section 4 discusses the implementation of ORWELL in the MCAPL framework. Section 5 discusses a case study we undertook to model check some properties in a number of different multi-agent systems using the organisation.

2   ORWELL **Programming Normative Agent Organisations**

This section briefly explains the basic concepts involved in the approach to constructing normative multi-agent organisations and how they can be programmed in ORWELL. A more detailed description of its formal syntax and operational semantics together with an example involving a conference management system can be found in [9].

A multi-agent system, as we conceive it, consists of a set of heterogeneous agents interacting with a normative organisation (henceforth organisation). Figure 1 depicts a snapshot of such a multi-agent system. As mentioned before, by heterogeneous we mean that agents are potentially implemented in different agent programming languages by unknown programmers. An organisation encapsulates a domain specific state and function, for instance, a database in which papers and reviews are stored and accompanying functions to upload them. The domain specific state is modeled by a set of *brute facts*, taken from Searle [18]. The agents perform actions that change the brute state to interact with the organisation and exploit its functionality. The general structure of a multi-agent system we adopt is indeed inspired by the agents and artifacts approach of Ricci et al. [17] in which agents exploit artifacts to achieve their design objectives.

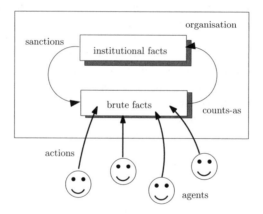

Fig. 1. Agents interacting with a normative organisation

An important purpose of an organisation is to coordinate the behavior of its interactants and to guide them in interacting with it in a meaningful way. This is achieved through normative component that is defined by a simple account of *counts-as rules* as defined by Grossi [12]. Counts-as rules normatively assess the brute facts and label a state with a normative judgment marking brute states as, for example, good or bad. An uploaded paper that exceeds the page limit would, for instance, be assessed as an undesirable state. The normative judgments about the brute state are stored as *institutional facts*, again taken from Searle [18]. To motivate the agents to abide by the norms, certain normative judgments might lead to sanctions which are imposed on the brute state, for example rejecting a paper that violates the page limit by removing it from the database.

In what follows we explain all these constructs using the agent variant of the famous dining philosophers problem in which five spaghetti-eating agents sit at a circular table and compete for five chopsticks. The sticks are placed in between the agents and each agent needs two sticks to eat. Each agent can only pickup the sticks on her immediate left and right. When not eating the agents are deliberating. It is important to emphasize that in this example the chopsticks are metaphors for shared resources and the problem touches upon many interesting problems that commonly arise in the field of concurrent computing, in particular deadlock and starvation. The problem in all its simplicity is, however, also interesting in the context of multi-agent systems (which are characterised by distribution and concurrency) in general, and organisation-oriented approaches in particular. Solutions of how the agents can efficiently share the resources can be considered protocols, which as will be shown naturally translate into norms. There are many known solutions to the dining philosophers problem and it is not our intention to come up with a novel solution. We merely use it to illustrate the ORWELL language.

The ORWELL implementation of the dining agents is listed in code fragment 2.1 (and continued in code fragment 2.2.) The initial brute state of the organisation is specified by the facts component. The agents named $ag1,\ldots,ag5$ are numbered one to five clockwise through facts of the form $agent(A,I)$. Sticks are also identified by a number such that the right stick of an agent numbered I is numbered I and its left stick is numbered $I\%5+1$[1]. The fact that an agent I is holding a stick is modeled by $hold(I,X)$ with $X \in \{r,l\}$ in which r denotes the right and l the left stick. The fact that a stick I is down on the table is denoted by $down(I)$ and a fact $food(I)$ denotes that there is food on the plate of agent I. We assume that initially no agent is holding a stick (all sticks are on the table) and all agents are served with food. The initial situation of the dining agents is shown graphically in figure 2. The specification of the initial brute state is depicted in lines 1-4.

The brute facts change under the performance of actions by agents. The effects describe how the brute state may evolve under the performance of actions. They are used by the organization to determine the resulting brute state after performance of the action. They are defined by triples of the form $\{Pre\}a\{Post\}$, intuitively meaning that when action a is executed and set of facts Pre is derivable by the current brute state, the set of facts denoted by $Post$ is to be accomodated in it. We use the notation ϕ to indicate that a belief holds in the precondition, or should be added in the postcondition and $-\phi$ to indicate that a belief does not hold (precondition) or should be removed (postcondition). Actions a are modeled by predicates of the form $does(A,Act)$ in which Act is a term denoting the action and A denotes the name of the agent performing it. The dining agents, for example, can perform actions to pick up and put down their (left and right) sticks and eat. The effect rules defining these actions are listed in lines 6-54[2]. An agent can only pickup a stick if the stick is on the table (e.g. lines 7-9 defining the action of picking up a right stick), can only put down a stick when it is holding it (e.g. line 11 defining the action of putting down a right stick) and can eat when it has lifted both

---

[1] Where % is arithmetic modulus.

[2] It should be noted that the current ORWELL prototype has limited ability to reason about arithmetic in rule preconditions. Hence the unecessary proliferation of some rules in this example.

Code fragment 2.1 Dining agents implemented in ORWELL.

```
:Brute Facts:                                                              1
down(1)  down(2)  down(3)  down(4)  down(5)                                2
food(1)  food(2)  food(3)  food(4)  food(5)                               3
agent(ag1,1)  agent(ag2,2)  agent(ag3,3)  agent(ag4,4)  agent(ag5,5)      4
                                                                          5
:Effect Rules:                                                            6
{agent(A,I),  down(I)}                                                    7
   does(A,pur)                                                            8
{-down(I),  hold(I,r),  return(u)}                                        9
                                                                         10
{agent(A,I),  -down(I)}  does(A,pur)  {return(d)}                        11
                                                                         12
{agent(A,  I),  hold(I,r)}  does(A,pdr)  {down(I),  -hold(I,r)}          13
                                                                         14
{agent(ag1,1),  down(2)}                                                 15
   does(ag1,pul)  {-down(2),  hold(1,1),  return(u)}                     16
{agent(ag1,1),  -down(2)}  does(ag1,pul)  {return(d)}                    17
                                                                         18
{agent(ag2,2),  down(3)}                                                 19
   does(ag2,pul)  {-down(3),  hold(2,1),  return(u)}                     20
{agent(ag2,2),  -down(3)}  does(ag2,pul)  {return(d)}                    21
                                                                         22
{agent(ag3,3),  down(4)}                                                 23
   does(ag3,pul)  {-down(4),  hold(3,1),  return(u)}                     24
{agent(ag3,3),  -down(4)}  does(ag3,pul)  {return(d)}                    25
                                                                         26
{agent(ag4,4),  down(5)}                                                 27
   does(ag4,pul)  {-down(5),  hold(4,1),  return(u)}                     28
{agent(ag4,4),  -down(5)}  does(ag4,pul)  {return(d)}                    29
                                                                         30
{agent(ag5,5),  down(1)}                                                 31
   does(ag5,pul)  {-down(1),  hold(5,1),  return(u)}                     32
{agent(ag5,5),  -down(1)}  does(ag5,pul)  {return(d)}                    33
                                                                         34
{agent(ag1,1),  hold(1,1)}                                               35
   does(ag1,pdl)  {down(2),  -hold(1,1)}                                 36
                                                                         37
{agent(ag2,2),  hold(2,1)}                                               38
   does(ag2,pdl)  {down(3),  -hold(2,1)}                                 39
                                                                         40
{agent(ag3,3),  hold(3,1)}                                               41
   does(ag3,pdl)  {down(4),  -hold(3,1)}                                 42
                                                                         43
{agent(ag4,4),  hold(4,1)}                                               44
   does(ag4,pdl)  {down(5),  -hold(4,1)}                                 45
                                                                         46
{agent(ag5,5),  hold(5,1)}                                               47
   does(ag5,pdl)  {down(1),  -hold(5,1)}                                 48
                                                                         49
{agent(A,I),  hold(I,r),  hold(I,1),  food(I)}                           50
   does(A,eat)                                                           51
{-food(I),  return(yes)}                                                 52
                                                                         53
{agent(A,I),  -food(I)}  does(A,eat)  {return(no)}                       54
```

Code fragment 2.2 Dining agents implemented in ORWELL(cont.)

```
:CountsAs Rules:                                                              1
{−hold(1,r), hold(1,l), food(1)} {True} => {viol(1)}                          2
{hold(2,r), −hold(2,l), food(2)} {True} => {viol(2)}                          3
{−hold(3,r), hold(3,l), food(3)} {True} => {viol(3)}                          4
{hold(4,r), −hold(4,l), food(4)} {True} => {viol(4)}                          5
{−hold(5,r), hold(5,l), food(5)} {True} => {viol(5)}                          6
{agent(A,I),−food(I),−hold(I,r),−hold(I,l)} {True} => {reward(I)}             7
                                                                             8
:Sanction Rules:                                                             9
{viol(A)} => {−food(A), punished(A)}                                        10
{reward(A)} => {food(A), rewarded(A)}                                       11
```

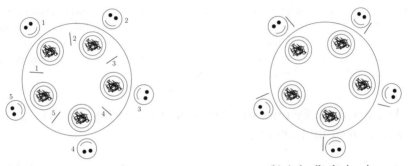

(a) The initial table arrangement.   (b) A deadlock situation.

Fig. 2. The dining agents problem

sticks and has food on its plate (lines 50-52). Actions might have different effects depending on the particular brute state. To inform agents about the effect of an action we introduce special designated unary facts starting with predicate return to pass back information (terms) to the agent performing the action. These facts are not asserted to the brute state. Picking up a stick will thus return u (up) in case the stick is successfully lifted (line 9) and d (down) otherwise (e.g. line 11). Similarly, the succes of performing an eat action is indicated by returning yes (line 52) or no (line 54). Note that we assume that agents will only perform the eat action in case they have lifted their stick. Ways for returning information (and handling failure) were not originally described in [9] and are left for future research.

When every agent has decided to eat, holds a left stick and waits for a right stick, we have a deadlock situation (see figure 2b for a graphical representation). One (of many) possible solutions to prevent deadlocks is to implement a protocol in which the odd numbered agents are supposed to pick-up their right stick first and the even numbered agents their left. Because we cannot make any assumptions about the internals of the agents we need to account for the sub-ideal situation in which an agent does not follow the protocol. To motivate the agents to abide by the protocol we implement norms to detect undesirable (violations) and desirable behaviour (code fragment 2.2). The norms in our framework take on the form of elementary counts-as rules relating a set of brute facts with a set of institutional facts (the normative judgment). The rules listed in lines 2, 4 and 6 state that a situation in which an odd numbered agent holds her left stick and not her right while there is food on her plate counts as a violation. Rules listed in lines 3 and 5 implement the symmetric case for even numbered agents. The last rule marks a state in which an agent puts down both sticks when there is no food on her plate as good behaviour. It is important to emphasize that in general hard-wiring the protocol by the action specification (in this case effect rules) such that violations are not possible severely limits the agent's autonomy [2]. It should also be noted that the antecedent of a counts-as rule can also contain institutional facts (in this example these are irrelevant and the institutional precondition is True).

Undesirable behaviour is punished and good behaviour is rewarded. This is expressed by the sanction rules (lines 9-11) of code fragment 2.2. Sanction rules are expressed as a kind of inverted counts-as rules relating a set of institutional facts with a set of brute facts to be accommodated in the brute state. Bad behaviour, that is not abiding by the protocol, is thus punished by taking away the food of the agent such that it cannot successfully perform the eat action. Good behaviour, i.e. not unnecesarily keeping hold of sticks, is rewarded with food.

3   The MCAPL Framework for Model Checking Agent Programming Languages

The MCAPL framework is intended to provide a uniform access to model-checking facilities to programs written in a wide range of BDI-style agent programming languages. The framework is outlined in [10] and described in more detail in [3].

Fig. 3 shows an agent executing within the framework. A program, originally programmed in some agent programming language and running within the MCAPL Framework is represented. It uses data structures from the Agent Infrastructure Layer (AIL) to store its internal state comprising, for instance, an agent's belief base and a rule library. It also uses an interpreter for the agent programming language that is built using AIL classes and methods. The interpreter defines the reasoning cycle for the agent programming language which interacts with a model checker, essentially notifying it when a new state is reached that is relevant for verification.

The Agent Infrastructure Layer (AIL) toolkit was introduced as a uniform framework [11] for easing the integration of new languages into the existing execution and verification engine. It provides an effective, high-level, basis for implementing operational semantics [16] for BDI-like programming languages. An operational semantics describes the behavior of a programming language in terms of transitions between program configurations. A configuration describes a state of the program and a transition is a transformation of one configuration γ into another configuration γ', denoted by $\gamma \to \gamma'$. The transitions that can be derived for a programming language are defined by a set of derivation rules of the form $\frac{P}{\gamma \to \gamma'}$ with the intuitive reading that transition $\gamma \to \gamma'$ can be derived when premise P holds. An execution trace in a transition system is then a sequence of configurations that can be generated by applying transition rules to an initial configuration. An execution thus shows a possible behavior of the system at

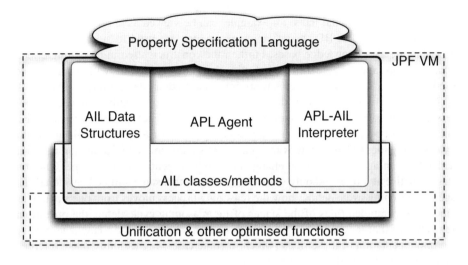

Fig. 3. Outline of Approach

hand. All possible executions for an initial configuration show the complete behavior. The key *operations* of many (BDI-)languages together with a set of standard transition rules form the AIL *toolkit* that can be used by any agent programming language in its own AIL-based interpreter. Of course, it is possible to add custom rules for specific languages.

The agent system runs in the Java Pathfinder (JPF) virtual machine. This is a JAVA virtual machine specially designed to maintain backtrack points and explore, for instance, all possible thread scheduling options (that can affect the result of the verification) [22]. Agent JPF (AJPF) is a customisation of JPF that is optimised for AIL-based interpreters. Common to all language interpreters implemented using the AIL are the AIL-agent data structures for beliefs, intentions, goals, etc., which are accessed by the model checker and on which the modalities of a property specification language are defined. For instance the belief modality of the property specification language is defined in terms of the way logical consequence is implemented within the AIL.

The AIL can be viewed as a platform on which agents programmed in different programming languages co-exist. Together with AJPF this provides uniform model checking techniques for various agent-oriented programming languages and even allows heterogeneous settings [11].

4 Modified Semantics for ORWELL for Implementation in the AIL

In this work we apply the MCAPL framework to the ORWELL language and experiment with the model checking of organisations. Although ORWELL is an organisational language rather than an agent programming language many of its features show a remarkable similarity to concepts that are used in BDI agent programming languages. The brute and insitutional facts, for example, can be viewed as knowledge bases. The belief bases of typical BDI agent languages, which are used to store the beliefs of an agent, are also knowledge bases. Further, the constructs used in modelling effects, counts-as and sanctions are all types of rules that show similarities with planning rules used by agents. This made it relatively straightforward to model ORWELL in the AIL.

The AIL framework assumes that agents in an agent programming language all possess a *reasoning cycle* consisting of several (≥ 1) stages. Each stage describes a coherent activity of an agent, for example, generating plans for achieving goals and acting by executing these plans. Moreover, each stage is a disjunction of transition rules that define how an agent's state may change during the execution of that stage. Only one stage is active at a time and only rules that belong to that stage will be considered. The agent's reasoning cycle defines how the reasoning process moves from one stage to another. The combined rules of the stages of the reasoning cycle define the operational semantics of that language. The construction of an interpreter for a language involves the implementation of these rules (which in some cases might simply make reference to the pre-implemented rules) and a reasoning cycle.

Standard ORWELL [9] does not explicitly consider a reasoning cycle, but what can be considered its reasoning cycle consists of one single transition rule that describes the organisation's response to actions performed by interacting agents. In words, when an action is received, the application of this transition rule;

1. applies one effect rule,
2. then applies all applicable counts-as rules until no more apply and
3. then applies all applicable sanction rules.

The application of this rule thus performs a sequence of modifications to the agent state which the AIL would most naturally present as separate transitions. We needed to reformulate the original rule as a sequence of transition rules in a new form of the operational semantics and include a step in which the organisation perceived the actions taken by the agents interacting with it. Determining all the effects of applying the counts-as rules, for example, was explained in [9] by the definition of a mathematical closure function which was then used in its single transition rule. Although mathematically correct, such a closure function is too abstract to serve as a basis for an actual implementation and needed to be redefined in terms of transition rules for a natural implementation in the AIL.

Figure 4 shows the reworked reasoning cycle for ORWELL. It starts with a perception phase in which agent actions are perceived. Then it moves through two stages which apply an effect rule (B & C), two for applying counts-as rules (D & E) and two for applying sanction rules (F & G). Lastly there is a stage (H) where the results of actions are returned to the agent taking them.

The splitting of the rule phases into two was dictated by the default mechanisms for applying rules[3] in the AIL, in which a set of applicable rules are first generated and then one is chosen and processed. It would have been possible to combine this process

---

[3] Called plans in the AIL terminology.

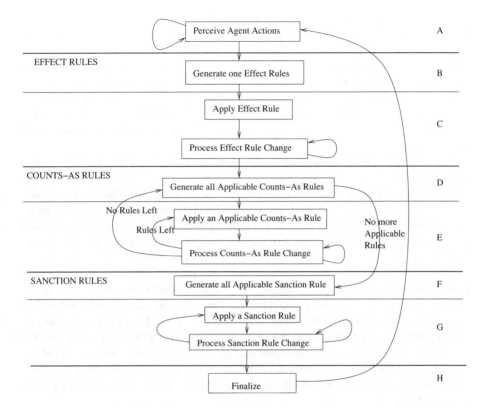

Fig. 4. The ORWELL Reasoning Cycle in the AIL

into one rule, but it was simpler, when implementing this prototype, to leave it in this form, although it complicates the semantics.

Figures 5 to 8 show the operational semantics of ORWELL, reworked for an AIL interpreter and simplified slightly to ignore the effects of unification. The state of an organisation is represented by a large tuple of the form $\langle i, I, BF, IF, ER, CAR, SR, AP, A, RS \rangle$ in which:

- i is the "current intention";
- I is a set of additional "intentions";
- BF is a set of brute facts;
- IF is a set of institutional facts;
- ER is a set of effect rules;
- CAR is a set of counts-as rules;
- SR is a set of sanction rules;
- AP is a set of applicable rules;
- A is a list of actions taken by the agents in the organisation;
- RS is an atomic formula with predicate name `return` for storing the result of the action.

We extend this tuple with one final element to indicate the phase of the reasoning cycle from figure 4 that is currently in focus. This element will always occur as last element of the tuple. In order to improve readability, we show *only* those parts of the agent tuple actually changed or referred to by a transition rule. We use the naming conventions just outlined to indicate which parts of the tuple we refer to, priming the names on the right hand side of the transition where the value has changed. Where there may be confusion we also show their value as an equality – i.e. $i = (a, \epsilon)$ means the current intention is (a, ϵ), if this is changed to *null* then we will write $i' = null$ on the right hand side of the transition..

The concept of intention is common in many BDI-languages and is used to indicate the *intended means* for achieving a goal or handling an event. Within the AIL, intentions are data structures which associate events with the plans generated to handle that event (including any instantiations of variables appearing in those plans). As plans are executed the intention is modified accordingly so that it only stores that part of the plan yet to be processed. Of course, the concept of intention is not originally used in ORWELL. We slightly abuse this single agent concept to store the instantiated plans associated with any applicable rules. Its exact meaning depends on which type of rule (effect, counts-as or sanction) is considered. When an effect rule is applicable, an intention stores the (unexecuted) postconditions of the rule associated with the action that triggered the rule. When a counts-as or sanction rule is applicable an intention stores its (unexecuted) postconditions together with a record of state that made the rule applicable (essentially the conjunction of its instantiated preconditions). Also the concepts of applicable rules denoting which (effect, counts-as or sanction) rules are applicable (their precondition is satisfied) in a specific situation are AIL specific and are not originally part of ORWELL.

$$\frac{}{\langle i, A = a;A', \mathbf{A} \rangle \rightarrow \langle i' = (a, \epsilon), A', \mathbf{B} \rangle} \tag{1}$$

Fig. 5. The Operational Semantics for ORWELL as implemented in the AIL (Agent Actions)

Figure 5 shows the semantics for the initial stage. As agents take actions, these are stored in a queue, A, within the organisation for processing[4]. The organisation processes one agent action at a time. The reasoning cycle starts by selecting an action, a, for processing. This is converted into an intention tuple (a, ϵ) where the first part of the tuple stores the action (in this case) which created the intention and the second part of the tuple stores the effects of any rule triggered by the intention, i.e. the brute facts to be asserted and retracted. Initially the effects are indicated by a distinguished symbol ϵ, which indicates that no effects have yet been calculated. We believe that when this rule fires the current intention will be empty (i.e. all its effects will have been processed) but we have not proved this fact.

Figure 6 shows the semantics for processing effect rules. These semantics are very similar to those used for processing counts-as rules and sanction rules and, in many

---

[4] We use ; to represent list cons.

$$\frac{\{(a, Post) \mid \{Pre\}a\{Post\} \in ER \land BF \models Pre\} = \emptyset}{\langle BF, i = (a, \epsilon), AP, \mathbf{B} \rangle \rightarrow \langle BF, i' = \mathbf{null}, AP' = \emptyset, \mathbf{H} \rangle} \quad (2)$$

$$\frac{\{(a, Post) \mid \{Pre\}a\{Post\} \in ER \land BF \models Pre\} = AP' \quad AP' \neq \emptyset}{\langle BF, i = (a, \epsilon), AP, \mathbf{B} \rangle \rightarrow \langle BF, i' = (a, \epsilon), AP', \mathbf{C} \rangle} \quad (3)$$

$$\frac{(a, Post) \in AP}{\langle i = (a, \epsilon), AP, \mathbf{C} \rangle \rightarrow \langle i' = (a, Post), AP' = \emptyset, \mathbf{C} \rangle} \quad (4)$$

$$\frac{}{\langle BF, i = (a, +bf;Post), \mathbf{C} \rangle \rightarrow \langle BF' = BF \cup \{bf\}, i' = (a, Post), \mathbf{C} \rangle} \quad (5)$$

$$\frac{}{\langle BF, i = (a, -bf;Post), \mathbf{C} \rangle \rightarrow \langle BF' = BF/\{bf\}, i' = (a, Post), \mathbf{C} \rangle} \quad (6)$$

$$\frac{}{\langle i = (a, []), \mathbf{C} \rangle \rightarrow \langle i' = (a, []), \mathbf{D} \rangle} \quad (7)$$

Fig. 6. The Operational Semantics for ORWELL as implemented in the AIL (Effect Rules)

cases the implementation uses the same code, simply customised to choose from different sets of rules depending upon the stage of the reasoning cycle. Recall that an effect rule is a triple $\{Pre\}a\{Post\}$ consisting of a set of preconditions Pre, an action a taken by an agent and a set of postconditions $Post$.

If the action matches the current intention and the preconditions hold , written $BF \models Pre$ (where BF are the brute facts of the organisation), then the effect rule is applicable. Rule 2 pertains to the case in which no effect rule can be applied. This could happen when no precondition is satisfied or if the action is simply undefined. The brute state will remain unchanged, so there is no need for normatively assessing it. Therefore, the organisation cycles on to stage **H** were an empty result will be returned. Applicable effect rules are stored in the set of applicable rules AP (rule 3), of which one applicable rule is chosen (rule 4) and its postconditions are processed (rules 5 and 6). The postconditions consist of a stack of changes to be made to the brute facts, $+bf$ indicates that the fact bf should be added and $-bf$ indicates that a fact should be removed. These are processed by rules 5 and 6 in turn until no more postconditions apply (rule 7). Then it moves on to the next stage (stage **D**) in which the resulting brute state is normatively assessed by the counts-as rules.

Figure 7 shows the semantics for handling counts-as rules. These are similar to the semantics for effect rules except that the closure of all counts-as rules are applied. The set G, is used to track the rules that have been applied. All applicable counts as rules are made into intentions, these are selected one at a time and the rule postconditions are processed. As mentioned before, a counts-as rule may contain institutional facts in its precondition. Thus the application of a counts-as rule might trigger another counts-as rule that was not triggered before. Therefore, when all intentions are processed the stage returns to stage **D**, in order to see if any new counts-as rules have become applicable.

Figure 8 shows the rules governing the application of sanction rules. These are similar to the application of counts-as rules however, since sanction rules consider only

$$\frac{\{(\bigwedge Pre, Post) \mid \{Pre\} \Rightarrow \{Post\} \in CAR/G \wedge BF \cup IF \models Pre\} = \emptyset}{\langle BF, IF, AP, G, \mathbf{D}\rangle \rightarrow \langle BF, IF, AP' = \emptyset, G' = \emptyset, \mathbf{F}\rangle} \tag{8}$$

$$\frac{\{(\bigwedge Pre, Post) \mid \{Pre\} \Rightarrow \{Post\} \in CAR/G \wedge BF \cup IF \models Pre\} = AP' \quad AP' \neq \emptyset}{\langle BF, IF, AP, G, \mathbf{D}\rangle \rightarrow \langle BF, IF, AP', G' = AP' \cup G, \mathbf{E}\rangle} \tag{9}$$

$$\frac{AP \neq \emptyset}{\langle org, I, AP, \mathbf{E}\rangle \rightarrow \langle org, I' = AP \cup I, AP' = \emptyset, \mathbf{E}\rangle} \tag{10}$$

$$\frac{}{\langle org, i = (\bigwedge Pre, []), I = i';I', \mathbf{E}\rangle \rightarrow \langle org, i', I', \mathbf{E}\rangle} \tag{11}$$

$$\frac{}{\langle org, IF, i = (\bigwedge Pre, +if;Post), \mathbf{E}\rangle \rightarrow \langle org, IF' = IF \cup \{if\}, i' = (\bigwedge Pre, Post), \mathbf{E}\rangle} \tag{12}$$

$$\frac{}{\langle org, IF, i = (\bigwedge Pre, -if;Post), \mathbf{E}\rangle \rightarrow \langle org, IF' = IF/\{if\}, i' = (\bigwedge Pre, Post), \mathbf{E}\rangle} \tag{13}$$

$$\frac{I = \emptyset}{\langle org, i = (\bigwedge Pre, []), I, \mathbf{E}\rangle \rightarrow \langle org, i' = (\bigwedge Pre, []), I, \mathbf{D}\rangle} \tag{14}$$

Fig. 7. The Operational Semantics for ORWELL as implemented in the AIL (Counts-As Rules)

$$\frac{\{(\bigwedge Pre, Post) \mid \{Pre\} \Rightarrow \{Post\} \in SR \wedge IF \models Pre\} = \emptyset}{\langle IF, I, AP, \mathbf{F}\rangle \rightarrow \langle IF, I' = \emptyset, \mathbf{H}\rangle} \tag{15}$$

$$\frac{\{(\bigwedge Pre, Post) \mid \{Pre\} \Rightarrow \{Post\} \in SR \wedge IF \models Pre\} = AP' \quad AP' \neq \emptyset}{\langle IF, AP, \mathbf{F}\rangle \rightarrow \langle IF, AP', \mathbf{G}\rangle} \tag{16}$$

$$\frac{AP \neq \emptyset}{\langle I, AP, \mathbf{G}\rangle \rightarrow \langle I' = AP \cup I, AP' = \emptyset, \mathbf{G}\rangle} \tag{17}$$

$$\frac{}{\langle i = (\bigwedge Pre, []), I = i';I', \mathbf{G}\rangle \rightarrow \langle i', I', \mathbf{G}\rangle} \tag{18}$$

$$\frac{}{\langle BF, i = (\bigwedge Pre, +bf;Post), \mathbf{G}\rangle \rightarrow \langle BF' = BF \cup \{bf\}, i' = (\bigwedge Pre, Post), \mathbf{G}\rangle} \tag{19}$$

$$\frac{}{\langle BF, i = (\bigwedge Pre, -bf;Post), \mathbf{G}\rangle \rightarrow \langle BF' = BF/\{bf\}, i' = (\bigwedge Pre, Post), \mathbf{G}\rangle} \tag{20}$$

$$\frac{I = \emptyset}{\langle i = (\bigwedge Pre, []), I, \mathbf{G}\rangle \rightarrow \langle i = (\bigwedge Pre, []), I, \mathbf{H}\rangle} \tag{21}$$

Fig. 8. The Operational Semantics for ORWELL as implemented in the AIL (Sanction Rules)

$$\frac{return(X) \in BF \quad RS = []}{\langle org, BF, RS, \mathbf{H} \rangle \rightarrow \langle org, BF' = BF/\{\mathbf{return(X)}\}, RS' = [\mathbf{X}], \mathbf{A} \rangle} \quad (22)$$

$$\frac{return(X) \notin BF \quad RS = []}{\langle org, BF, RS, \mathbf{H} \rangle \rightarrow \langle org, BF, RS' = [\mathbf{none}], \mathbf{A} \rangle} \quad (23)$$

Fig. 9. The Operational Semantics for ORWELL as implemented in the AIL (Finalise)

institutional facts and alter only brute facts there is no need to check for more applicable rules once they have all applied.

Lastly, figure 9 shows the rules of the final stage. The final stage of the semantics returns any results derived from processing the agent action. It does this by looking for a term of the form $return(X)$ in the Brute Facts and placing that result, X, in the result store. The result store is implemented as a blocking queue, so, in this implementation, the rules wait until the store is empty and then place the result in it. When individual agents within the organisation take actions these remove a result from the store, again waiting until a result is available.

Many of these rules are reused versions of customisable rules from the AIL toolkit. For instance the AIL mechanims for selecting applicable "plans" were easily customised to select rules and was used in stages $\mathbf{B}, \mathbf{D}$ and $\mathbf{F}$. Similarly we were able to use AIL rules for adding and removing beliefs from an agent belief base to handle the addition and removal of brute and institutional facts. We modeled ORWELL's fact sets as belief bases and extended the AIL's belief handling methods to deal with the presence of multiple belief bases.

It became clear that the ORWELL stages couldn't be simply presented as a cycle. In some cases we needed to loop back to a previous stage. We ended up introducing rules to control phase changes explicitly (e.g. rule (21)) but these had to be used via an awkward implementational mechanism which involved considering the rule that had last fired. In future we intend to extend the AIL with a generic mechanism for doing this.

It was outside the scope of our exploratory work to verify that the semantics of OR-WELL, as implemented in the AIL, conformed to the standard language semantics as presented in [9]. However our aim is to discuss the verification of normative organisational programs and this implementation is sufficient for that, even if it is not an exact implementation of ORWELL.

5   Model Checking Normative Agent Organisations

We implemented the ORWELL Organisation for the dining philosophers system shown in code fragment 2.1 but modified, for time reasons, to consider only three agents rather than five. We integrated this organisation into three multi-agent systems.

The first system (System A) consisted of three agents implemented in the GOAL language. Part of the implementation of one of these agents is shown in code fragment 5.1. This agent has a goal to have eaten (line 4), but initially believes it has not eaten (line 7). It also believes that its left and right stick are both down on the table (also line 7). The agent has capabilities (lines 9-14) to perform all actions provided by the organisation.

Code fragment 5.1 A protocol abiding GOAL agent.

```
: name :  ag1                                                    1
                                                                 2
: Initial  Goals :                                              3
eaten ( yes )                                                    4
                                                                 5
: Initial  Beliefs :                                            6
eaten ( no )  left ( d )  right ( d )                            7
                                                                 8
: Capabilities :                                                9
pul  pul  {True}  {−left ( d ),  left ( R )}                    10
pur  pur  {True}  {−right ( d ),  right ( R )}                  11
pdl  pdl  {True}  {−left ( u ),  left ( d )}                    12
pdr  pdr  {True}  {−right ( u ),  right ( d )}                  13
eat  eat  {True}  {−eaten ( no ),  eaten ( R )}                14
                                                                15
: Conditional  Actions :                                       16
G  eaten ( yes ),  B  left ( d ),  B  right ( d )  |>  do ( pur )   17
G  eaten ( yes ),  B  left ( d ),  B  right ( u )  |>  do ( pul )   18
G  eaten ( yes ),  B  left ( u ),  B  right ( u )  |>  do ( eat )   19
B  eaten ( yes ),  B  left ( u )  |>  do ( pdl )               20
B  eaten ( yes ),  B  right ( u )  |>  do ( pdr )              21
```

The return value of the organisation is accessed through the special designated variable term R that can be used in the postcondition of the capability specification. The beliefs of the agent will thus be updated with the effect of the action. The conditional actions define what the agent should do in achieving its goals and are the key to a protocol implementation. Whenever the agent has a goal to have eaten and believes it has not to have lifted either stick it will start by picking up its right stick first (line 17). Then it will pick up its left (line 18) and start eating when both are acquired (line 19). Note that if the eat action is successfully performed the agent has accomplished its goal. When the agent believes it has eaten and holds its sticks it will put them down again (lines 20 and 21). Other protocol abiding agents are programmed in a similar fashion provided that ag2 will pick up their left stick first instead of their right. Our expectation was, therefore, that this multi-agent system would never incur any sanctions within the organisation.

System B used a similar set of three GOAL agents, only in this case all three agents were identical (i.e. they would all pick up their right stick first). We anticipated that this group of agents would trigger sanctions.

Lastly, for System C, we implemented three Black Box agents which performed the five possible actions almost at random[5]. The random agents could take no more than five actions in a run of the program, though actions could be repetitions of previous

---

[5] In order to reduce search we constrained the agents a little internally, so that they could not perform a put down action before a pick up action, and they couldn't eat until after they had performed both pick up actions. The agents had no perceptions of the outside world and so the actions were not necessarily successful.

ones. This system did not conform to the assumption that once an agent has picked up a stick it will not put it down until it has eaten.

We investigated the truth of three properties evaluated on these three multi-agent systems. In what follows $\Box$ is the LTL operator, always. Thus $\Box\phi$ means that ϕ holds in all states contained in every run of the system. $\diamond$ is the LTL operator, eventually or finally. $\diamond\phi$ means that ϕ holds at some point in every run of a system. The modal operator $\mathcal{B}(ag, \phi)$ stands for "ag believes ϕ" and is used by AJPF to interrogate the knowledge base of an agent. In the case of ORWELL this interrogates the fact bases.

Property 1 states that it is always the case that if the organisation believes (i.e. stores as a brute fact in its knowledge base) all agents are holding their right stick (or all agents are holding their left stick) – i.e., the system is potentially in a deadlock – then at least one agent believes it has eaten (i.e., one agent is about to put down it's stick and deadlock has been avoided).

$$\Box((\bigwedge_i \mathcal{B}(org, hold(i, r)) \vee \bigwedge_i \mathcal{B}(org, hold(i, l))) \Rightarrow \bigvee_i \mathcal{B}(ag_i, eaten(yes))) \quad (24)$$

Property 2 states that it is not possible for any agent which has been punished to be given more food.

$$\Box \bigwedge_i \neg(\mathcal{B}(org, punished(i)) \wedge \mathcal{B}(org, food(i))) \quad (25)$$

Property 3 states after an agent violates the protocol it either always has no food or it gets rewarded (for putting its sticks down). This property was expected to hold for all systems irrespective of whether the agents wait until they have eaten before putting down their sticks or not.

$$\Box \bigwedge_i (\mathcal{B}(org, hold(i, l)) \wedge \neg\mathcal{B}(org, hold(i, r)))$$
$$\Longrightarrow \quad (26)$$
$$(\Box\neg\mathcal{B}(org, food(i)) \vee \diamond\mathcal{B}(org, rewarded(i)))$$

The results of model checking the three properties on the three systems are shown below. We give the result of model checking together with the time taken in hours (h), minutes (m) or seconds (s) as appropriate and the number of states (st) generated by the model checker:

	System A	System B	System C
Property 1	True (40m, 8214 st)	False (2m, 432st)	False (16s, 46st)
Property 2	True (40m, 8214st)	True (30m, 5622st)	False (11s, 57st)
Property 3	True (1h 7m , 9878st)	True (1h 2m, 10352st)	True (15h, 256049 st)

It should be noted that transitions between states within AJPF generally involve the execution of a considerable amount of JAVA code in the JPF virtual machine since the system only branches the search space when absolutely necessary. There is scope, within the MCAPL framework for controlling how often properties are checked. In our case we had the properties checked after each full execution of the ORWELL reasoning cycle. This was a decision made in an attempt to reduce the search space further. So in some cases above a transition between two states represents the execution of all the rules from stages **A** to **H** of the ORWELL reasoning cycle. Furthermore the JPF virtual machine is slow, compared to standard JAVA virtual machines, partly because of the extra burden it incurs maintaining the information needed for model checking. This accounts for the comparatively small number of states examined for the time taken when these results are compared with those of other model checking systems. Even though we excluded as much as possible of the internal state of our random agents there was clearly a much larger search space associated with them. We attribute this to the much higher number of "illogical" states that occur - (when an agent tries to perform an impossible action). We believe it likely that verifying an organisation containing agents with known internal states will prove considerably more computationally tractable than verifying organisations that contain entirely random agents.

In the process of conducting this experiment we discovered errors, even in the small program we had implemented. For instance we did not, initially, return a result when an agent attempted to pick up a stick which was held by another agent. This resulted in a failure of the agents to instantiate the result variable and, in some possible runs, to therefore assume that they had the stick and to attempt to pick up their other stick despite that being a protocol violation. This showed the benefit of model checking an organisation with reference to agents that are assumed to obey its norms.

The experiments also show the benefits of allowing access to an agent's state when verifying an organisation in order to, for instance, check that properties hold under assumptions such as that agents do not put down sticks until after they have eaten. The more that can be assumed about the agents within an organisation the more that can be proved and so the behaviour of the organisation with respect to different kinds of agent can be determined.

6   Conclusions

In this paper we have explored the verification of multi-agent systems running within a normative organisation. We have implemented a normative organisational language, ORWELL, within the MCAPL framework for model checking multi-agent systems in a fashion that allows us to model check properties of organisations.

We have investigated a simple example of an organisational multi-agent system based on the dining philosophers problem and examined its behaviour in settings where we make very few assumptions about the behaviour of the agents within the system and in settings where the agents within the system are white box (i.e., the model checker has full access to their internal state). We have been able to use these systems to verify properties of the organisation, in particular properties about the way in which the organisation handles norms and sanctions.

An interesting result of these experiments has been showing that the use of white box agents allows us to prove a wider range of properties about the way in which the organisation behaves with respect to agents that obey its norms, or agents that, even if they do not obey its norms, respect certain assumptions the organisation embodies about their operation. In particular the white box system enabled us to detect a bug in the organisational code which revealed that the organisation did not provide agents which did obey its norms with sufficient information to do so. This bug would have been difficult to detect in a system where there was no information about the internal state of the constituent agents, since the property that revealed it did not hold in general.

In more general terms the verification of organisations containing white box agents enables the verification that a given multi-agent system respects the norms of an organisation.

References

1. Aştefănoaei, L., Dastani, M., Meyer, J.-J., Boer, F.S.: A verification framework for normative multi-agent systems. In: Bui, T.D., Ho, T.V., Ha, Q.T. (eds.) PRIMA 2008. LNCS (LNAI), vol. 5357, pp. 54–65. Springer, Heidelberg (2008)
2. Aldewereld, H.: Autonomy versus Conformity an Institutional Perspective on Norms and Protocols. PhD thesis, Utrecht University, SIKS (2007)
3. Bordini, R.H., Dennis, L.A., Farwer, B., Fisher, M.: Automated Verification of Multi-Agent Programs. In: Proc. 23rd IEEE/ACM International Conference on Automated Software Engineering (ASE), pp. 69–78 (2008)
4. Bordini, R.H., Fisher, M., Visser, W., Wooldridge, M.: Model Checking Rational Agents. IEEE Intelligent Systems 19(5), 46–52 (2004)
5. Bordini, R.H., Fisher, M., Visser, W., Wooldridge, M.: Verifying Multi-Agent Programs by Model Checking. Journal of Autonomous Agents and Multi-Agent Systems 12(2), 239–256 (2006)
6. Bordini, R.H., Hübner, J.F., Wooldridge, M.: Programming Multi-Agent Systems in AgentSpeak Using Jason. Wiley Series in Agent Technology. John Wiley & Sons, Chichester (2007)
7. Cliffe, O., Vos, M.D., Padget, J.A.: Answer set programming for representing and reasoning about virtual institutions. In: Inoue, K., Satoh, K., Toni, F. (eds.) CLIMA 2006. LNCS (LNAI), vol. 4371, pp. 60–79. Springer, Heidelberg (2007)
8. Dastani, M.: 2APL: a practical agent programming language. Autonomous Agents and Multi-Agent Systems 16(3), 214–248 (2008)
9. Dastani, M., Tinnemeier, N.A.M., Meyer, J.-J.C.: A programming language for normative multi-agent systems. In: Dignum, V. (ed.) Multi-Agent Systems: Semantics and Dynamics of Organizational Models, ch. 16. IGI Global (2008)
10. Dennis, L.A., Farwer, B., Bordini, R.H., Fisher, M.: A Flexible Framework for Verifying Agent Programs. In: Proc. 7th International Conference on Autonomous Agents and Multiagent Systems (AAMAS). ACM Press, New York (2008) (Short paper)
11. Dennis, L.A., Fisher, M.: Programming verifiable heterogeneous agent systems. In: Hindriks, K.V., Pokahr, A., Sardina, S. (eds.) ProMAS 2008. LNCS, vol. 5442, pp. 27–42. Springer, Heidelberg (2009)
12. Grossi, D.: Designing Invisible Handcuffs. Formal Investigations in Institutions and Organizations for Multi-agent Systems. PhD thesis, Utrecht University, SIKS (2007)
13. Hindriks, K.V., de Boer, F.S., van der Hoek, W., Meyer, J.-J.C.: Agent programming with declarative goals. In: Castelfranchi, C., Lespérance, Y. (eds.) ATAL 2000. LNCS (LNAI), vol. 1986, pp. 228–243. Springer, Heidelberg (2001)
14. Huguet, M.-P., Esteva, M., Phelps, S., Sierra, C., Wooldridge, M.: Model checking electronic institutions. In: MoChArt 2002, pp. 51–58 (2002)
15. Kacprzak, M., Lomuscio, A., Penczek, W.: Verification of Multiagent Systems via Unbounded Model Checking. In: Proc. 3rd International Joint Conference on Autonomous Agents and Multiagent Systems (AAMAS), pp. 638–645. IEEE Computer Society, Los Alamitos (2004)

16. Plotkin, G.D.: A structural approach to operational semantics. Technical Report DAIMI FN-19, University of Aarhus (1981)
17. Ricci, A., Viroli, M., Omicini, A.: Give agents their artifacts: the A&A approach for engineering working environments in MAS. In: AAMAS (2007)
18. Searle, J.R.: The Construction of Social Reality. Free Press, New York (1995)
19. Shoham, Y.: Agent-oriented programming. AI 60(1), 51–92 (1993)
20. Vázquez-Salceda, J., Aldewereld, H., Grossi, D., Dignum, F.: From human regulations to regulated software agents' behavior. AI & Law 16(1), 73–87 (2008)
21. Viganò, F.: A framework for model checking institutions. In: Edelkamp, S., Lomuscio, A. (eds.) MoChArt IV 2006. LNCS (LNAI), vol. 4428, pp. 129–145. Springer, Heidelberg (2007)
22. Visser, W., Havelund, K., Brat, G.P., Park, S., Lerda, F.: Model Checking Programs. Automated Software Engineering 10(2), 203–232 (2003)

Operational Semantics for BDI Modules
in Multi-agent Programming

Mehdi Dastani and Bas R. Steunebrink

Utrecht University
The Netherlands
{mehdi,bass}@cs.uu.nl

Abstract. This paper proposes an operational semantics for BDI modules that can be incorporated in multi-agent programming languages. The introduced concept of modules facilitates the implementation of agents, agent roles, and agent profiles. Moreover, the introduced concept of modules enables common programming techniques such as encapsulation and information hiding for BDI-based multi-agent programs. This vision is applied to a BDI-based multi-agent programming language to which specific programming constructs are added to allow the implementation of modules. The syntax and operational semantics of this programming language are provided and some properties of the module related programming constructs are discussed. An example is presented to illustrate how modules can be used to implement BDI-based multi-agent systems.

1   Introduction

Modularity is an essential principle in structured programming in general and in agent programming in particular. This paper focuses on the modularity principle applied to BDI-based agent programming languages. There have been some proposals for supporting modules in BDI-based programming languages, e.g., [2,3,5,8]. In these proposals, modularization is considered as a mechanism to structure an individual agent's program in separate modules, each encapsulating cognitive components such as beliefs, goals, and plans that together model a specific functionality and can be used to handle specific situations or tasks. However, the way the modules are used in these programming approaches are different.

For example, in Jack [3] and Jadex [2], modules (which are also called capabilities) are employed for information hiding and reusability by encapsulating different cognitive components that together implement a specific capability/functionality of the agent. In these approaches, the encapsulated components are used during an agent's execution to process the events received by the agent. In other approaches [5,8], modules are used to realize a specific policy or mechanism in order to control agent execution. More specifically, modules in GOAL [5] are considered as the 'focus of execution', which can be used to disambiguate the application and execution of plans. This is done by assigning a mental state condition (beliefs and/or goals) to each module. The modules whose conditions are satisfied form the focus of an agent's execution such that only plans from these modules are applied and executed. Finally, in 3APL [8] a module can be associated with a specific goal indicating which planning rules can be applied to achieve the

J. Dix, M. Fisher, and P. Novák (Eds.): CLIMA X, LNAI 6214, pp. 83–101, 2010.

goal. In other words, a module implements specific means for achieving specific goals. It should also be noted that the concept of module as used in [6] is different than in other approaches. A module in [6] is considered as one specific cognitive component (e.g., an agent's beliefs) and not as a functionality modeled by different cognitive components.

In these proposals, most module-related decisions such as when and how modules should be used during an agent's execution are controlled by the agent's execution strategy, usually implemented in the agent's interpreter (i.e., agent deliberation cycle). An agent programmer can control the use of modules during an agent's execution indirectly and implicitly either based on the predetermined functionality given to the modules or through conditions assigned to them. For example, in Jack [3] and Jadex [2] the agent's interpreter uses modules to process the received events. In [5], belief or goal conditions are assigned to modules such that an agent's interpreter uses the modules when the respective conditions hold. Finally, in [8] a programmer has only a limited control over the modules by indicating which modules (i.e., which planning rules) should be used to achieve a goal.

Like in other approaches, we consider a module as an encapsulation of different cognitive components that together implement a specific agent functionality. However, the added value of our approach is that a programmer can perform a wide range of operations on modules. These module-related operations enable a programmer to directly and explicitly control *when* and *how* modules are used. Thus, in contrast to the abovementioned approaches, we propose a set of generic programming constructs that can be used by an agent programmer to perform a variety of operations on modules. The proposed notion of module can be used to implement a variety of agent concepts such as agent role and agent profile. In fact, in our approach a module can be used as a mechanism to specify a role that can be enacted by an agent during its execution. We also explain how the proposed notion of modules can be used to implement agents that can represent and reason about other agents. In section 2, we explain our module based programming vision, present its syntax, and provide an example. The operational semantics of the programming language are presented in section 3. In section 4, we discuss how the proposed notion of modules can be used to implement agent roles and agent profiles. Finally, in section 5, we conclude the paper and indicate some future research directions.

2   BDI Programming with Modules

Programming a BDI-based individual agent amounts to specifying its initial (cognitive) state in terms of beliefs (information), goals (objectives), and plans (means). In programming terminology, the beliefs, goals, and plans can be considered as (cognitive) data structures specifying the state of the agent program. The execution of a BDI-based agent program, which is supposed to modify the state of the agent program, is based on a cyclic process called *deliberation cycle* (sense-reason-act cycle). Each iteration of this process starts with sensing the environment (i.e., receive events and messages), reasoning about its state (i.e., update the state with received events and messages, and generate plans to either achieve goals or to react to events), and performing actions (i.e., perform actions of the generated plans). Similar BDI ingredients and deliberation cycles are used in existing BDI-based programming languages such as Jason [1], 2APL [4], Jadex [7], and Jack [9].

Without losing generality and committing to a specific knowledge representation scheme, we assume in the rest of the paper a BDI-based agent programming language with (cognitive) data structures and a similar deliberation process. Moreover, we consider structuring a BDI-based agent program in separate modules as encapsulation of cognitive data that together model a specific functionality (when the deliberation process operates on them). A multi-agent program consists of a set of modules with unique names, each specifying a state in terms of cognitive concepts. Initially, a subset of these modules is identified as the specification of the initial state of individual agents. The execution of a multi-agent program is then the instantiation of this subset of modules followed by performing a deliberation process on each module instance. In this way, an instance of a module forms the initial state of an individual agent. It should be emphasized that a module instance specifies the cognitive state of an agent while the agent itself is the deliberation process working on the cognitive state.

2.1   Syntax

We do not present here the complete syntax of a modular BDI-based agent programming language as we aim at focusing on modules and module-related actions. In fact, we assume that a module is just like an agent program specifying a cognitive state by means of programming constructs (for beliefs, goals, and plans) of existing BDI-based programming languages extended with module-related actions. Moreover, we assume that the proposed module-related actions can be added to any existing BDI-based agent programming language [1,4,7,9].

For the sake of presenting an example, however, we consider an agent's beliefs being implemented by a set of Horn-clauses. An agent's goals are assumed to be implemented by a set of conjunctive ground atoms, where each conjunction represents a situation the agent wants to realize. An agent is assumed to be capable of performing different types of actions such as update actions (to modify beliefs and adopt and drop goals), belief and goal test actions (to query beliefs and goals), and actions to send messages and to change the state of external environments. Moreover, an agent is assumed to generate plans at runtime by applying rules. These rules can be used to generate plans based on either the agent's beliefs and goals, or the received internal and external events including messages from other agents. Rules have the form $trigger \mid guard \rightarrow plan$, where $trigger$ is either a goal or an event query of the form $G(\varphi)$ or $E(\varphi)$, respectively, and the $guard$ is a belief query of the form $B(\varphi)$. Finally, $plan$ is the plan to be generated and added to the set of plans if both $trigger$ and $guard$ hold. Similar BDI related programming constructs occur in many existing BDI-based agent programming languages such as Jason [1], Jadex [7], Jack [9], and 2APL [4].

The first module-related action is $\texttt{create}(mod\text{-}name, ins\text{-}ident)$, which can be used to create an instance of the module specification named $mod\text{-}name$. The name that is assigned to the created module instance is given by the second argument $ins\text{-}ident$. The creating module instance (also called the owner of the created module instance or simply the owner) can use this name to perform further operations on the created module instance (also called the owned module instance). One module specification can be instantiated more than once by one or more module instances. In such a case, the creating module instance should assign a unique name to each created module instance. A module instance with identifier m can be released by its owner by means of the release(m) action. The released module instance m will be removed/lost.

It is also possible that one and the same module instance is used by two different module instances. For this purpose, a special type of module, called singleton module, is introduced. While the ownership of a singleton module instance can be changed through create and release operations performed by different modules instances, the state of the singleton module instance remain unchanged, i.e., the state of a singleton module instance is maintained after one module instance release it and another one owns it again.

A module instance m can be executed by its owner through the execute(m, *test*) action. The execution of a module instance, performed by its owner, has two effects: 1) it suspends the execution of the owner module instance, and 2) it starts the execution of the owned module instance. The execution of the owner module instance will be resumed as soon as the execution of the owned module instance is terminated. In a sense, an agent that executes an owned module instance, stops deliberating on its current cognitive state and starts deliberating on a new cognitive state.

The termination of the owned module instance[1] is based on the mandatory test condition (i.e., the second argument of the execute action). As soon as this condition holds, a stop event is sent to the owned module instance. The module instance can then use the received event and start a cleaning operation after which it should broadcast a return event. For this we introduce an action return that can be executed by an owned module instance after which its execution is terminated and the execution of the owner module instance is resumed.

The owner of a module instance can access, query, and update the internals of the instance. In particular, the owner can test whether certain beliefs and goals are entailed by the beliefs and goals of its owned module instance m through action test(m, φ, f), where φ consists of belief and goal queries of the form B(φ) and G(φ), and f is a boolean flag indicating whether the query φ is positively answered (in which case a, possibly empty, substitution is resulted) or is negatively answered (in which case an empty substitution is resulted). It is important to note that argument m and φ of the test action are input parameters while argument f is an output parameter. Also, the beliefs and goals of a module instance m can be updated by means of the actions updateB(m, φ) and updateG(m, φ), respectively. Here φ can consist of multiple terms to be added, separated by commas; however, terms preceded by a minus sign are removed from the beliefs/goals.

A typical life cycle of a module in terms of these operations is illustrated in Figure 1, which proceeds as follows. A module instance i can create a new module instance j from a specification file. The module instance i can modify j's internal state using update actions. The module instance i can transfer the execution control to the module instance j by the execute action. The execution of j continues until j performs a return action. The module instance i can specify a stopping condition φ, causing j to receive a

---

[1] The owner cannot force the owned module instance's execution to stop because its own execution has been suspended.

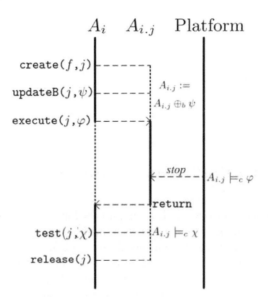

Fig. 1. A typical life cycle of a module

stop event when φ is satisfied, in response to which it can perform clean-up operations before returning execution control back to the module instance i. When i is active again, it can query j's internal state by the test action and release (remove) it.

2.2 An Example of a Multi-agent Program

The following example is provided to illustrate the idea of module-related constructs and their use to implement an agent's role. This example is not intended to demonstrate the practical use of the constructs for which we may need substantially more space. Suppose we need to build a multi-agent system in which one single manager and three workers cooperate to collect gold items in an environment called gridworld. The manager coordinates the activities of the three workers by asking them either to play the explorer role to detect the gold items in the gridworld environment or to play the carrier role to carry the detected gold items to a depot and store them. For this example, which can be implemented as the program illustrated in Figure 2, the module declaration includes a manager module (i.e., `manager.mod`) which specifies the initial state of the manager agent with the name m (the implementation of the manager module is presented in Figure 3). Note that only one manager agent will be initialized and created (line 7). Moreover, the worker module (`worker.mod`; see Figure 4) specifies the initial state of three worker agents. The names of the worker agents in the implemented multi-agent system is assumed to be indexed with numbers, i.e., there will be three worker agents with names w1, w2, and w3 (line 8). Finally, two additional modules are declared to implement the explorer and carrier functionalities (line 4, 5). As we will see, these functionalities/roles will be played by the worker agents at runtime. Note that both functionalities/roles can access the 'gridworld' environment and that the internals

```
1  Modules:
2    manager.mod
3    worker.mod
4    explorer.mod  @gridworld
5    carrier.mod   @gridworld
6  Agents:
7    m manager 1
8    w worker 3
```

Fig. 2. The multi-agent program of the running example

of these module instances (roles in this example) need not to be known to their owner module instances (information hiding aspects of modules).

The manager module can be implemented as in Figure 3. The goal of the manager m is to find and have gold items (line 10). Moreover, it has one initial plan through which it sends a request to worker w3 to explore the gridworld environment (line 11). We assume that the manager is aware of the three created workers, i.e., it has the identities of the workers. This assumption can be relaxed by making a query to a possibly existing agent management system to get the identifier of a worker.

The first rule of the manager agent (lines 13-17) indicates that the goal to have a gold item (i.e., G(haveGold())) can be achieved if the agent believes that there is a gold item at position POS not assigned to any (worker) agent yet and that there is a worker agent A having no assigned task (i.e., collecting gold items) yet (i.e., B(gold(POS) && -assigned(POS,_) && worker(A) && -assigned(_,A))). The plan to achieve this goal sends a message to the free agent asking to play the carrier role to collect the gold item. This is followed by the action ModOwnBel(assigned(POS,A)) by means of which the manager agent modifies its own beliefs to record the fact that the free agent is not free anymore (i.e., after this action the manager agent believes that agent A has an assigned task).

The second rule of the manager agent (lines 19-23) indicates that the goal to find a gold item can be achieved if the agent does not have any beliefs about goal items and that there is a worker agent A having no assigned task yet (i.e., B(-gold(_) && -worker(A) && -assigned(_,A))). The plan to achieve this goal sends a message to the free agent asking to play the explorer role to find a gold item. This is followed by the action ModOwnBel(assigned(_,A)) by means of which the manager agent modifies its own beliefs to record the fact that the free agent is not free anymore.

The third rule (lines 25-27) indicates that whenever the manager receives an event (message) containing the information about the position of a gold item (i.e., gold(POS)), it updates its own beliefs with this information (line 26). The fourth rule (lines 29-31) indicates that when a worker informs the manager that it has done its task (i.e., collected and carried its assigned gold items to the depot), the manager updates its own beliefs (atoms preceded by a minus sign are removed) with the fact that the gold item is removed and that the worker is ready to carry new gold items again. Finally, the fifth rule (lines 33-35) indicates that when a worker informs the manager

```
 9  Beliefs = { worker(w1), worker(w2), worker(w3) }
10  Goals = { findGold() and haveGold() }
11  Plans = { send( w3, play(explorer) ); }
12  Rules = {
13    G( haveGold() ) | B( gold(POS) && -assigned(POS, _) &&
14                           worker(A) && -assigned(_, A)     ) ->
15          { send( A, play(carrier, POS) );
16            ModOwnBel( assigned(POS, A) );
17          },
18
19    G( findGold() ) | B( -gold(_) && worker(A) &&
20                         -assigned(_, A)                 ) ->
21          { send( A, play(explorer) );
22            ModOwnBel( assigned(_, A) );
23          },
24
25    E( receive( A, gold(POS) ) ) | B( worker(A) ) ->
26          { ModOwnBel( gold(POS) );
27          },
28
29    E( receive( A, done(POS) ) ) | B( worker(A) ) ->
30          { ModOwnBel( -assigned(POS, A), -gold(POS) );
31          },
32
33    E( receive( A, error(POS) ) ) | B( worker(A) ) ->
34          { ModOwnBel( -assigned(_,A) );
35          }
36  }
```

Fig. 3. The code of the manager module

that it has failed to collect and carry the gold item from the designated position, the manager updates its own beliefs with the fact that the worker is free and ready to do perform a new task.

The worker agent, as implemented in Figure 4, is an agent that waits for requests to play either the explorer or the carrier role. When it receives a request to play the explorer role from the manager (line 39), it creates an explorer module instance and executes it (line 40-41). Note that the stopping condition of this module instance is the belief that gold has been found. When the execution of the module instance halts, the worker agent sends the position of the detected gold item to the manager (line 43), and finally releases the explorer module instance (line 44). It is important to note that for the worker agent the creation of an explorer module instance and executing it is the same as playing the explorer role. The worker agent plays this role until the goal of the role (i.e., finding gold items) is believed to be achieved. Note the use of the test action. This action results in a substitution that assigns a value to variable POS, making the position of the found gold item accessible to the testing module instance. Also, the

```
37  Beliefs = { manager(m) }
38  Rules = {
39    E( receive( A, play(explorer) ) ) | B( manager(A) ) ->
40          { create( "explorer.mod", myexp );
41            execute( myexp, B( gold(_) ) );
42            test( myexp, B( gold(POS) ), F);
43            If F=true then send( A, gold(POS) );
44            release( myexp );
45          },
46
47    E( receive( A, play(carrier, POS) ) ) | B( manager(A) ) ->
48          { create( "carrier.mod", mycar );
49            updateB( mycar , gold(POS) );
50            execute( mycar, B( done() or error() ) );
51            test( mycar , B(done()) , F);
52            if F=true then send( A, done(POS) )
53                  else send( A, error(POS) );
54            release( mycar );
55          }
56  }
```

Fig. 4. The code of the worker module

output parameter F will in this case have the value true as the query gold(POS) will be answered positively. This is because the query is used as the stopping condition of the preceding execute action. Therefore, the test F=true in line (line 43) is not necessary (this test is added to stress the use of the output parameter). The second rule of the worker agent (line 47) is responsible for carrying gold items by creating a carrier module instance (line 48), adding the gold item information to its beliefs (line 49), and executing it until either it has found the gold items (done() condition) or an error has occurred (error() condition); see line 50. The final four lines of this code (51-54) is to inform the manager agent about the success or failure of carrying the gold item and releasing the carrier module instance after this communication. In other words, this second rule indicates when the worker agent should play the carrier role. Note that the code of the manager agent has no rule to react to the failure message; for the running implementation such a rule should be added. The use of the output parameter F in this rule is essential as checking its value is necessary to generate different responses.

The explorer module (i.e., the implementation of the explorer role), as implemented in Figure 5, has the goal to find gold items (line 58). In order to achieve this goal, it proceeds to a random location in the gridworld, performs a sense gold action there and, if successful, adds the position of the detected gold item (i.e., gold(POS)) to its own local beliefs (line 63). Note that this belief information satisfies the stopping condition of the module instance (see line 41) since the goal foundGold() is achieved as soon as gold(POS) is added to its beliefs (line 57). In this example, the final rule (line 66) is to react to the stop event which is broadcasted when the explorer's stopping condition holds. The reception of this event causes the explorer module to perform a return action, which in turn causes the execution to be handed back to the worker module instance.

```
57 Beliefs = { foundGold() :- gold(_) };
58 Goals = {foundGold()}
59 Rules = {
60    G( foundGold() ) | true ->
61            { @gridworld( goToRandomPosition() );
62              @gridworld( senseGold() , POS );
63              if POS != nil then ModOwnBel( gold(POS) );
64            },
65
66    E( stop ) | true -> { return; }
67 }
```

Fig. 5. The code of the explorer module

Finally, the carrier module (i.e., the implementation of the carrier role) as implemented in Figure 6 has a goal to store a gold item (line 69). This goal can be achieved by fetching the gold item, storing it in the depot, and removing that gold item from its own local beliefs (lines 72-74). Similar to the explorer module, the carrier module performs a return action when it receives a stop event (line 77). The third rule (line 80) adds error information (i.e., error()) to its own local beliefs when the execution of an action in the gridworld environment fails. Note that error() in the beliefs was one of the stopping conditions to stop the execution of the carrier module instance (line 50). It is also important to note that it is up to the gridworld programmer to determine when the execution of a gridworld action fails.

In this example, we did not use any singleton modules. However, for applications where the cognitive state of the explorer or carrier module instances are considered as important and useful for the next time these roles are played, then one may consider to define them as singleton.

3   Semantics

The semantics of the proposed actions are defined in terms of a transition system, which consists of a set of transition rules for deriving transitions. A transition specifies a single computation/execution step by indicating how one configuration can be transformed into another. In this paper, we first present the multi-agent system configuration, which consists of the configurations of module instances/individual agents and the state of the external shared environments. Then, we present transition rules from which possible execution steps for multi-agent programs can be derived. Here, we focus only on the semantics of module-related constructs.

```
68  Beliefs = { goldStored() :- not gold(_) }
69  Goals = { goldStored()}
70  Rules = {
71    G( goldStored() ) | B( gold(POS) ) ->
72          { @gridworld( fetchGold(POS) );
73            @gridworld( storeGold() );
74            ModOwnBel( -gold(POS), done() );
75          },
76
77    E( stop ) | true -> { return; },
78
79    E( fail( @gridworld(_) ) ) | true ->
80          { ModOwnBel( error() );} }
```

Fig. 6. The code of the carrier module

3.1 Multi-agent System Configuration

The configuration of a multi-agent program is defined in terms of the configuration of active modules instances (some module instances are individual agents), inactive ones, and the state of their shared external environments. The configuration of a module instance includes 1) the cognitive state of the module instance (beliefs, goals, plans) with a unique name, and 2) a stopping condition for the module instance.

We denote the configuration of the cognitive state of an agent (or a module instance) with name i as A_i. We write A_i^B and A_i^G to denote the beliefs and goals of agent A_i, respectively. Moreover, we assume suitable definitions of $\models_b$, $\models_g$, $\oplus_b$, and $\oplus_g$ such that beliefs and goals can be queried and updated, respectively. We then define $\models_c$ as a test on a single agent (or module instance) configuration A_i as: $A_i \not\models_c \bot$; $A_i \models_c \mathrm{B}(\varphi) \Leftrightarrow A_i^B \models_b \varphi$; and $A_i \models_c \mathrm{G}(\varphi) \Leftrightarrow A_i^G \models_g \varphi$. To simplify keeping track of which module instance owns which, their names are composed using periods. For example, a module instance named 1.4.7 is owned by module instance 1.4, which is owned by the 'top-level' module instance 1. More formally, we define the sets Bid of 'basic identifiers' and Cid of 'composed identifiers'; the function $prefix$ returns all prefixes of a composed name (e.g., $prefix(1.4.7) = \{1.4.7, 1.4, 1\}$):

$$Bid = \mathbb{N}$$
$$Cid = Bid \cup \{ c.b \mid c \in Cid, b \in Bid \}$$
$$prefix(i) = \begin{cases} \{i\} & \text{if } i \in Bid \\ \{i\} \cup prefix(j) & \text{if } i = j.k \text{ for some } j \in Cid, k \in Bid \end{cases}$$

When writing $A_{i.j}$, it is assumed that $i \in Cid$ and $j \in Bid$.

The configuration of a multi-agent system is a tuple $\langle \mathcal{A}, \mathcal{I}, \mathcal{S}, \chi \rangle$, where $\mathcal{A}$ is a set of configurations of *active* module instances (including module instances that implement individual agents), $\mathcal{I}$ is a set of configurations of *inactive* module instances, $\mathcal{S}$ is a set of configurations of *released singleton* module instances, and χ is the state of the shared environments. The initial configuration of each individual agent is determined by the declared module that is assigned to the agent in the multi-agent program. In particular, for each individual agent with initial configuration A, a module instantiation $(A, \perp)$ is created and added to the set of active module instances $\mathcal{A}$. Thus, module instances created when the multi-agent program is started will have $\perp$ as stopping condition. Also, all environments from the multi-agent system program are collected in the set χ. The initial state of the shared external environment is set by the programmer, e.g., the programmer may initially place gold or obstacles at certain positions in a grid-world environment. Finally, in the initial configuration the sets of inactive module instances $\mathcal{I}$ and released singletons $\mathcal{S}$ are empty.

The idea behind the distinction between $\mathcal{A}$, $\mathcal{I}$, and $\mathcal{S}$ is that only module instance contained in $\mathcal{A}$ are subject to deliberation and thus subject to making transitions. The inactive module instances are kept in $\mathcal{I}$ and the released instances of singleton modules are kept in $\mathcal{S}$. The module instances in $\mathcal{I}$ may at run-time be (re)activated (i.e. transferred to $\mathcal{A}$) or removed from $\mathcal{I}$. The module instances in $\mathcal{S}$ may at run-time be (re)created by another module instance, i.e., a module instance can become the (new) owner of a release instance of a singleton module. A singleton module instance can never be removed once it is created.

Given a multi-agent configuration $\langle \mathcal{A}, \mathcal{I}, \mathcal{S}, \chi \rangle$, two convenience functions are defined for looking up all ancestors and descendants using the name of a module instance, as follows:

$$anc_{\mathcal{I}}^{\mathcal{A}}(i) = \{ (A_j, \psi) \in \mathcal{A} \cup \mathcal{I} \mid j \in prefix(i) \}$$
$$desc_{\mathcal{I}}^{\mathcal{A}}(i) = \{ (A_j, \psi) \in \mathcal{A} \cup \mathcal{I} \mid i \in prefix(j) \}$$

Note that the module instance with the given name (i) is included as its own ancestor and descendant.

The execution of a multi-agent program modifies its initial configuration by means of transitions that are derivable from the transition rules presented in the following subsection. In fact, each transition rule indicates which execution step (i.e., transition) is possible from a given configuration. It should be noted that for a given configuration there may be several transition rules applicable. An interpreter is a deterministic choice of applying transition rules in a certain order.

3.2 Transition Rules for Module Actions

We provide the transition rules for deriving multi-agent system transitions based on the execution of a module-related actions. Since module related actions, which are performed by individual module instances, have global effects at the multi-agent system level, we use individual module transitions cause by module related actions to define global multi-agent system transitions. For this reason, we use $A_i \xrightarrow{\alpha!} A_i'$ to indicate that the module instance A_i can make a transition to module instance A_i' by performing action α. The performance of the action *broadcasts* event $\alpha!$. When $\alpha?$ is used, instead of $\alpha!$, A_i *receives* the event $\alpha?$. Finally, we use $\alpha!?$ to indicate that A_i performs action α with some output parameters. The performance of such an action broadcasts event $\alpha!$ and waits for receiving the values of the output parameters.

The first transition indicates the effect of the $\texttt{create}(f,j)$ action performed by the module instance A_i, where f is the identifier of a module specification (typically a file name) and j is the name that will be associated with the created module instance. This transition rule indicates that a module instance can be created by another module instance if the creating module instance is active, i.e., $(A_i, \varphi) \in \mathcal{A}$. The result is that the set of module instances $\mathcal{A}$, $\mathcal{I}$, and $\mathcal{S}$ in the multi-agent system configuration are modified. In particular, the creating module instance is modified as it has performed the $\texttt{create}$ action. This results in a set of active module instance $\mathcal{A}'$ which is the same as $\mathcal{A}$ except that the creating module instance A_i is changed to A_i'. The modification of $\mathcal{I}$ and $\mathcal{S}$ depend, however, on whether the module f is a singleton module or not. If f is a singleton module and there exists already an instance of this module in the set of released singleton module instances $\mathcal{S}$, then the creation of the instance will remove the released instance from $\mathcal{S}$ and add it to the set of inactive module instances $\mathcal{I}$. Otherwise, if either f is not a singleton module or no instance of f is created yet, then an instance of module f is created and added to the set of inactive module instances $\mathcal{I}$. The set of released singleton module instances remains unchanged. In the following, we write $spec(A) = f$ to indicate that A is an instance of module f. We also use A as referring to the module instance $A_{i.j}$, i.e., A is the same module instance as $A_{i.j}$ without the name $i.j$.

$$\frac{(A_i, \varphi) \in \mathcal{A} \qquad A_i \xrightarrow{create(f,j)!} A_i' \qquad (A_{i.j}, \bot) \notin \mathcal{I}}{\langle \mathcal{A}, \mathcal{I}, \mathcal{S}, \chi \rangle \longrightarrow \langle \mathcal{A}', \mathcal{I}', \mathcal{S}', \chi \rangle} \tag{1}$$

where $\mathcal{A}' = (\mathcal{A} \setminus \{(A_i, \varphi)\}) \cup \{(A_i', \varphi)\}$ and $\mathcal{I}'$ and $\mathcal{S}'$ are determined as follows:

- if f is a singleton module and $\exists A \in \mathcal{S} : spec(A) = f$, then $\mathcal{S}' = \mathcal{S} \setminus \{A\}$ and $\mathcal{I}' = \mathcal{I} \cup \{(A_{i.j}, \bot)\}$
- otherwise, $\mathcal{S}' = \mathcal{S}$, $A_{i.j}$ is a new configuration with name $i.j$ created from specification f, and $\mathcal{I}' = \mathcal{I} \cup \{(A_{i.j}, \bot)\}$.

The newly created module's execution stopping condition is set to $\bot$ (as an arbitrary initial value). This is because the stopping condition should be set when the module instance is executed. We would like to emphasize that a module is only allowed to create another non-singleton module twice (or more) if different names are used to identify it. This will result in two different instances of the non-singleton module, each with its own name and state. Otherwise the create action blocks.

A module A_i that owns another module named j (i.e. $(A_{i.j}, \bot) \in \mathcal{I}$) can release (delete) it. It can do this by performing the action $\texttt{release}(j)$. As a result, this module configuration is removed from $\mathcal{I}$. If $A_{i.j}$ does not exist, the release action blocks. Moreover, if $A_{i.j}$ is an instance of a singleton module, then the module instance will be added to the set of released singleton module instances $\mathcal{S}$.

$$\frac{(A_i, \varphi) \in \mathcal{A} \qquad A_i \xrightarrow{release(j)!} A_i' \qquad (A_{i.j}, \bot) \in \mathcal{I}}{\langle \mathcal{A}, \mathcal{I}, \mathcal{S}, \chi \rangle \longrightarrow \langle \mathcal{A}', \mathcal{I}', \mathcal{S}', \chi \rangle} \tag{2}$$

where $\mathcal{A}' = (\mathcal{A} \setminus \{(A_i, \varphi)\}) \cup \{(A_i', \varphi)\}$ and $\mathcal{I}' = \mathcal{I} \setminus desc_{\mathcal{I}}^{\mathcal{A}}(i.j)$. Note that all descendants of $A_{i.j}$ (including $A_{i.j}$) must be removed from the set of inactive module instances, otherwise any unreleased (inactive) module instances owned by $A_{i.j}$ would be kept dangling. All singleton descendants of $A_{i.j}$ are then saved in $\mathcal{S}'$. This is done by collecting all descendants A_k of $A_{i.j}$ whose specification f (i.e., $spec(A_k) = f$) is singleton (i.e., $singleton(f)$). So the new set of saved singleton module instances becomes $\mathcal{S}' = \mathcal{S} \cup \{ A \mid (A_k, \psi) \in desc_{\mathcal{I}}^{\mathcal{A}}(i.j), singleton(spec(A)) \}$. Note that the names assigned to the saved singletons (e.g., k above) are removed, and that it is possible that $\mathcal{S}' = \mathcal{S}$ if neither $A_{i.j}$ nor any of its descendants were defined as singletons.

An instance of a non-singleton module is always created privately for the creating module instance (or agent). Therefore, a non-singleton module instance will not retain its state when it is released and created again. Also, the creating module instance (agent) is the only one that can release and thereby delete the module instance. However, if the released instance is an instance of a singleton module, then its owned module instances will remain inactive in $\mathcal{I}$. If the singleton module instance is created and executed once again, then these module instances may be activated too.

A module instance that owns another module instance can execute it, meaning that the owned module instance is transferred from $\mathcal{I}$ to $\mathcal{A}$ so that it can perform actions by itself. In doing so, the owning module instance is transferred from $\mathcal{A}$ to $\mathcal{I}$, i.e. its execution is halted. In effect, control is 'handed over' from the owner module instance to the owned module instance. As part of the execute action, a stopping condition ψ is provided with which the owner module instance can specify when it wants control returned, i.e., as soon as the owned module instance satisfies the stopping condition ($A_{i.j} \models_c \psi$; a transition rule for this case is provided next).

$$\frac{(A_i, \varphi) \in \mathcal{A} \qquad A_i \xrightarrow{execute(j, \psi)!} A_i' \qquad (A_{i.j}, \perp) \in \mathcal{I}}{\langle \mathcal{A}, \mathcal{I}, \mathcal{S}, \chi \rangle \longrightarrow \langle \mathcal{A}', \mathcal{I}', \mathcal{S}, \chi \rangle} \qquad (3)$$

where $\mathcal{A}' = (\mathcal{A} \setminus \{(A_i, \varphi)\}) \cup \{(A_{i.j}, \psi)\}$ and $\mathcal{I}' = (\mathcal{I} \setminus \{(A_{i.j}, \perp)\}) \cup \{(A_i', \varphi)\}$.

As soon as the stopping condition of an executing module instance holds ($A_i \models_c \varphi$), it will receive a *stop* event from the multi-agent level requesting it to stop its execution, possibly after first performing some cleanup operations. Note that it is assumed that a module instance is always able to receive a *stop* event ($A_i \xrightarrow{stop?} A_i'$). It is not guaranteed by the system that a module instance will actually ever stop; it must perform a return action (see below) itself in order to have it transferred back to $\mathcal{I}$.

$$\frac{(A_i, \varphi) \in \mathcal{A} \qquad A_i \models_c \varphi \qquad A_i \xrightarrow{stop?} A_i'}{\langle \mathcal{A}, \mathcal{I}, \mathcal{S}, \chi \rangle \longrightarrow \langle \mathcal{A}', \mathcal{I}, \mathcal{S}, \chi \rangle} \qquad (4)$$

where $\mathcal{A}' = (\mathcal{A} \setminus \{(A_i, \varphi)\}) \cup \{(A_i', \varphi)\}$. Note that by definition, $A_i \not\models_c \perp$. This means that 1) top-level module instances (i.e. those created at initialization of the multi-agent configuration, i.e. those with a non-composed name) never receive a stop event because they have $\perp$ as stopping condition, and 2) module instances executed with $\perp$ as stopping condition (e.g. execute($j, \perp$)) never receive a stop event either; it is up to the programmer to ensure that the executed module instance performs a return action (see below) at some point to return control to its owning module instance.

A module instance can return control to its parent module instance by performing a return action. This will cause them to 'switch places' again with respect to $\mathcal{A}$ and $\mathcal{I}$. Only module instances with a parent can return control, which is enforced below requiring that the module instance performing a `return` action has a composite name $i.j$. It is up to the programmer to ensure that a `return` action is performed by a module instance in response to a *stop* event. It should be noted that a module's execution has to be finished before it can be released, because the owning module instance must be in $\mathcal{A}$ to be able to perform a `release` action.

$$\frac{(A_{i.j}, \psi) \in \mathcal{A} \quad A_{i.j} \xrightarrow{return!} A'_{i.j} \quad (A_i, \varphi) \in \mathcal{I}}{\langle \mathcal{A}, \mathcal{I}, \mathcal{S}, \chi \rangle \longrightarrow \langle \mathcal{A}', \mathcal{I}', \mathcal{S}, \chi \rangle} \tag{5}$$

where $\mathcal{A}' = (\mathcal{A} \setminus \{(A_{i.j}, \psi)\}) \cup \{(A_i, \varphi)\}$ and $\mathcal{I}' = (\mathcal{I} \setminus \{(A_i, \varphi)\}) \cup \{(A'_{i.j}, \bot)\}$. This mechanism allows a module instance to respond to a stop event by performing clean up operations and then returning. Finally, note that the state of $A'_{i.j}$ is saved (in $\mathcal{I}$) with the default $\bot$ as stopping condition.

Next we consider several actions that a module instance can perform on a module instance that it owns. These actions do not pertain to control, but to the state of the owned module instance. Specifically, a module instance can query the beliefs and goals of an owned module instance, update the beliefs of an owned module instance, and adopt and drop goals in an owned module instance. First we consider the belief and goal queries. A module instance A_i that owns another module instance named j, which is currently inactive (i.e. $(A_{i.j}, \bot) \in \mathcal{I}$), can perform a (belief/goal) query ψ on $A_{i.j}$ by means of a test action. The query can be answered positively and returns substitution θ if $A_{i.j} \models_c \psi\theta$, or it fails returning an empty substitution. The following transition rule captures this.

$$\frac{(A_i, \varphi) \in \mathcal{A} \quad A_i \xrightarrow{test(j,\psi,f)!?} A'_i\theta \quad (A_{i.j}, \bot) \in \mathcal{I}}{\langle \mathcal{A}, \mathcal{I}, \mathcal{S}, \chi \rangle \longrightarrow \langle \mathcal{A}', \mathcal{I}, \mathcal{S}, \chi \rangle} \tag{6}$$

where $\mathcal{A}' = (\mathcal{A} \setminus \{(A_i, \varphi)\}) \cup \{(A'_i\theta, \varphi)\}$ and $f = \top$ if $A_{i.j} \models_c \psi\theta$ or $f = \bot$ and $\theta = \emptyset$ if $A_{i.j} \not\models_c \psi$. In this transition rule, we assume $A'_i\theta$ to be the same as A_i except that the test action has been processed and the substitution θ is applied. How these operations are performed depends on the corresponding agent transition rules from which the transition $A_i \longrightarrow A'_i$ can be derived. Note that $A_{i.j}$ is not changed by the test and that only direct descendants can be tested (and updated; see below). As the test action has an output parameter, it will broadcast event `test(`$j, \psi, $`f)` `!` and wait for the value of the output parameter `f`. This is the reason for using the notation `test(`$j, \psi, $`f)` `!?`.

We now consider belief and goal updates. It is assumed that a formula ψ can represent a belief/goal and that $A_{i.j} \oplus_{b/g} \psi$ yields a configuration where the beliefs/goals have been updated with ψ. Note that if ψ contains any negated terms, these will be deleted from $A_{i.j}$. Similar to the transition rule for queries above, the owned module instance on which the belief or goal update is performed must be contained in the set of inactive module instances $\mathcal{I}$. With slight abuse of notation (using a slash), the following transition rule captures both the `updateB` and `updateG` actions, respectively.

$$\frac{(A_i, \varphi) \in \mathcal{A} \quad A_i \xrightarrow{updateB/G(j,\psi)!} A'_i \quad (A_{i.j}, \bot) \in \mathcal{I}}{\langle \mathcal{A}, \mathcal{I}, \mathcal{S}, \chi \rangle \longrightarrow \langle \mathcal{A}', \mathcal{I}', \mathcal{S}, \chi \rangle} \tag{7}$$

where $\mathcal{A}' = (\mathcal{A}\setminus\{(A_i,\varphi)\})\cup\{(A_i',\varphi)\}$ and $\mathcal{I}' = (\mathcal{I}\setminus\{(A_{i.j},\perp)\})\cup\{(A_{i.j}\oplus_{b/g}\psi,\perp)\}$.

One module instance can send a message to another module instance if both the sender and receiver exist as active module instances (i.e. are elements of $\mathcal{A}$). It is assumed a *receive* event is always successful.

$$\frac{(A_i,\varphi)\in\mathcal{A}\quad A_i\xrightarrow{send(j,\psi)!}A_i'\quad (A_j,\varphi')\in\mathcal{A}\quad A_j\xrightarrow{receive(i,\psi)?}A_j'}{\langle\mathcal{A},\mathcal{I},\mathcal{S},\chi\rangle\longrightarrow\langle\mathcal{A}',\mathcal{I},\mathcal{S},\chi\rangle} \quad (8)$$

where $\mathcal{A}' = (\mathcal{A}\setminus\{(A_i,\varphi),(A_j,\varphi')\})\cup\{(A_i',\varphi),(A_j',\varphi')\}$. Note that only active module instances can exchange messages, meaning that they can never send messages to ancestors or descendants. If the intended receiver does not exist as an active module instance, the message is 'bounced' back to the sender. Again, it is assumed an *undelivered* event is always successful. Note that sending a message to a module instance that was once active but has since stopped or been released will fail.

$$\frac{(A_i,\varphi)\in\mathcal{A}\quad A_i\xrightarrow{send(j,\psi)!}A_i'\quad (A_j,\varphi')\notin\mathcal{A}\quad A_i'\xrightarrow{undelivered(j,\psi)?}A_i''}{\langle\mathcal{A},\mathcal{I},\mathcal{S},\chi\rangle\longrightarrow\langle\mathcal{A}',\mathcal{I},\mathcal{S},\chi\rangle} \quad (9)$$

where $\mathcal{A}' = (\mathcal{A}\setminus\{(A_i,\varphi)\})\cup\{(A_i'',\varphi)\}$. Thus we assume that the recipient of a message must be fully and correctly specified for it to be delivered. A different choice could be to always address messages to the top-level parent and look up which module instance of the receiving agent is currently active and deliver the message there. An objection to this would be that each module instance encapsulates a certain functionality and that a message sent to a specific module instance of an agent may make little sense to another module instance of the same agent.

Finally, a general transition rule is needed for all actions α not equal to one of the module-specific ones introduced actions above (e.g. 'normal' actions such as assignments, function calls, etc.). Note that the execution of action α possibly leads to a change in the environment χ (as expressed by the subscript χ').

$$\frac{(A_i,\varphi)\in\mathcal{A}\quad A_i\xrightarrow{\alpha!}_{\chi'}A_i'}{\langle\mathcal{A},\mathcal{I},\mathcal{S},\chi\rangle\longrightarrow\langle\mathcal{A}',\mathcal{I},\mathcal{S},\chi'\rangle} \quad (10)$$

where $\mathcal{A}' = (\mathcal{A}\setminus\{(A_i,\varphi)\})\cup\{(A_i',\varphi)\}$.

3.3 Properties

In this section we describe several properties (**P1-P6**) of the proposed module system. A proof sketch is provided after each property. All properties below assume a given multi-agent configuration $\langle\mathcal{A},\mathcal{I},\mathcal{S},\chi\rangle$.

P1: If the names of all *initial* agents (i.e., those module instances with a basic, non-composed name from Bid) are unique, then *all* module names that are generated at runtime are unique as well:

$$\left[\forall(A_i,\varphi)\neq(A_j,\psi)\in\mathcal{A}\cup\mathcal{I}:i,j\in Bid\Rightarrow i\neq j\right]\Rightarrow$$
$$\left[\forall(A_i,\varphi)\neq(A_j,\psi)\in\mathcal{A}\cup\mathcal{I}:i\neq j\right]$$

Proof (sketch). This property follows from (a) the fact that transition rule (1) for the `create` action does not allow a module instance to create two modules with the same name, and (b) the fact that when different module instances create new module instances using equal names, they are still assigned unique names because their given names are composed with their ancestors' names.

P2: All children of an active module instance have $\perp$ (a default value) as stopping condition:

$$\forall (A_i, \varphi) \in \mathcal{A} : \forall (A_{i.j}, \psi) \in \mathcal{I} : \psi = \perp$$

Proof (sketch). Whenever a module instance A_i creates a new module instance $A_{i.j}$ (by rule (1)) or an active module instance $A_{i.j}$ is halted (because it performed a `return` action; rule (5)), the stopping condition of $A_{i.j}$ is/becomes irrelevant and is set to $\perp$ as a default value. The only other transition rule that sets a stopping condition (except (1) and (5)) is rule (3) for the `execute` action; however, performing an `execute` action transfers the owner module to $\mathcal{I}$ and the owned module to $\mathcal{A}$, whereas the property above quantifies over all pairs of module instances where the owner is in $\mathcal{A}$ and the owned module instance is in $\mathcal{I}$, so the property still holds.

P3: All proper ancestors and descendants of an active module instance are themselves inactive:

$$\forall (A_i, \varphi) \in \mathcal{A} : (anc_{\mathcal{I}}^{\mathcal{A}}(i) \cup desc_{\mathcal{I}}^{\mathcal{A}}(i)) \setminus \{(A_i, \varphi)\} \subseteq \mathcal{I}$$

Proof (sketch). When a module instance activates another module instance by performing an `execute` action (rule (3)), it becomes inactive itself; when a module instance performs a `return` action (rule (5)), it becomes inactive and its parent becomes active again. No other transition rules add or remove module instances from $\mathcal{A}$. Therefore only one module instance can be active at the time in a line of ancestors and descendants.

P4: If an *inactive* module instance has a stopping condition not equal to $\perp$, then all its ancestors must be inactive and it must have one active descendant:

$$\forall (A_i, \varphi) \in \mathcal{I} : \varphi \neq \perp \Rightarrow \left[anc_{\mathcal{I}}^{\mathcal{A}}(i) \subseteq \mathcal{I} \;\&\; |desc_{\mathcal{I}}^{\mathcal{A}}(i) \cap \mathcal{A}| = 1 \right]$$

Proof (sketch). Initially, $\mathcal{I} = \emptyset$, so if $(A_i, \varphi) \in \mathcal{I}$ then A_i must have been added to $\mathcal{I}$ by one of the transition rules. Now if $\varphi \neq \perp$, A_i cannot have been added to $\mathcal{I}$ by performing a `return` action (rule (5)), because then its stopping condition would have been set to $\perp$. So when a module instance has a stopping condition not equal to $\perp$ yet it is inactive, it must be the case that it has created (rule (1)) and executed (rule (3)) another module instance. But this descendant may have done the same thing, and so on. Nevertheless, some where down the line of descendants of A_i (including A_i), one module instance must be active (i.e., $|desc_{\mathcal{I}}^{\mathcal{A}}(i) \cap \mathcal{A}| = 1$). Because all of A_i's ancestors must have performed an `execute` action they are all inactive (i.e., $anc_{\mathcal{I}}^{\mathcal{A}}(i) \subseteq \mathcal{I}$).

P5: For each initial agent there is always exactly one active descendant (possibly itself):

$$\forall (A_i, \varphi) \in \mathcal{A} \cup \mathcal{I} : i \in Bid \Rightarrow |desc_{\mathcal{I}}^{\mathcal{A}}(i) \cap \mathcal{A}| = 1$$

Proof (sketch). A module instance A_i is an initial agent if $i \in Bid$, i.e., if its name is non-composed. Each initial agent can only pass control to other module instances by becoming inactive itself (see rule (3)), and the same holds for every module instance down the line of descendants. So only one descendant of A_i (including A_i) can be active, i.e., $|desc_{\mathcal{I}}^{\mathcal{A}}(i) \cap \mathcal{A}| = 1$.

This leads to the following corollary.

P6: $|\mathcal{A}|$ is constant.

Proof (sketch). It is easy to see from the previous property that the number of active module instances (i.e., $|\mathcal{A}|$) will always be equal to the number of initial agents. This property can also be verified by examining all provided transition rules and seeing that for every module instance removed from $\mathcal{A}$, one other is put in its place.

4   Roles, Profiles, and Task Encapsulation

The proposed approach for modular programming is general enough to be used for the implementation of several agent-oriented programming topics. These include taking on different roles, making profiles of other agents, and the general programming technique of task encapsulation. We will provide an example for each of these topics in the following subsections.

4.1   Roles

A module specification can be considered as the specification of a role. In this way, a role specifies a set of objectives (goals) to be achieved by the agent that plays the role, power that the agent gets when its plays the role (actions and plans), information that becomes accessible to the role playing agent (beliefs), and strategies of how to achieve objectives or react to events (rules). The runtime creation and execution of a module instance can then be used to implement the activation and enactment of a role. The file that is used to create the new module instance is then the specification of the role that is to be played. In particular, the action create(*role*, *name*) can be seen as the activation of a role, by which the activating agent acquires a lock on the activated role, i.e. it becomes the role's owner and gains the exclusive right to manipulate the activated role. If *role* has been declared as *singleton*, this property of locking is important, because other agents may attempt the acquire the *role* as well. If *role* is not singleton, the role is created new and private to the creating agent anyway. Upon releasing a singleton role, the role is not deleted but retained with a blank owner, so that another agent may activate (using create(*role*, *name'*)) and use it.

An agent that has successfully performed the action create(*role*, *name*) may *enact/play* this role using execute(*name*, φ), where φ is a stopping condition, i.e., a composition of belief and goal queries. The owner agent is then put on hold until the role satisfies the terminating condition, at which point control is returned to the owner agent. In this way, an agent can only play one role at each moment of time. In principle, it is allowed for a role to activate and enact a new role, and repeat this without (theoretical) depth limits. However, this is usually not allowed in literature on roles. We assume that it is up to the programmer to prevent roles from enacting other roles.

4.2   Agent Profiles

As agents can be specified in terms of beliefs, goals and plans, we can use modules to represent agents. An agent can thus create and maintain profiles of other agents by creating module instances. For example, assume agent `mary` executes the actions `create("profile_template.mod", chris)` and `create("profile_template.mod", john)`, i.e., it uses a single template to initialize profiles of the (hypothetical) agents `chris` and `john`. These profiles can be updated by `mary` using, e.g., `updateB(chris, $\varphi$)` and `adoptgoal(john, $\psi$)` when appropriate. `mary` can even 'wonder' what `chris` would do in a certain situation by setting up that situation using belief and goal updates on `chris` and then performing `execute(chris, $\varphi$)` with a suitable stopping condition φ. The resulting state of `chris` can be queried afterwards to determine what `chris` 'would have done'.

4.3   Task Encapsulation

Modules can also be used for the common programming techniques of encapsulation and information hiding. Modules can encapsulate certain tasks, which can be performed by its owning agent if it performs an `execute` action on that module instance. Such a module can thus hide its internal state and keep it consistent for its task(s). An important difference between *creating* a module (in the sense proposed here) and *including* a module (in the sense of [3,2,4]) is that the contents of an *included* module instance are simply added to the including agent, whereas the contents of a *created* module instance are kept in a separate scope. So when using the `create` action, there can be no (inadvertent) clashes caused by equal names being used in different files for beliefs, goals, actions, and rules. Also, by creating and executing a module instance the focus of execution will be on the rules and the state of the created module instance such that the effect of executing a module instance remains local and limited to the state of that module.

5   Conclusions and Future Work

This paper introduced a mechanism to implement modules in BDI-based agent programming languages. The operational semantics for module-related actions such as creating, executing, testing, updating and releasing module instances are provided. It should be noted that these module-related actions are already added to the implemented 2APL interpreter such that 2APL multi-agent programs *with modules* can be developed and executed. We have also explained how modules can be used to facilitate the implementation of notions relevant to agent programming; namely, the implementation of agent roles and agent profiles. It should be noted that modularity in programming languages is not new. Our proposed notion of modules is inspired on the concepts found in many languages, particularly object-oriented languages. As a consequence some properties are the same, e.g. modules instances have an owner, which dictate the life cycle of the module. Also a module is designed with a particular task in mind, hiding the details from the owner.

For future work, there are several extensions to this work on modularization that can make it more powerful for encapsulation and implementation of roles and agent profiles. Firstly, the `execute` action may not be entirely appropriate for the implementation of profile execution, i.e., when an agent wonders "what would agent X (of which I have a profile) do in such and such a situation?". This is because executing a profile should not have consequences for the environment and other agents, so a module representing an agent profile should not be allowed to execute external actions or send messages. Also, the execute action can be generalized to allow the simultaneous execution of multiple module instances. Doing so one may be able to implement agents that can play several roles simultaneously.

Secondly, the notion of module can be generalized by introducing the possibility of specifying a minimum and maximum amount of instances of a module that can be active at one time. This can be used for ensuring that, e.g., there must always be three to five agents in the role of security guard. Additionally, one may want to be able to pass ownership of a module instance from one agent to another (especially when the module in question models a role) without losing its internal state.

Thirdly, additional actions such as `updateP` and `updateR` can be introduced that accept as arguments a module instance and a plan or rule, so that all types of contents of module instances can be modified during runtime. In particular, by creating an empty module instance and using `update*` actions, modules instances can be created from scratch with custom components available at runtime. A related issue is the access to the internals of module instances by means of test and update actions. In order to manage the access to the internals of module instances, modules can be specified as private or public allowing restricted access to the internals of modules.

References

1. Bordini, R.H., Wooldridge, M., Hübner, J.F.: Programming Multi-Agent Systems in AgentSpeak using Jason. Wiley Series in Agent Technology. John Wiley & Sons, Chichester (2007)
2. Braubach, L., Pokahr, A., Lamersdorf, W.: Extending the Capability Concept for Flexible BDI Agent Modularization. In: Bordini, R.H., Dastani, M.M., Dix, J., El Fallah Seghrouchni, A. (eds.) PROMAS 2005. LNCS (LNAI), vol. 3862, pp. 139–155. Springer, Heidelberg (2006)
3. Busetta, P., Howden, N., Ronnquist, R., Hodgson, A.: Structuring BDI Agents in Functional Clusters. In: Jennings, N., Lesperance, Y. (eds.) Intelligent Agents VI: Theories, Architectures and Languages, pp. 277–289 (2000)
4. Dastani, M.: 2APL: a practical agent programming language. International Journal of Autonomous Agents and Multi-Agent Systems (JAAMAS) 16(3), 214–248 (2008)
5. Hindriks, K.V.: Modules as policy-based intentions: Modular agent programming in GOAL. In: Dastani, M.M., El Fallah Seghrouchni, A., Ricci, A., Winikoff, M. (eds.) ProMAS 2007. LNCS (LNAI), vol. 4908, pp. 156–171. Springer, Heidelberg (2008)
6. Novák, P., Dix, J.: Modular BDI architecture. In: Proceedings of the AAMAS (2006)
7. Pokahr, A., Braubach, L., Lamersdorf, W.: Jadex: A BDI reasoning engine. In: Multi-Agent Programming: Languages, Platforms and Applications. Kluwer, Dordrecht (2005)
8. van Riemsdijk, M.B., Dastani, M., Meyer, J.-J.C., de Boer, F.S.: Goal-Oriented Modularity in Agent Programming. In: Proceedings of AAMAS 2006, pp. 1271–1278 (2006)
9. Winikoff, M.: JACK^{TM} intelligent agents: An industrial strength platform. In: Multi-Agent Programming: Languages, Platforms and Applications. Kluwer, Dordrecht (2005)

InstQL: A Query Language for Virtual Institutions Using Answer Set Programming

Luke Hopton, Owen Cliffe⋆, Marina De Vos∗, and Julian Padget∗

Department of Computer Science
University of Bath, BATH BA2 7AY, UK
lch21@bath.ac.uk, {occ,mdv,jap}@cs.bath.ac.uk

Abstract. Institutions provide a mechanism to capture and reason about "correct" and "incorrect" behaviour within a social context. While institutions can be studied in their own right, their real potential is as instruments to govern open software architectures like multi-agent and service-oriented systems. Our domain-specific action language for normative frameworks, Inst*AL* aims to help focus designers' attention on the expression of issues such as permission, violation and power but does not help the designer in verifying or querying the model they have specified. In this paper we present the query language Inst*QL* which includes a number of powerful features including temporal constraints over events and fluents that can be used in conjunction with Inst*AL* to specify those traces that are of interest in order to investigate and reason over the underlying normative models. The semantics of the query language is provided by translating Inst*QL* queries into *AnsProlog*, the same computational language as Inst*AL*. The result is a simple, high-level query and constraint language that builds on and uses the reasoning power of ASP.

1 Introduction

Institutions [21, 23, 6], also known as normative frameworks or organisations in the literature, are a specific class of multi-agent systems where agent behaviour is governed by social norms and regulations. Within institutions it is possible to monitor the permissions, empowerment and obligations of participants and to indicate violations when norms are not followed. The change of the state over time as a result of these actions provides participants with information about each others behaviour. The information can also be used by the designer to query and verify normative properties, effects and expected outcomes in an institution. The research on institutions such as electronic contracts, and rules of governance over the last decade has demonstrated that they are powerful mechanism to make agent interactions more effective, structured and efficient. As with human regulatory settings, institutions become useful when it is possible to *verify* that particular properties are satisfied for all possible scenarios.

Answer set programming [3, 14], a logic programming paradigm, permits, in contrast to related techniques like the event calculus [19] and $\mathcal{C}^+$[11], the specification of

---

⋆ This work has been supported in part by the European Commission, project FP7-215890 (ALIVE).

J. Dix, M. Fisher, and P. Novák (Eds.): CLIMA X, LNAI 6214, pp. 102–121, 2010.

both problem and query as an executable program, thus eliminating the gap between specification and verification language. But perhaps more importantly, the specification language and implementation language are identical, allowing for more straightforward verification and validation.

In [6], we introduced a formal model for institutions, which admits reasoning about them by mapping to *AnsProlog*, logic programs under answer set semantics. To make the reasoning process more accessible to users, in [7] we developed an action language named Inst*AL* that allows a developer to design an institution in a more straightforward manner. Inst*AL* is then translated into *AnsProlog*, resulting in the same program as the formal description would have provided. While Inst*AL* allowed the designer to specify the institution, it provided little to no support for verifying the institution and its design—indeed, as it stands queries must be written directly in *AnsProlog*, thereby undoing most of the benefits of specifying in Inst*AL*.

In this paper, we present Inst*QL*: a query language designed to complement Inst*AL*. Its semantics is provided by ASP and it is used together with a description of an institution either in Inst*AL* or *AnsProlog*. Inst*QL* can be used in two ways: as a tool to select certain transitions in the state space of the institution or to model-check a certain path. For temporal queries we describe how queries expressed in the widely used temporal logic LTL may be expressed (via simple transformations) in our query language. A brief summary of the Inst*QL* language appears in [17]. In this paper we provide an extended account of the language, illustrations of its capabilities and applications and situate it firmly in the context of multi-agent systems.

2 Answer Set Programming

In *answer set programming* ([3]) a logic program is used to describe the requirements that must be fulfilled by the solutions of a certain problem. Answer set semantics is a model-based semantics for normal logic programs. Following the notation of [3], we refer to the language over which the answer set semantics is defined as *AnsProlog*.

An *AnsProlog* program consists of a set of rules of the form $a : -B$, **not** C. with a being an atom and B, C being (possibly empty) sets of atoms. a is called the head of the rule, while $B \cup$ **not** C is the body. The rule can be read as: "if we know all atoms in B and we do not know any atom in C, then we must know a". Rules with an empty body are called facts, as the head is always considered known. An interpretation is a truth assignment to all atoms in the program. Often only those literals that are considered true are mentioned, as all the other are false by default (negation as failure).

The semantics of programs without negation (effectively horn clauses) are simple and uncontroversial, the T_p (immediate consequence) operator is iterated until a fixed point it reached. The *Gelfond-Lifschitz* reduct is used to deal with negation as failure. This takes a candidate set and reduces the program by removing any rule that depends on the negation of an atom in the set and removing all remaining negated atoms. *Answer Sets* are candidate sets that are also models of the corresponding reduced programs. The uncertain nature of negation-as-failure gives rise to several answer sets, which are all solutions to the problem that has been modelled.

Algorithms and implementations for obtaining answer sets of logic programs are referred to as *answer set solvers*. Some of the most popular and widely used solvers are DLV [8], SMODELS [20] and CLASP [13].

3 Institutions

In this section, we give an informal description of institutions and their mapping to ASP. A more in-depth description can be found in [6, 7].

The concept of normative systems has long been used in economics, legal theory and political science to refer to systems of regulation which enable or assist human interaction at a high-level. The same principles could be applied to multi-agent systems.

The model we use is based on the concept of *exogenous events* that describe salient events of the physical world—"shoot somebody"—and *normative events* that are generated by the normative framework—"murder"—but which only have meaning within a given social context. While exogenous events are clearly observable, normative ones are not, so how do they come into being? Searle [18] describes the creation of a normative state of affairs through *conventional generation*, whereby an event in one context *counts as* or *generates* the occurrence of another event in a second context. Taking the physical world as the first context and by defining conditions in terms of states, normative events may be created that count as the presence of states or the occurrence of events in the normative world.

Thus, we model an institution as a set of *normative states* that evolve over time subject to the occurrence of *events*, where a normative state is a set of *fluents* that may be held to be true at some instant. Furthermore, we may separate such fluents into *domain* fluents, that depend on the institution being modelled and *normative fluents* that are common to all specifications and may be classified as follows:

– **Permission:** A permission fluent captures the property that some event may occur without violation. If an event occurs, and that event is not permitted, then a *violation event* is generated.
– **Normative Power:** This represents the normative capability for an event to be brought about meaningfully, and hence change some fluents in the normative state. Without normative power, the event may not be brought about and has no effect; for example, a marriage ceremony will only bring about the married state, if the person performing the ceremony is empowered so to do.
– **Obligation:** Obligation fluents are modelled as the dual of permission. They state that a particular event must occur before a given deadline event (such as a time-out) and is associated with a specified violation. If an obligation fluent holds and the necessary event occurs then the obligation is said to be satisfied. If the corresponding deadline event occurs then the obligation is said to be violated and the specified violation event is generated. Such a violation event can then be dealt with perhaps by a participating agent or the normative framework itself.

Each event, being exogenous or normative, when generated could have an impact on the next state. For example, the event could trigger a violation or it could result in permissions being granted or retracted (e.g. once you obtain your driving licence, you obtain the permission to drive a car, but, if you are convicted of a driving offence you lose that permission). The effects of events are modelled by the consequence relation.

Thus we represent the normative framework by these five components: (i) the initial state—the set of fluents which are true when the institution is created, (ii) the set of fluents that capture the essential facts about the normative state, (iii) the set of events (both exogenous and normative) that can occur, (iv) the conventional generation relation, and (v) the consequence relation.

All state changes in a system stem from the occurrence of exactly one exogenous event. When such an event occurs, the transitive closure of the conventional generation function computes all empowered normative events that are directly or indirectly caused by the occurrence of the underlying event. This may include violations for unsatisfied obligations or unpermitted events. The consequences of each of these events with respect to the current state is computed using the consequence relationship. The combination of added and deleted fluents results in the new normative state. The semantics of this framework are defined over traces of exogenous events. Each trace induces a sequence of normative states, called a model or scenario.

In [6], it was shown that the formal model of an institution could be translated to $AnsProlog$ program such that the answer sets of the program correspond exactly to the traces of the institution. A detailed description of the mapping can be found there.

The mapping uses the following atoms: ifluent(P) to identify fluents, evtype(E, T) to describe the type of an event, event(E) to denote the events, instant(I) for time instances, final(I) for the last time instance in a trace, next(I1, I2) to establish time ordering, occurred(E, I) to indicate that the event happened at time I, observed(E, I) that the event was observed at that time, holdsat(P, I) to state that the institutional fluent holds at I, initiated(P, I) and terminated(P, I) for fluents that are initiated and terminated at I.

When modelling traces, we need to monitor the domain over a period of time (or a sequence of states). We model time using instant(I) and an ordering on instances established by next(I1, I2), with the final instance defined as final(I). Following convention, we assume that the truth of a fluent $F \in \mathcal{F}$ at a given state instance I is represented as holdsat(F, I), while an event or an action $E \in \mathcal{E}$ is modelled as occurred(E, I).

In [5] we developed InstAL, an action language inspired by action languages such as $\mathcal{C}^+$ and $\mathcal{A}$ [11]. The use of the action language makes generating the $AnsProlog$ code less open to human coding errors, and perhaps more importantly, easier to understand and create by narrowing the semantic gap without losing either expressiveness or a formal basis for the language.

Institutions specifications could give rise to a vast number of valid traces and associated histories. Often not all of them are equally useful for the task at hand and selection criteria have to be applied. Through InstQL, we aim to offer the designer the same sort of abstraction for queries as is provided by InstAL for the specification.

4   The Dutch Auction: A Motivating Example

4.1   The Case Study

As a case study we will look a fragment of the Dutch auction protocol with only one round of bidding. Protocols such as this have been extensively studied in the area of agent-mediated electronic commerce, as they are particularly suited to computer implementation and reasoning.

In this protocol a single agent is assigned to the role of auctioneer, and one or more agents play the role of bidders. The purpose of the protocol as a whole is either to determine a winning bidder and a valuation for a particular item on sale, or to establish that no bidders wish to purchase the item. Consequently, conflict—where two bids are received "simultaneously"—is treated as an in-round state which takes the process back to the beginning. The protocol is summarised as follows:

1. Round starts: auctioneer selects a price for the item and informs each of the bidders present of the starting price. The auctioneer then waits for a given period of time for bidders to respond.
2. Bidding: upon receipt of the starting price, each bidder has the choice whether to send a message indicating their desire to bid on the item at that price or not.
3. Single Bid: at the end of the prescribed period of time, if the auctioneer has received a single bid from a given agent, then the auctioneer is obliged to inform each of the participating agents that this agent has won the auction.
4. No bids: if no bids are received at the end of the prescribed period of time, the auctioneer must inform each of the participants that the item has not been sold.
5. Multiple bids: if more than one bid was received then the auctioneer must inform every agent that a conflict has occurred.
6. Termination: the protocol completes when an announcement is made indicating that an item is sold or that no bids have been received.
7. Conflict resolution: in the case where a conflict occurs then the auctioneer must re-open the bidding and re-start the round in order to resolve the conflict.

Based on the protocol description above, the following agent actions are defined: the auctioneer announces a price to a given bidder (`annprice`), the bidder bids on the current item (`annbid`), the auctioneer announces a conflict to a given bidder (`annconf`) and the auctioneer announces that the item is sold (`annsold`) or not sold (`annunsold`) respectively. In addition to the agent actions we also include a number of time-outs indicating the three external events—that are independent of agents' actions—that affect the protocol. For each time-out we define a corresponding protocol/institutional event suffixed by dl indicating a deadline in the protocol. The differentiation between time-out and deadline events allow a finer and more abstract control structure. While we do not want or can restrict the behaviour of an external clock (time-out) we can control the behaviour of the institution to the occurrence of the these events.

`priceto`, `pricedl`: A time-out indicating the deadline by which the auctioneer must have announced the initial price of the item on sale to all bidders.

`bidto`, `biddl`: A time-out indicating the expiration of the waiting period for the auctioneer to receive bids for the item.

`decto`, `decdl`: A time-out indicating the deadline by which the auctioneer must have announced the decision about the auction to all bidders

When the auctioneer violates the protocol, an event `badgov` occurs and the auction dissolves.

Figure 1 gives the Inst*AL* specification of the third phase of the protocol. The excerpt shows how internal events are generated and how fluents are initiated or

```
annsold(A,B) generates sold(A,B);                                    (DAR-1)
annunsold(A,B) generates unsold(A,B);                                (DAR-2)
annconf(A,B) generates conf(A,B);                                    (DAR-3)
biddl terminates pow(bid(B,A));                                      (DAR-4)
biddl initiates pow(sold(A,B)),pow(unsold(A,B)),
        pow(conf(A,B)), pow(notified(B)),perm(notified(B));         (DAR-5)
biddl initiates perm(annunsold(A,B)),perm(unsold(A,B)),
        obl(unsold(A,B),desdl,badgov) if not havebid;               (DAR-6)
biddl initiates perm(annsold(A,B)),perm(sold(A,B)),
        obl(sold(A,B), desdl, badgov) if havebid, not conflict;     (DAR-7)
biddl initiates perm(annconf(A,B)),perm(conf(A,B)),
        obl(conf(A,B), desdl, badgov) if havebid, conflict;         (DAR-8)
unsold(A,B) generates notified(B);                                  (DAR-9)
sold(A,B) generates notified(B);                                    (DAR-10)
conf(A,B) generates notified(B);                                    (DAR-11)
notified(B) terminates pow(unsold(A,B)), perm(unsold(A,B)),
  pow(sold(A,B)), pow(conf(A,B)), pow(notified(B)),
  perm(sold(A,B)), perm(conf(A,B)), perm(notified(B)),
  perm(annconf(A,B)),perm(annsold(A,B)),perm(annunsold(A,B));       (DAR-12)
desdl generates finished if not conflict;                           (DAR-13)
desdl terminates havebid,conflict,perm(annconf(A,B));               (DAR-14)
desdl initiates pow(price(A,B)), perm(price(A,B)),
  perm(annprice(A,B)), perm(pricedl),pow(pricedl),
  obl(price(A,B),pricedl,badgov) if conflict;                       (DAR-15)
```

Fig. 1. A partial Inst*AL* specification for the Dutch Auction Round Institution

terminates depending on the current state and the occurrence of events. Normative fluents of power, permission and obligation are represented as pow, per) and obl respectively. The full specification can be found on [5]. Figure 2 shows the translation of the first seven Inst*AL* specification rules of Figure 1 translated in *AnsProlog* and grounded for one auctioneer and one bidding agent. The entire program contains about 1500 rules. Although the program can be written by hand, we believe that this process is rather tiresome and error prone.

Figure 3 shows the state transition diagram for an auctioneer and a single bidder. Every path in the graph is a valid trace.

4.2 Queries

To guide the development of our query language Inst*QL* for institutional models written in Inst*AL*, five types of existing queries which were directly encoded in *AnsProlog* were considered.

The first case is a simple constraint involving event occurrence. An example would be a query to obtain those traces in which the auctioneer violates the protocol. This query states that answer sets corresponding to traces in which the event badgov occurs at any point should be excluded. The key part of this condition is that an event can occur at **any** time.

$$\begin{aligned} \text{bad} &\leftarrow \text{occurred(badgov, I), instant(I)}. \\ \bot &\leftarrow \text{bad}. \end{aligned}$$ (Q1)

```
occured(sold(a,b),I) :-
    occured(annsold(a,b),I),holdsat(pow(dutch_auction_round,sold(a,b)),I),instant(I).
occured(unsold(a,b),I) :-
    occured(annunsold(a,b),I),holdsat(pow(dutch_auction_round,unsold(a,b)),I),instant(I).
occured(conf(a,b),I) :-
    occured(annconf(a,b),I),holdsat(pow(dutch_auction_round,conf(a,b)),I),instant(I).

terminated(pow(dutch_auction_round,bid(b,a)),I) :-
    occured(bidd1,I),holdsat(live(dutch_auction_round),I),instant(I).

initiated(pow(dutch_auction_round,sold(a,b,b)),I) :-
    occured(bidd1,I),holdsat(live(dutch_auction_round),I),instant(I).
initiated(pow(dutch_auction_round,unsold(a,b)),I) :-
    occured(bidd1,I),holdsat(live(dutch_auction_round),I),instant(I).
initiated(pow(dutch_auction_round,conf(a,b)),I) :-
    occured(bidd1,I),holdsat(live(dutch_auction_round),I),instant(I).
initiated(pow(dutch_auction_round,ntified(b)),I) :-
    occured(bidd1,I),holdsat(live(dutch_auction_round),I),instant(I).
initiated(perm(alterted(b)),I) :-
    occured(bidd1,I),holdsat(live(dutch_auction_round),I),instant(I).

initiated(perm(annunsold(a,b)),I) :-
    occured(bidd1,I),not holdsat(havebid,I),holdsat(live(dutch_auction_round),I),instant(I).
initiated(perm(unsold(a,b)),I) :-
    occured(bidd1,I),not holdsat(havebid,I),holdsat(live(dutch_auction_round),I),instant(I).
initiated(obl(unsold(a,b),desd1,badgov),I) :-
    occured(bidd1,I),not holdsat(havebid,I),holdsat(live(dutch_auction_round),I),instant(I).

initiated(perm(annconf(a,b)),I) :-
    occured(bidd1,I),holdsat(havebid,I),holdsat(conflict,I),
    holdsat(live(dutch_auction_round),I),instant(I).
initiated(perm(conf(a,b)),I) :-
    occured(bidd1,I),holdsat(havebid,I),holdsat(conflict,I),
    holdsat(live(dutch_auction_round),I),instant(I).
initiated(obl(conf(a,b),desd1,badgov),I) :-
    occured(bidd1,I),holdsat(havebid,I),holdsat(conflict,I),
    holdsat(live(dutch_auction_round),I),instant(I).

occured(notified(b),I) :-
    occured(unsold(a,b),I),holdsat(pow(dutch_auction_round,alterted(b)),I),instant(I).

occured(notified(b),I) :-
    occured(sold(a,b,b),I),holdsat(pow(dutch_auction_round,notified(b)),I),instant(I).

occured(notified(b),I) :-
    occured(conf(a,b),I),holdsat(pow(dutch_auction_round,alterted(b)),I),instant(I).
```

Fig. 2. The first seven DAR-Inst*AL* specification rules translated into *AnsProlog* and grounded for one auctioneer and bidding agent

Similarly, the second query involves a fluent being true at **any** time during the execution. This time, only those answer sets corresponding to traces that satisfy the condition should be included. As an example, we have a query that selects those traces in which a conflict occurs, i.e. more than one bidder submits a timely bid.

$$
\begin{aligned}
\text{hadconflict} &\leftarrow \text{holdsat(conflict, I), instant(I).} \\
\bot &\leftarrow \textbf{not}\ \text{hadconflict.}
\end{aligned}
\tag{Q2}
$$

In the third case, the query condition is for an event to occur **at the same time** as a fluent holds. Again, only answer sets in which the condition is satisfied should be included. An example of such a query would be selecting those traces in which at the occurrence of the desd1-event we also have a conflict between two or more bidders.

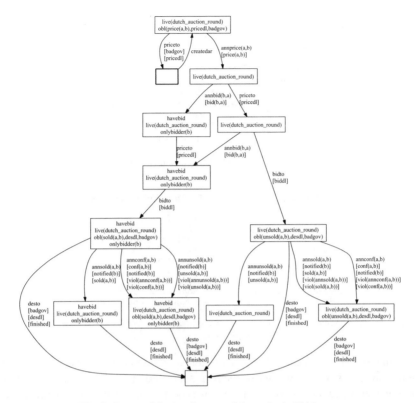

Fig. 3. States of the auction round for a single bidder

$$\text{restarted} \leftarrow \text{occurred(desdl, I), holdsat(conflict, I),}$$
$$\text{instant(I).} \qquad \text{(Q3)}$$
$$\bot \leftarrow \textbf{not} \text{ restarted.}$$

The fourth case declares a parameterised condition. Whilst earlier we considered conditions that are true/false for a whole model, this case declares a condition `startstate` that is true for a particular fluent. In addition, this query requires that the fluent is true in the state **after** an event occurs. The use of parameterised conditions is illustrated in the following statement that enumerates all the fluents that are true when the protocol has just started, which is indicated by the occurrence of the event `createdar`:

$$\text{startstate(F)} \leftarrow \text{holdsat(F, I1), occurred(createdar, I0),}$$
$$\text{next(I0, I1), ifluent(F).} \qquad \text{(Q4)}$$

The fifth query can be used to verify the protocol. This query features the use of previously declared conditions in subsequent conditions. (Note that one of these, `startstate(F)`, is the condition specified in query (Q4).) The protocol states that if more than one bidder bids for the good, the protocol needs to restart completely. This implies that all the fluents from the beginning of the protocol need to be reinstated and all others have to be terminated. The query checks this has been done, but if we still obtain a trace with this query we know something has gone wrong.

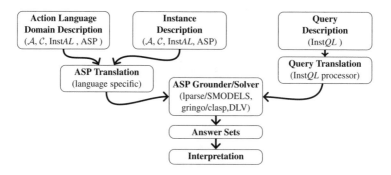

Fig. 4. The Data Flow of for Designing Institutions

```
startstate(F) ← holdsat(F, I1), occurred(createdar, I0),
                next(I0, I1), ifluent(F).
restartstate(F) ← holdsat(F, I1), occurred(desdl, I0),
                holdsat(conflict, I0),
                next(I0, I1), ifluent(F).                        (Q5)
    missing(F) ← startstate(F), not restartstate(F), ifluent(F).
      added(F) ← restartstate(F), not startstate(F), ifluent(F).
      invalid ← missing(F), ifluent(F).
      invalid ← added(F), ifluent(F).
            ⊥ ← not invalid.
```

From the above, it is clear that it is possible to express these queries in *AnsProlog*, but it requires a solid knowledge of the formalism and implementation detail to get the order of events and fluents correct. Inst*QL* was designed to remove these difficulties and allow designers to write queries in a language more closely related to natural language.

5   Inst*QL*

In this section we introduce the query language, Inst*QL*, that can either be used in conjunction with Inst*AL* or directly with an *AnsProlog* program representing the institution, whether the program is derived from the formal description or Inst*AL*.

Figure 4 shows the flow chart of the relationships between the various components. A designer will first have to specify the institution. This can either be written directly in *AnsProlog* or using Inst*AL* by providing the domain description and the institutional description which are then translated into *AnsProlog*. For verification, queries on the traces are specified in Inst*QL* and then translated into *AnsProlog*. Both programs are then merged and passed to the grounder and solver. The returned answer sets are then interpreted. A possible course of action might be that the description of the institution needs to be changed or that a new query is required.

The Inst*QL* queries act as filters on the valid traces of the institutions. Instead of returning all traces we use the queries to return only the queries that satisfy the query, in a similar way as, for example, SQL queries.

Inst*QL* has two basic concepts: (i) *constraint:* an assertion of a property that must be satisfied by a valid trace (for example, a restriction on which traces are considered), and (ii) *condition:* a specification of properties that may hold for a given trace. Conditions can be declared in relation to other conditions and constraints can involve declared conditions. Table 1 summarises the syntax of the language, while the remainder of this section discusses in detail the elements of the language and their semantics.

5.1 Syntax

Inst*QL* provides two *predicates* that form the basis of all Inst*QL* queries. The first is `happens(Event)`, meaning that the specified event should occur at some point during the lifetime of the institution. The second is `holds(Fluent)`, which means that the specified fluent is true at any point during the lifetime of the institution. That is:

```
| <predicate> ::= happens( <identifier> ) | holds(<identifier>)
```

where the *identifier* corresponds to an event e (in the first case) or a fluent f (in the second case).

Negation (as failure) is provided by the unary operator `not`:

```
| <literal> ::= not <predicate> | <predicate>
```

To construct complex queries, it is often easier to break them up into sub-queries, or in Inst*QL* terminology, sub-conditions. For example, suppose we have defined a condition called `my_cond` which specifies some desired property. We can then join this with other criteria e.g. "`my_cond and happens(e)`". Sub-conditions may be referenced within rules as *condition literals*:

```
| <condition_literal> ::= not <identifier> | <identifier>
```

Note that this allows for parameterised conditions to be defined by the definition of an *identifier*.

The building block of query conditions is the *term*:

```
| <term> ::= <after_expr> | <condition_literal>
```

The after expression also allows for the simpler constructs of `<literal>` and `<while_expr>`. *Terms* may be grouped and connected by the connectives `and` and `or` which provide logical conjunction and disjunction.

```
| <conjunction> ::= <term> and <conjunction> | <term>
| <disjunction> ::= <term> or <disjunction>  | <term>
```

On its own, this does not allow us create arbitrary combinations of *predicates* and named conditions and the logical operators `and`, `or`, `not`. To do so we need to be able to declare conditions:

```
| <condition_decl> ::=   condition <identifier> : <disjunction>
|                      | condition <identifier> : <conjunction>;
```

This construction defines a `condition` with the specified name to have a value equal to the specified `disjunction` or `conjunction`. This allows the `condition` name to be used as a `condition_literal`.

Constraints specify properties of the trace that must be true:

```
| <constraint> ::= constraint <disjunction> | <conjunction> ;
```

For example, consider the following Inst*QL* query:

```
| constraint happens(e);
```

This indicates that only traces in which event `e` occurs should be considered.

Table 1. Inst*QL* Syntax

Expression	Definition
`<variable>`	`::= [A-Z][a-zA-Z0-9_]*`
`<variable_list>`	`::= <variable> , <variable_list>	<variable>`
`<name>`	`::= [a-z][a-zA-Z0-9_]*`
`<param_list>`	`::= ( <variable_list> )`
`<identifier>`	`::= <name> <param_list>	<name>`
`<predicate>`	`::= happens(<identifier>)	holds(<identifier>)`
`<literal>`	`::= not <predicate>	<predicate>`
`<while_literal>`	`::= <literal>|<condition_literal>`
`<while_expr>`	`::= <while_literal> while <while_expr>	<while_literal>`
`<after>`	`::= after(<integer>)	after`
`<after_expr>`	`::= <while_expr> <after> <after_expr> |`
	`<while_expr>`
`<condition_literal> ::=`	`not <identifier>	<identifier>`
`<term>`	`::= <after_expr>	<condition_literal>`
`<conjunction>`	`::= <term> and <conjunction>	<term>`
`<disjunction>`	`::= <term> or <disjunction>	<term>`
`<condition_decl>`	`::= condition <identifier> : <disjunction>; |`
	`condition <identifier> : <conjunction>;`
`<constraint>`	`::= constraint <disjunction> ; |`
	`constraint <conjunction>;`

To illustrate how this language is used to form queries, consider a simple light bulb action domain. The fluent `on` is true when the bulb is on. The event `switch` turns the light on or off. We can require that at some point the light is on:

```
constraint holds(on);
```

We can require that the light is never on:

```
condition light_on: holds(on);
constraint not light_on;
```

There is some subtlety here in that `light_on` is true if at any instant `on` is true. Therefore, if `light_on` is not true, there cannot be an instant at which `on` was true. And what if the bulb is broken—the switch is pressed but the light never comes on? This can be expressed as:

```
constraint not light_on and happens(switch);
```

Using condition names, we can create arbitrary logical expressions. The statement that event $e1$ and either event $e2$ or $e3$ should occur can be expressed as follows:

```
condition disj: happens(e2) or happens(e3);
condition conj: happens(e1) and disj;
```

We may wish to specify queries of the form "X and Y happen at the same time". That is, we may wish to talk about events occurring at the same time as one or more fluents are true, simultaneous occurrence of events or combinations of fluents being simultaneously true (and/or false). For this situation, Inst*QL* has the keyword `while` to indicate that literals are true *simultaneously*. Such `while` expressions are only defined over literals constructed from predicates (that is, `happens` and `holds`) or condition literals involving condition names. A while expression is defined as follows:

```
<while_literal} ::= <literal> | <condition_literal>
<while_expr>    ::= <literal> while <while_expr> | <literal>
```

The `while`-operator has higher precedence than `and` and `or`.

Returning to the light bulb example, we can now specify that we want only traces where the light was turned off at some point:

```
| constraint happens(switch) while holds(on);
```

Or that at some point the light was left on:

```
| constraint holds(on) while not happens(switch);
```

The language allows for the expression of orderings over events. This is done with the `after` keyword. This allows statements of the form:

```
| holds(f1) while not holds(f2) after happens(e1)
|                                after happens(e2)
```

This should be read as: (i) at some time instant k the event `e2` occurs (ii) at some other time instant j the event `e1` occurs (iii) at some other time instant i the fluent `f1` is true but the fluent `f2` is not true (iv) these time instants are ordered such that $i > j > k$ (that is, k is the earliest time instant). However, in some cases we need to say not only that a given literal holds after some other literal, but that this is precisely one time instant later. Rather than just providing the facility to specify a literal occurs/holds in the next time instant, this is generalised to say that a literal holds n time instants after another. That is, for a fluent that does (not) hold at time instant t_i or an event that occurs between t_i and t_{i+1}, we can talk about literals that hold at t_{i+n} or occur between t_{i+n} and t_{i+n+1}. The syntax of an `after` expression is:

```
<after> ::= after | after( <integer> )
<after_expr> ::= <while_expr> <after> <after_expr> |
                 <while_expr>
```

An `after` expression may contain only the `after` operator or the `after(n)` operator, depending on how precisely the gap between the two operands is to be specified.

Once again returning to the light bulb example, we can now specify a query which requires the light to be switched twice (or more):

```
| constraint happens(switch) after happens(switch);
```

Or that once that light has is on, it cannot be switched off again:

```
| condition switch_off: happens(switch) after holds(on);
| constraint not switch_off;
```

5.2   Semantics

The semantics of an Inst*QL* query is defined by the translation function T which translates Inst*QL* into *AnsProlog*. This function takes a fragment of Inst*QL* and generates a set of (partial) *AnsProlog* rules. Typically, this set is a singleton; only expressions involving disjunctions generate more than one rule. The semantics of predicates are defined as follows:

$$T(\texttt{happens(e)}) = \texttt{occurred(e, I)}, \texttt{event(e)}$$
$$T(\texttt{holds(f)}) = \texttt{holdsat(f, I)}, \texttt{ifluent(f)}$$

For a literal of the form `not P` (where `P` is a predicate) the semantics is:

$$T(\texttt{not } P) = \texttt{not } T(\texttt{P})$$

while for a condition literal they are:

$$T(\texttt{conditionName}) = \texttt{conditionName(I)}$$
$$T(\texttt{not conditionName}) = \texttt{not conditionName(I)}$$

and a conjunction of terms is:

$$T(c_1 \text{ and } c_2 \text{ and} \cdots \text{ and } c_n) = T(c_1), T(c_2), \dots, T(c_n)$$

A disjunction translates to more than one rule. However, this is defined slightly differently depending on whether it is part of a condition declaration or a constraint.

$$T(\texttt{condition conditionName}: \; c_1 \text{ or } c_2 \text{ or } \cdots \text{or } c_n;) =$$
$$\{\texttt{conditionName} \leftarrow T(c_i). \mid 1 \le i \le n\}$$
$$T(\texttt{constraint} \qquad c_1 \text{ or } c_2 \text{ or } \cdots \text{or } c_n;) =$$
$$\{\texttt{newName} \leftarrow T(c_i). \mid 1 \le i \le n\} \cup$$
$$\{\perp \leftarrow \texttt{not newName.}\}$$

The *AnsProlog* term `newName` denotes any identifier that is unique within the *Ans-Prolog* program that is the combination of the query and the action program. This atom becomes true if one of the sub-queries in the disjunction becomes true. In order to satisfy the entire query at least one the sub-queries not to be true, as expressed by the constraint. In addition, each time instant `I` generated in the translation of a predicate represents a name for a time instant that is unique within the Inst*QL* query. Recall that a condition name may be parameterised: since an Inst*QL* variable translates to a variable in Smodels, no additional machinery is required. For example, the condition "`condition ever(E): happens(E);`" (which just defines an alias for `happens`) is translated to "`ever(E) ← occurred(E, I), instant(I), event(E).`".

Notice that so far only the translation of constraint and condition provide a specification for time (`instance`). Because of the grammar of our language, the translation of other terms results in a set of literals which will appear in a rule that already include this atom.

The semantics for `while` is:

$$T(L_1 \text{ while } L_2 \text{ while } \cdots \text{ while } L_n) = T(L_1), T(L_2), \dots, T(L_n), \texttt{instant(I)}$$

We give the semantics for the binary operator `after(n)`. This readily generalises for sequences of `after(n)` operators mixed with `after` operators.

$$T(W_i \text{ after(n) } W_j) = T(W_i), \; T(W_j), \; \texttt{after}(t_i, t_j, n)$$

Where t_i and t_j are the time instants generated by W_i and W_j respectively. This is defined such that we require $n > 0$.

We now provide a concrete example of the translation of an `after` expression to illustrate this process:

$$T \,(\texttt{happens(e) while holds(f) after happens(d) after(3) holds(g)}) =$$
$$\texttt{occurred}(e, t_i), \texttt{event}(e), \texttt{holdsat}(f, t_i), \texttt{ifluent}(f),$$
$$\texttt{instant}(t_i), \texttt{occurred}(d, t_j), \texttt{event}(d), \texttt{instant}(t_j),$$
$$\texttt{holdsat}(g, t_k), \texttt{ifluent}(g), \texttt{instant}(t_k),$$
$$\texttt{after}(t_i, t_j), \texttt{after}(t_j, t_k, 3).$$

5.3 The Dutch Auction Queries

Having defined the query language Inst*QL*, we return to the example queries for the Dutch auction from Section 4.

For (Q1) the following InstQL query is equivalent:

```
condition bad: happens(badgov);
constraint not bad;
```

Alternatively, we could look at all the traces in which the protocol is never violated by one of the bidders.

```
    condition bad: happens(viol(E));
    constraint not bad;
```

An InstQL query that is equivalent to (Q2) is:

```
constraint holds(conflict);
```

The following query is equivalent to (Q3):

```
constraint happens(desdl) while holds(conflict);
```

For (Q4), the following InstQL query is equivalent:

```
condition startstate(F): holds(F) after(1) happens(createdar);
```

For (Q5) the following InstQL query is equivalent:

```
condition startstate(F): holds(F) after(1) happens(createdar);
condition restartstate(F): holds(F) after(1) happens(desdl)} while holds(conflict);
condition missing(F): startstate(F) and not restartstate(F);
condition added(F): restartstate(F) and not startstate(F);
constraint missing(F) or added(F);
```

While queries 1-5 demonstrate the capabilities of our query language they might not be the only queries a designer of the Dutch Auction would pose.

The following query verifies it is never the case that an agent has permission to perform an action while not having the power. A correct protocol will return no traces.

```
condition permission(F): holds(perm(F)) while not holds(pow(F));
constraint permission(F);
```

The following query returns traces containing violations that have not been detected.

```
condition violation(F): not happens(badgov) after happens(viol(F));
constraint violation(F);
```

As a designer you also want to verify the order of the important events that need to take place. The following query verifies that the two deadlines occur in the correct order and that the corresponding obligations are fulfilled.

```
condition order: pricedl after desdl;
condition obl: not holds(obligation(E,D,V)) while
               not happens(V) after holds(obligation(E,D,V));
constraint: order and not happens(badgov) and obl;
```

6   Reasoning

6.1   Common Reasoning Tasks

Following the description of InstQL in the preceding section, we now illustrate how it can be used to perform three common tasks [24] in computational reasoning: prediction, postdiction and planning.

Prediction is the problem of ascertaining the resulting state for a given (partial) sequence of events/actions and initial state. That is, suppose some transition system is in state $s \in S$ with S the set of all possible states of the system and a sequence $A = a_1, \ldots, a_n$ of actions/events occurs. Then the prediction problem (s, A) is to decide the set of states $\{S' \subseteq S\}$ which may result. Postdiction is the converse problem: if a system is in state s' and we know that $A = a_1, \ldots, a_n$ have occurred, then the problem (A, s') is to decide the set $\{S \subseteq S\}$ of states that could have held before

A. The planning problem (s, s') is to decide which sequence(s) of actions, $\{A' \subseteq \mathcal{A}\}$, with $\mathcal{A}$ all possible sequences of actions/events, will bring about state s' from state s.

Identifying States: A state is described by the set of fluents that are true $s = \{f_1, \ldots, f_n\}$ where f_i are the fluents. States containing or not containing given fluents may be identified in InstQL using the `while` operator:

```
holds(f_1) while ... while holds(f_n) while
not holds(g_1) while ... while not holds(g_k)
```

where $f_{1 \ldots k}$ are fluents which must hold in the matched state and $g_{1 \ldots k}$ are those fluents that do not.

Describing Event Ordering: A sequence of events $E = e_1, \ldots, e_n$ may be encoded as an `after` expression. If we have complete information, then we know that e_1 occurred, then e_2 at the next time instant and so on up to e_n with no other events occurring in between. In this case, we can express E as follows:

```
happens(e_n) after(1) ... after(1) happens(e_1)
```

This can be generalised to the case where e_{i+1} occurs after e_i with some known number $k \geq 0$ of events happening in between:

```
happens(e_i+1) after(1) ... after(k+1) happens(e_i)
```

Alternatively if we do not know k (that is, we know that e_{i+1} happens later than e_i but zero or more events occur in between) we can express this as:

```
happens(e_i+1) after happens(e_i)
```

We can combine these cases throughout the formulation of E to represent the amount of information available.

The Prediction Problem: Given an initial state s and a sequence of events E, the prediction problem (s, E) can be expressed in InstQL as:

```
constraint E after(1) s;
```

This query limits traces to those in which at some point s holds after which the events of E occur in sequence. The answer sets that satisfy this query will then contain the states $\{S' \subseteq \mathcal{S}\}$.

The Postdiction Problem: Given a sequence of events E and a resulting state s', the postdiction problem (E, s') can be expressed as:

```
constraint s' after(1) E;
```

This requires s' to hold in the next instant following the final event of E.

The Planning Problem: Given a pair of states s and s' the planning problem (s, s') can be expressed in InstQL as:

```
constraint s' after s;
```

This allows any non-empty sequence of events to bring about the transition from s to s'. If we want to consider plans of length k (i.e. $E = e_1, \ldots, e_k$) then we express this:

```
constraint s' after(k) s;
```

Reasoning with institutions: There are two distinct types of reasoning about institutions. The first is the verification and exploration of normative properties. After specifying an institutions, queries can be used to determine that desired properties of the model are present or to elicit emergent properties that were perhaps not intended. The second kind is for the participants/agents within that institution to use the available information in their decision processes. The participants could, using the current state and the specification apply prediction to determine previous actions of other participants, postdiction to evaluate possible effects of their actions or planning to determine the actions necessary to achieve certain goals. Using *AnsProlog* as the underlying formalism, designers and institutional participants can use partial information to reason about the institution itself of other participants.

6.2 Modelling Linear Temporal Logic

LTL [22] is a commonly used temporal logic used for model checking transitions systems. In this section we show that LTL style reasoning can also modelled using our Inst*QL*. We opted for LTL since it shares the same linear time structure as our model and also allows complex expressions of temporal properties between states. Traditional LTL syntax is often considered difficult to write and we believe that Inst*QL* would be a valuable alternative, especially if one wants to reason about events and fluents at the same time.

Linear Temporal Logic: (LTL) [22] provides us with a formalism for reasoning about paths of state transition systems. In LTL, we have a set AP of *atomic propositions*. The syntax of LTL [10] is defined as follows: (i) $p \in AP$ is a formula of LTL (ii) $\neg f$ is a formula if f is a formula (iii) $f \vee g$ is a formula if f and g are formulae (iv) $f \wedge g$ is a formula if f and g are formulae (v) $\Diamond f$ is a formula if f is a formula ("sometimes f") (vi) fUg is a formula if f and g are formulae ("f until g"). We abbreviate $\neg\Diamond\neg f$ by $\Box f$ ("always f").

The semantics of LTL is given with respect to a structure $M = (\mathbf{S}, \mathbf{X}, \mathbf{L})$ and a path of state transitions. M contains a non-empty set of *states*, $\mathbf{X}$ a non-empty set of *paths* and $\mathbf{L} : \mathbf{S} \rightarrow \mathbb{P}(AP)$ a *labelling function* which assigns to each state a set of propositions true in that state. A path is a non-empty sequence of states $x = s_0 s_1 s_2 \ldots$. We denote by x^k the suffix of path x starting with the kth state. In addition, we use $first(x)$ to denote the first state in path x.

The semantics of LTL is defined inductively in terms of interpretations (paths) over a linear structure (time) by the relation $\models$ [10, 9, 25, 16, 4]. Without loss of generality we use the natural numbers $\mathcal{N}$ as our structure. An interpretation is a function $\pi : \mathcal{N} \rightarrow \mathbb{P}(AP)$, which assigns a truth value to each element of AP at every instant $i \in \mathcal{N}$.

Let M be a structure and $x \in \mathbf{X}$, then:

$$
\begin{aligned}
\pi, i &\models p \in AP &&\Longleftrightarrow p \in \pi(i) \\
\pi, i &\models \neg f &&\Longleftrightarrow p, i \not\models f \\
\pi, i &\models f \vee g &&\Longleftrightarrow \pi, i \models f \text{ or } \pi, i \models g \\
\pi, i &\models f \wedge g &&\Longleftrightarrow \pi, i \models f \text{ and } \pi, i \models g \\
\pi, i &\models \Diamond f &&\Longleftrightarrow \exists j \geq i \cdot \pi, j \models f \\
\pi, i &\models fUg &&\Longleftrightarrow \exists j \geq i \cdot \pi, j \models g \wedge (\forall i \leq k < j \cdot \pi, k \models f)
\end{aligned}
$$

Where the structure is understood, we will omit it from the relation and write $x \models f$.

In principle LTL (originally) only refers to states, and as a general observation, the merging of actions and fluents inside LTL is non-trivial as you are merging state-relative and transition-relative concepts. With institutions we want to reason about both fluents and events, so $AP = \mathcal{E} \cup \mathcal{F}$.

Expressing LTL in Inst*QL* : There is an important difference between LTL and Inst*QL* in the sense that Inst*QL* is not designed for model checking but for model generation. Given a query, it will generate those paths that satisfy the criteria. If π is the path given to LTL for verification, Inst*QL* will return all traces that satisfy the query which may or may not include the path given for verification. To solve this problem one can provide the path itself as a constraint to the Inst*QL* query. This can be easily done using a combination of `while` and `after` in the same way as be defined event ordering above. This will restrict the search space to those traces in which the path is satisfied. If the path itself is invalid (e.g. two observed events during the same time, fluents that are in a state while they should not be), then the query will automatically not be satisfied.

The LTL query itself can then be expressed in Inst*QL*. We will briefly describe how the various formulae may be expressed as conditions in Inst*QL*. Each sub-formula S of the formula F that is to be checked is translated as a condition with a unique name `cond-S`. To make a formula F effective (i.e. only compute traces for which F is true) we add a constraint to the query that specifies the condition for F must hold: "`constraint cond-F;`". Atomic elements a of AP and their negation simply become conditions with `happens(a)` or `holds(a)` or their negation depending on the type of a. Consequently, LTL disjunction can be handled be handled as a disjunction in Inst*QL*. Conjunction is LTL is like our Inst*QL* while as all sub-formulas need to be evaluated over the same time instant.

For formulae of the form "$\Diamond F$" we define the conditions:

```
condition diamond-F: cond-F;
```

Although it might seem similar to the encoding of atomic elements, this encoding guarantees a possible different time instance.

Defining until (FUG) is more subtle. Naïvely, we could define "F until G" as:

```
condition false_before(cond-F,cond-G): cond-F after not cond-G;
condition cond-FUG: & not false_before(cond-F, cond-G);
```

However, translating this into *AnsProlog* we see that the condition is too strong. To make the example easier assume that F is a fluent and G an event and that we skip the encoding for the sub-formula:

$$\text{false\_before}(F, E) \leftarrow \text{occurred}(E, I), \text{event}(E), \text{instant}(I),$$
$$\text{not holdsat}(F, J), \text{ifluent}(F), \text{instant}(J), \text{after}(I, J).$$
$$\text{until}(F, E) \leftarrow \text{not false\_before}(F, E).$$

We can satisfy `false_before(f, e)` if we can find time instants t_i and t_j such that $t_j < t_i$, e happens at t_i and at t_j f is false. That is, f cannot be false before any occurrence of e. The correct semantics of until is that f cannot be false before the *first* occurrence of e [16].

In order to achieve the correct semantics, we need to introduce new fluents `happened(e)` to the domain for each event $e \in \mathcal{E}$ to indicate that e occurred for the first time. This is done automatically when we translate Inst*QL* to *AnsProlog* to indicate when an event has happened at any time in the past during the current trace.

holdsat(happened(E), I) ← occurred(E, I), event(E), instant(I).

holdsat(happened(E), I) ← occurred(E, J), after(I, J),

event(E), instant(I), instant(J).

To allow for this we need for each event E that is part of the query and the until statement the condition condition con-E: holds(happened(E));.

This allows us to then specify FUG as follows:

```
condition fb(cond-F, cond-G): not cond-F while not cond_G;
    condition cond-FUG: not fb(cond-F, cond-G) and cond-E
                                and cond-F;
```

6.3 Institutional Designer and Reasoning Tools: Inst*Suite*

Both Inst*QL* and Inst*AL* were designed and implemented to make representing and reasoning about institutions more intuitive and effective. While they were designed to work together they can be used independently from each other. Inst*AL* and Inst*QL* specifications can be written in any text processor and then translated into an answer set program and passed on to an answer set solver that computes the requested traces and models. To provide normative designer more support, we have developed an integrated development environment Inst*Edit* with syntax highlighting. Together they are referred to as Inst*Suite* , which source code, a combination of Java and perl, can be obtained from http://agents.cs.bath.ac.uk/InstSuite/

7 Discussion

Previous work in [2, 1] (using the action language $\mathcal{C}^+$ [11]), has shown that action languages are particularly suited to modelling normative domains, where actions in the language are equated with institutional events. In [7] we extend this approach with the language Inst*AL* which incorporates normative properties directly into the syntax of the language and operates by translating institutional specifications into *AnsProlog*. In this case we are able to directly leverage the reasoning capabilities inherent in the underlying logic programming platform to query properties of models. By building Inst*QL* upon this model we are able to offer an equivalent level of abstraction to Inst*AL* while at the same time remaining independent of the action language itself Inst*AL*.

Inst*QL* was designed for institutions, but it can be used a general query language for action domains, provided their descriptions can be mapped to *AnsProlog*. Compared to existing query languages for action domains, Inst*QL* allows for simultaneous actions and the definition of conditions which can then be used to create more complex queries.

In [15], the authors present four query languages: $\mathcal{P}, \mathcal{Q}, \mathcal{Q}_n, \mathcal{R}$. Queries expressed in those languages can also be expressed using Inst*QL*. The action query language $\mathcal{P}$ has only two constructs : now L and necessarily F after A1, ..., An, where L refers to a fluent or its negation, F is a fluent and where Ai are actions. These queries can be encoded in Inst*QL* using the techniques discussed in Section 6. now L can be written as constraint happens(An) after(1) ... after(1)

happens(A1) after(1) holds(L) while necessarily F after A1, ..., An
is expressed as holds(F) after(1) happens(An) after(1) ... after(1)
happens(A1). Similar techniques can be used for the query languages $\mathcal{Q}$, $\mathcal{Q}_n$ and
$\mathcal{R}$. Given the action ordering technique used, we can assign specific times to each of
the fluents. InstQL can express all the same kinds of queries as the query languages
above, but in addition InstQL is capable of modelling simultaneous actions and fluents,
which permits the expression of complex queries using disjunctions and conjunctions
of conditions and, above all, allows reasoning with incomplete information, thus fully
exploiting the reasoning power of answer set programming.

The Causal Calculator (CCALC) [12] is a versatile tool for modelling action domains. While queries are possible in CCALC, InstQL has been designed specifically as
a query language, providing constructs to make specifying queries more natural. Relative ordering of actions or states is much more difficult in CCALC than it is InstQL ,
nor does CCALC allow for the formulation of composite queries (condition literals).

As it stands InstQL is an intuitive and versatile query and abduction language for action domains. The language is succinct and without redundancy (i.e. no operator can be
expressed as a function of other operators). However, from a software engineering point
of view, we could make the language more accessible by providing commonly used
constructs as part of the language. To this end, we plan to incorporate constructs such
as eventually(F), never(F), always(F), before(F), before(E), and an
if-construct to express conditions on events or fluents. For the same reasons, we plan
to add time specific happens(E,I) and hold(F,I) predicates and the possibility to
construct general logical expression without the need for condition statements.

At the moment InstQL only supports linear time. For certain domains, other ways of
representing time might be more appropriate. While linear time assumes implicit universal quantification over all paths in the transition function, branching time allows for
explicit existential and universal quantification of all paths and alternating time offers
selective quantification over those paths that are possible outcomes. While linear and
branching time are natural ways of describing time in closed domains, alternating time
is more suited to open domains.

In [7] we introduced the concept of multi-institutions; groups of institutions that
can influence each others' state. In the near future we want to extend InstQL to multi-
institution specifications.

References

[1] Artikis, A., Sergot, M., Pitt, J.: Specifying electronic societies with the Causal Calculator.
    In: Giunchiglia, F., Odell, J.J., Weiss, G. (eds.) AOSE 2002. LNCS, vol. 2585, pp. 1–15.
    Springer, Heidelberg (2003)
[2] Artikis, A., Sergot, M., Pitt, J.: Specifying norm-governed computational societies. ACM
    Trans. Comput. Logic 10(1), 1–42 (2009)
[3] Baral, C.: Knowledge Representation, Reasoning and Declarative Problem Solving. Cam-
    bridge Press, Cambridge (2003)
[4] Calvanese, D., Vardi, M.Y.: Reasoning about actions and planning in LTL action theories.
    In: Proc. KR 2002 (2002)
[5] Cliffe, O.: Specifying and Analysing Institutions in Multi-Agent Systems using Answer Set
    Programming. PhD thesis, University of Bath (2007)

 [6] Cliffe, O., De Vos, M., Padget, J.: Answer set programming for representing and reasoning about virtual institutions. In: Inoue, K., Satoh, K., Toni, F. (eds.) CLIMA 2006. LNCS (LNAI), vol. 4371, pp. 60–79. Springer, Heidelberg (2007)

 [7] Cliffe, O., De Vos, M., Padget, J.: Specifying and reasoning about multiple institutions. In: Noriega, P., Vázquez-Salceda, J., Boella, G., Boissier, O., Dignum, V., Fornara, N., Matson, E. (eds.) COIN 2006. LNCS (LNAI), vol. 4386, pp. 63–81. Springer, Heidelberg (2007)

 [8] Eiter, T., Leone, N., Mateis, C., Pfeifer, G., Scarcello, F.: The KR system dlv: Progress report, comparisons and benchmarks. In: Cohn, A.G., Schubert, L., Shapiro, S.C. (eds.) KR 1998: Principles of Knowledge Representation and Reasoning, pp. 406–417. Morgan Kaufmann, San Francisco (1998)

 [9] Allen Emerson, E.: Temporal and modal logic. In: van Leeuwen, J. (ed.) Handbook of Theoretical Computer Science, pp. 995–1072. Elsevier, Amsterdam (1990)

[10] Emerson, E.A., Halpern, J.Y.: "sometimes" and "not never" revisited: on branching versus linear time temporal logic. Journal of the ACM 33(1), 151–178 (1986)

[11] Giunchiglia, E., Lee, J., Lifschitz, V., McCain, N., Turner, H.: Nonmonotonic causal theories. Artificial Intelligence 153, 49–104 (2004)

[12] Giunchiglia, E., Lee, J., Lifschitz, V., McCain, N., Turner, H.: Nonmonotonic causal theories. Artificial Intelligence 153, 49–104 (2004)

[13] Gebser, M., Kaufmann, B., Neumann, A., Schaub, T.: Conflict-Driven Answer Set Solving. In: Proceeding of IJCAI 2007, pp. 386–392 (2007)

[14] Gelfond, M., Lifschitz, V.: Classical negation in logic programs and disjunctive databases. New Generation Computing 9(3-4), 365–386 (1991)

[15] Gelfond, M., Lifschitz, V.: Action languages. Electron. Trans. Artif. Intell. 2, 193–210 (1998)

[16] Heljanko, K., Niemelä, I.: Bounded LTL model checking with stable models. In: Eiter, T., Faber, W., Truszczyński, M. (eds.) LPNMR 2001. LNCS (LNAI), vol. 2173, pp. 200–212. Springer, Heidelberg (2001)

[17] Hopton, L., Cliffe, O., De Vos, M., Padget, J. A.: Aql: A query language for action domains modelled using answer set programming. In: Erdem, E., Lin, F., Schaub, T. (eds.) LPNMR 2009. LNCS, vol. 5753, pp. 437–443. Springer, Heidelberg (2009)

[18] Searle, J.R.: The Construction of Social Reality. The Penguin Press, Allen Lane (1995)

[19] Kowalski, R.A., Sadri, F.: Reconciling the event calculus with the situation calculus. Journal of Logic Programming 31(1-3), 39–58 (1997)

[20] Niemelä, I., Simons, P.: Smodels: An implementation of the stable model and well-founded semantics for normal LP. In: Fuhrbach, U., Dix, J., Nerode, A. (eds.) LPNMR 1997. LNCS (LNAI), vol. 1265, pp. 420–429. Springer, Heidelberg (1997)

[21] Noriega, P.: Agent mediated auctions: The Fishmarket Metaphor. PhD thesis, Universitat Autonoma de Barcelona (1997)

[22] Pnueli, A.: The Temporal Logic of Programs. In: 19th Annual Symp. on Foundations of Computer Science (1977)

[23] Rodríguez, J.-A., Noriega, P., Sierra, C., Padget, J.: FM 96.5 A Java-based Electronic Auction House. In: Proceedings of 2nd Conference on Practical Applications of Intelligent Agents and MultiAgent Technology (PAAM 1997), pp. 207–224 (1997) ISBN 0-9525554-6-8

[24] Sergot, M.: $\mathcal{C}+^{++}$: An action language for modelling norms and institutions. Technical Report 8, Department of Computing, Imperial College, London (2004)

[25] Sistla, A.P., Clarke, E.M.: The complexity of propostional linear temporal logics. Journal of the ACM 32(3), 733–749 (1985)

Interacting Answer Sets

Chiaki Sakama[1] and Tran Cao Son[2]

[1] Department of Computer and Communication Sciences
Wakayama University, Sakaedani, Wakayama 640-8510, Japan
sakama@sys.wakayama-u.ac.jp
[2] Department of Computer Science
New Mexico State University, Las Cruces, NM 88003, USA
tson@cs.nmsu.edu

Abstract. We consider agent societies represented by logic programs. Four different types of social interactions among agents, *cooperation*, *competition*, *norms*, and *subjection*, are formulated as interactions between answer sets of different programs. Answer sets satisfying conditions of interactions represent solutions coordinated in a multiagent society. A unique feature of our framework is that answer set interactions are specified outside of individual programs. This enables us to freely change the social specifications among agents without the need of modifying individual programs and to separate beliefs of agents from social requirements over them. Social interactions among agents are encoded in a single logic program using constraints. Coordinated solutions are then computed using answer set programming.

1 Introduction

In a multiagent society, agents interact with one another to pursue their goals or perform their tasks. The behavior of one agent is often affected by other agents or constrained in a society he/she belongs to. To reach better states of affairs in a society, goals and behaviors of agents are to be coordinated through agent interactions. Agents interact differently depending on situations. For instance, agents work cooperatively to achieve a common goal, while they behave competitively when their goals are conflicting.

The purpose of this paper is to formulate various types of agent interactions using *answer set programming* (ASP) [1]. In answer set programming, the knowledge base of an agent is represented by a logic program and the belief state of an agent is represented by a collection of answer sets. In the presence of multiple agents, individual agents have their own programs and those programs have different collections of answer sets in general. Consider cooperative problem solving by multiple agents. Each agent has a logic program representing his/her local problem, and computes its answer sets as local solutions. Those solutions are finally integrated to a solution of the global problem in a society. To have successful cooperative problem solving, agents are often required to follow some conditions. We illustrate the situation using an example.

There is a graph G and two robots, say P_1 and P_2, try to cooperatively solve the graph-coloring problem on G. They make a plan such that P_1 paints the left-half of the graph $l(G)$ and P_2 paints the right-half $r(G)$. There are some nodes on the border

J. Dix, M. Fisher, and P. Novák (Eds.): CLIMA X, LNAI 6214, pp. 122–140, 2010.

$b(G)$ and these nodes can be painted by each robot independently. The robots solve the problem using their logic programs and produce candidate solutions, respectively. At this point, some controls over the behaviors of robots are required.

- Every node on the border must have a unique color. That is, if a node n in the area $b(G)$ is painted with a color c by P_1, the node must also be painted with the same color by P_2, and vice versa.
- Every node which is not on the border must be painted by one of the two robots. That is, each node n in the area $l(G)$ (resp. $r(G)$) is painted by P_1 (resp. P_2) but not by P_2 (resp. P_1).
- Every node in the graph G must be painted by either P_1 or P_2.

These requirements can be expressed as conditions over answer sets of the programs of P_1 and P_2 as follows. Let S be an answer set of a program P_1 and T an answer set of a program P_2. S and T represent local coloring solutions devised by individual robots. The three conditions presented above are rephrased as follows: (i) S contains $paint(n, c)$ iff T contains $paint(n, c)$ for any node n in $b(G)$, (ii) S contains $paint(n, c)$ iff T does not contain $paint(n, c)$ for any node n in $l(G)$ or $r(G)$, (iii) for every node n in G, $paint(n, c)$ must be included in either S or T. Condition (i) represents that the two robots have to *cooperate* to paint nodes lying on the border. By contrast, (ii) represents that nodes in each area are *competitive*, that is, each node in the left-half or the right-half of the graph is painted by only one robot. Condition (iii) represents that painting nodes in the entire graph is *norms* of the two robots. Next consider that each node on the border is painted by two robots, but P_1 is prior to P_2 to make a decision on the color. So if P_1 paints a node n on the border with a color c, then P_2 must accept it. The situation is characterized by changing the condition (i) to implication: (iv) if S contains $paint(n, c)$ for any n in $b(G)$, then T contains $paint(n, c)$. Condition (iv) represents a *subjection* relation between local solutions of two robots.

Cooperation, competition, norms, and subjection are different types of interactions among agents and are frequently used in multiagent systems [15]. To develop multiagent systems in logic programming, the above example illustrates the need of formulating interaction among answer sets to coordinate belief states of multiple agents in a society. The goal of this paper is to provide a computational logic for various types of social interactions among agents. We suppose an agent society in which individual agents have knowledge bases represented by logic programs. Social interactions among agents are then captured as interactions among answer sets of programs. Answer sets satisfying conditions of interactions represent solutions coordinated in a multiagent society. Answer set interactions are extended in various ways and social attitudes of agents are formulated within the framework. Next, by combining different programs into a single joint program, social interactions are specified as constraints over the joint program. Solutions satisfying the requirements of those interactions are then computed as the answer sets of the joint program.

The rest of this paper is organized as follows. Section 2 reviews notions used in this paper. Section 3 formulates different types of interactions between answer sets. The framework is extended in various ways in Section 4. Section 5 provides computation of social interaction in answer set programming. Section 6 discusses related issues, and Section 7 concludes the paper.

2   Preliminaries

In this paper, we consider *extended disjunctive programs* as defined in [7]. An extended disjunctive program (EDP) is a set of *rules* of the form:

$$\ell_1 ; \cdots ; \ell_l \leftarrow \ell_{l+1}, \ldots, \ell_m, not\, \ell_{m+1}, \ldots, not\, \ell_n \quad (n \geq m \geq l \geq 0) \quad (1)$$

where each ℓ_i is a positive/negative literal. *not* is *negation as failure* (NAF) and *not* ℓ is called an *NAF-literal*. The left-hand side of the rule is the *head*, and the right-hand side is the *body*. For each rule r of the above form, $head(r)$, $body^+(r)$, and $body^-(r)$ denote the sets of literals $\{\ell_1, \ldots, \ell_l\}$, $\{\ell_{l+1}, \ldots, \ell_m\}$, and $\{\ell_{m+1}, \ldots, \ell_n\}$, respectively. A rule r is a *constraint* if $head(r) = \emptyset$; and r is a *fact* if $body^+(r) = body^-(r) = \emptyset$. An EDP is simply called a *program* hereafter. A program P is *NAF-free* if $body^-(r) = \emptyset$ for every rule r in P. A program, rule, or literal is *ground* if it contains no variable. A program containing variables is considered as a shorthand for the set of its ground instances, and this paper handles ground (propositional) programs.

The semantics of an EDP is defined by the *answer set semantics* [7]. Let Lit be the set of all ground literals in the language of a program. Suppose a program P and a set $S (\subseteq Lit)$ of ground literals. Then, the *reduct* P^S is the program which contains the ground rule $\ell_1 ; \cdots ; \ell_l \leftarrow \ell_{l+1}, \ldots, \ell_m$ iff there is a ground rule r of the form (1) in P such that $body^-(r) \cap S = \emptyset$. Given an NAF-free EDP P, let S be a set of ground literals which is (i) *closed* under P, i.e., for every ground rule r in P, $body^+(r) \subseteq S$ implies $head(r) \cap S \neq \emptyset$; and (ii) *logically closed*, i.e., it is either consistent or equal to Lit. An *answer set* of an NAF-free program P is a minimal set S satisfying both (i) and (ii). Given an EDP P and a set $S (\subseteq Lit)$ of ground literals, S is an *answer set* of P if S is an answer set of P^S. A program has none, one, or multiple answer sets in general. The set of all answer sets of P is written as $AS(P)$. An answer set is *consistent* if it is not Lit. A program P is *consistent* if it has a consistent answer set; otherwise, P is *inconsistent*. Throughout the paper, a program is assumed to be consistent unless stated otherwise.

We suppose an *agent* who has a knowledge base represented by a logic program with the answer set semantics. An agent is often identified with its logic program and we use those terms interchangeably throughout the paper. A *society* is a finite set of agents. We assume that individual agents have their respective programs over a common language and a shared ontology in a society. There are several *interactions* among agents in a society. Among them, we consider the following four interactions which are frequently used in multiagent systems.

Cooperation: an interaction among agents to work together to achieve a common goal.
Competition: an interaction such that a satisfactory result for one agent implies unsatisfactory results for others.
Norms: an interaction that directs an agent to meet expectations or obligations in a society.
Subjection: an interaction that restricts behavior of one agent relative to another agent.

In the next section, we formulate these interactions as well as various social attitudes of agents that would happen during interactions.

3 Answer Set Interactions

In this section, we consider a society that consists of two agents. Interactions between agents are then characterized as the problem of interactions between answer sets of two programs.

3.1 Cooperation

Cooperative agents interact with each other to achieve a common goal. We model the situation by considering that certain facts are held by answer sets of two programs.

Definition 3.1. (cooperation) Let P_1 and P_2 be two programs and $\Phi \subseteq Lit$. Two answer sets $S \in AS(P_1)$ and $T \in AS(P_2)$ *cooperate* on Φ if

$$S \cap \Phi = T \cap \Phi. \tag{2}$$

In this case, we also say that S and T make a *cooperation* on Φ.

Condition (2) requires that two answer sets $S \in AS(P_1)$ and $T \in AS(P_2)$ must include the same elements from Φ. This type of interaction is useful to specify agreement or a common goal in a society.

Example 3.1. John and Marry are planning to go to a restaurant. John prefers French and Mary prefers Italian, but they behave together anyway. Programs representing beliefs about restaurants and preferences for John (P_1) and Mary (P_2) are:

$$P_1 : preferred \leftarrow french, \qquad\qquad P_2 : preferred \leftarrow italian,$$
$$french\,;\,italian \leftarrow . \qquad\qquad\qquad french\,;\,italian \leftarrow .$$

P_1 has two answer sets $S_1 = \{\,french,\,preferred\,\}$ and $S_2 = \{\,italian\,\}$, while P_2 has two answer sets $T_1 = \{\,italian,\,preferred\,\}$ and $T_2 = \{\,french\,\}$. Putting $\Phi = \{\,french,\,italian\,\}$, we have that S_1 and T_2, and S_2 and T_1 cooperate on Φ.

Cooperation between answer sets is monotonic, namely, cooperation on Φ implies cooperation on its subset.

Proposition 3.1. *(monotonicity) If S and T cooperate on Φ, they cooperate on any Φ' such that $\Phi' \subseteq \Phi$.*

Note that any pair of answer sets cooperates on $\Phi = \emptyset$; and $S = T$ if S and T cooperate on $\Phi = Lit$.

When an answer set S of P_1 includes an answer set T of P_2, S can accept T as a part of beliefs of P_1. By contrast, when S is included in T, S can be extended to adapt to the beliefs of P_2.

Definition 3.2. (accept, adapt) $S \in AS(P_1)$ *accepts* $T \in AS(P_2)$ if $S \supseteq T$. If S accepts T, T *adapts* to S.

Acceptance and adaptation can be characterized by cooperation as follows.

Proposition 3.2. $S \in AS(P_1)$ *accepts* $T \in AS(P_2)$ *iff* S *and* T *cooperate on* T. S *adapts to* T *iff* S *and* T *cooperate on* S.

Proof. $S \supseteq T$ iff $S \cap T = T$ iff S and T cooperate on T. On the other hand, $S \subseteq T$ iff $S \cap T = S$ iff S and T cooperate on S. □

When $S \in AS(P_1)$ cannot accept nor adapt to $T \in AS(P_2)$, two agents might make a concession.

Definition 3.3. (concession) For any pair of answer sets $S \in AS(P_1)$ and $T \in AS(P_2)$, $\Phi = S \cap T$ is called a *concession* between P_1 and P_2. A *maximal concession* is a concession Φ such that there is no concession Φ' satisfying $\Phi \subset \Phi'$.

Example 3.2. Let $AS(P_1) = \{\{p, q\}, \{r\}\}$ and $AS(P_2) = \{\{p, r\}, \{s\}\}$. Then, $\{p\}$, $\{r\}$ and $\emptyset$ are three possible concessions between P_1 and P_2. Of which the first two sets are maximal concessions.

When there are multiple concessions, a maximal one characterizes a maximal agreement between agents. Concession and cooperation have the following relation.

Proposition 3.3. *If a set* Φ *is a concession between* P_1 *and* P_2, *then there are* $S \in AS(P_1)$ *and* $T \in AS(P_2)$ *which cooperate on* Φ.

Proof. If Φ is a concession between P_1 and P_2, then $\Phi = S \cap T$ for some $S \in AS(P_1)$ and $T \in AS(P_2)$. In this case, $S \cap \Phi = T \cap \Phi$ and the result holds. □

3.2 Competition

Competition between agents is a natural phenomenon that, in most cases, results in the satisfaction of one agent and the dissatisfaction of another agent on some issues. We model this phenomenon by considering that the presence (resp. absence) of certain facts in an answer set of one agent demonstrates the satisfaction (resp. dissatisfaction) of the agent with respect to the facts. This leads to the following definition.

Definition 3.4. (competition) Let P_1 and P_2 be two programs and $\Psi \subseteq Lit$. Two answer sets $S \in AS(P_1)$ and $T \in AS(P_2)$ are *competitive* for Ψ if

$$S \cap T \cap \Psi = \emptyset. \tag{3}$$

In this case, we also say that S and T are in a *competition* for Ψ.

Condition (3) requires that two answer sets $S \in AS(P_1)$ and $T \in AS(P_2)$ do not share any element belonging to Ψ. This type of interaction is useful to specify a limited resource or an exclusive right in a society.

Example 3.3. John and Mary share a car. John plans to go fishing if he can use the car, while Mary wants to go shopping if the car is available. Programs representing plans for John (P_1) and Mary (P_2) are:

$$P_1 : go\_fishing \leftarrow use\_car, \qquad\qquad P_2 : go\_shopping \leftarrow use\_car,$$
$$use\_car \, ; \, \neg use\_car \leftarrow . \qquad\qquad\qquad use\_car \, ; \, \neg use\_car \leftarrow .$$

P_1 has two answer sets $S_1 = \{go\_fishing, use\_car\}$ and $S_2 = \{\neg use\_car\}$, while P_2 has two answer sets $T_1 = \{go\_shopping, use\_car\}$ and $T_2 = \{\neg use\_car\}$. Putting $\Psi = \{use\_car\}$, we have that S_1 and T_2, S_2 and T_1, and S_2 and T_2 are competitive for Ψ.

The results of competition represent that a successful plan for John implies an unsatisfactory result for Mary, and vice versa.

Proposition 3.4. *(monotonicity) If S and T are competitive for Ψ, they are competitive for any Ψ' such that $\Psi' \subseteq \Psi$.*

As trivial cases, any pair of answer sets is competitive for $\Psi = \emptyset$; and S and T are competitive for Lit if $S \cap T = \emptyset$. Thus interesting cases of competition happen when $\Psi \neq \emptyset$ and $S \cap T \neq \emptyset$.

Definition 3.5. (benefit) Suppose that $S \in AS(P_1)$ and $T \in AS(P_2)$ are competitive for Ψ. Then, S has *benefit* over T wrt Ψ if $S \cap \Psi \neq \emptyset$.

Suppose that S and T are competitive for Ψ. When $S \cap \Psi \supseteq T \cap \Psi$, $S \cap T \cap \Psi = \emptyset$ iff $T \cap \Psi = \emptyset$. This means that in this case there is no chance for T to have benefit over S wrt Ψ. Such a precedence relation in competition is defined as follows.

Definition 3.6. (precedence) Suppose that $S \in AS(P_1)$ and $T \in AS(P_2)$ are competitive for Ψ. Then, S has *precedence* over T wrt Ψ if $S \cap \Psi \supseteq T \cap \Psi$.

Proposition 3.5. *If S has precedence over T wrt Ψ, T cannot have benefit over S wrt Ψ.*

Example 3.4. Suppose that there are two companies P_1 and P_2. P_1 has a right to mine both oil and gas, while P_2 has a right to mine either one of them. The situation is represented by answer sets of programs: $AS(P_1) = \{\{oil, gas\}\}$ and $AS(P_2) = \{\{oil\}, \{gas\}\}$. Then, $\{oil, gas\}$ and $\{gas\}$ are competitive for $\Psi = \{oil\}$, while $\{oil, gas\}$ and $\{oil\}$ are not. In this case, $\{oil, gas\}$ has precedence over $\{gas\}$ wrt $\{oil\}$. This means that if two companies coordinate their answer sets to be competitive for Ψ, there is no chance for P_2 to mine oil.

3.3 Norms

Norms represent expectations or obligations for agents to take some actions. We model the situation by considering that normative goals are included in one of the answer sets of two programs.

Definition 3.7. (norms) Let P_1 and P_2 be two programs and $\Theta \subseteq Lit$. Two answer sets $S \in AS(P_1)$ and $T \in AS(P_2)$ achieve *norms* for Θ if

$$(S \cup T) \cap \Theta = \Theta. \tag{4}$$

Condition (4) requires that two answer sets $S \in AS(P_1)$ and $T \in AS(P_2)$ should jointly include every element in Θ. This type of interaction is useful to specify duty or task allocation in a society.

Example 3.5. Mary is planning to have a home party. She asks her friends, John and Susie, to buy wine, juice and water. John will visit a liquor shop and can buy wine or water or both. Susie will visit a grocery store and can buy juice or water or both. Programs representing possible items for shopping by John (P_1) and Susie (P_2) are

$$P_1 : \ wine\,; \ \neg wine \leftarrow, \qquad\qquad P_2 : \ juice\,; \ \neg juice \leftarrow,$$
$$water\,; \ \neg water \leftarrow . \qquad\qquad\qquad water\,; \ \neg water \leftarrow .$$

Each program has four answer sets representing buying items. Of which, the following three pairs of answer sets achieve norms for $\Theta = \{\,wine, juice, water\,\}$: $S_1 = \{wine, water\}$ and $T_1 = \{juice, water\}$; $S_2 = \{wine, \neg water\}$ and $T_2 = \{juice, water\}$; and $S_3 = \{wine, water\}$ and $T_3 = \{juice, \neg water\}$.

Proposition 3.6. *(monotonicity) If S and T achieve norms for Θ, they achieve norms for any Θ' such that $\Theta' \subseteq \Theta$.*

As a special case, any pair of answer sets achieves norms for $\Theta = \emptyset$. To achieve norms, individual agents have their own roles. We formulate this below.

Definition 3.8. (responsible) Let $S \in AS(P_1)$, $T \in AS(P_2)$ and $\Theta \subseteq Lit$. We say that

- S is *individually responsible* for $\Theta \setminus T$;
- S has *no responsibility* if S is individually responsible for $\emptyset$; and
- S is *less responsible* than T if $\Theta \setminus T \subseteq \Theta \setminus S$.

The set $\Theta \setminus T$ is called an *individually responsible set* for S.

Proposition 3.7. *Let $S \in AS(P_1)$, $T \in AS(P_2)$ and $\Theta \subseteq Lit$.*

1. *S and T achieve norms for Θ if either S or T contains its individual responsible set.*
2. *If $S \subseteq T$ then S is less responsible than T.*
3. *If $T \supseteq \Theta$ then S has no responsibility.*

Proof. (1) If $S \supseteq \Theta \setminus T$, $S \cup T \supseteq (\Theta \setminus T) \cup T = \Theta$. Then, $(S \cup T) \cap \Theta = \Theta$. (2) $S \subseteq T$ implies $S \cap \Theta \subseteq T \cap \Theta$, which implies $\Theta \setminus T \subseteq \Theta \setminus S$. (3) $T \supseteq \Theta$ implies $\Theta \setminus T = \emptyset$.   □

An individual responsible set $\Theta \setminus T$ in Definition 3.8 represents the least task or obligation for S to achieve given norms. Undertaking individual responsibilities does not always achieve norms, however.

Example 3.6. In Example 3.5, $S_1 = \{wine, water\}$ and $T_1 = \{juice, water\}$ achieve norms for $\Theta = \{\,wine, juice, water\,\}$. Thus, S_1 is individually responsible for $\Theta \setminus T_1 = \{wine\}$ and T_1 is individually responsible for $\Theta \setminus S_1 = \{juice\}$, which means that the individual responsibility of John and Susie is to buy wine and juice respectively. It is easy to see that if John only buys wine and Susie only buys juice then they might not achieve norms for Θ. This is because $S_1' = \{wine, \neg water\}$ and $T_1' = \{juice, \neg water\}$ satisfy the individual responsibility for both John and Susie but do not achieve norms for Θ.

In the above example, John or Susie has to *voluntarily* buy water to achieve the norms. On the other hand, responsibility may change by taking a different pair of answer sets. In Example 3.5, S_2 and T_2 also achieve norms for Θ. But S_2 is responsible for $\Theta \setminus T_2 = \{wine\}$, while T_2 is responsible for $\Theta \setminus S_2 = \{juice, water\}$. So S_2 and T_2 achieve norms without voluntary actions. This leads us to the following definition.

Definition 3.9. (volunteer) Let $S \in AS(P_1)$, $T \in AS(P_2)$ and $\Theta \subseteq Lit$. We say that S and T *volunteer* for $S \cap T \cap \Theta$. For $S' \in AS(P_1)$ and $T' \in AS(P_2)$, we say that the pair (S, T) requires *less voluntary actions* than (S', T') if $(S \cap T \cap \Theta) \subseteq (S' \cap T' \cap \Theta)$.

By the definition, a voluntary action is required only if $S \cap T \neq \emptyset$.

Proposition 3.8. *Let $\Theta \subseteq Lit$, $\{S, S'\} \subseteq AS(P_1)$ and $\{T, T'\} \subseteq AS(P_2)$ such that S and T (resp. S' and T') achieve norms for Θ. Then, (S, T) requires less voluntary actions than (S', T') iff S and T have more individual responsibility than S' and T'.*

Proof. By $(\Theta \setminus S) \cup (\Theta \setminus T) = \Theta \cap \overline{S \cap T}$ and $(\Theta \setminus S') \cup (\Theta \setminus T') = \Theta \cap \overline{S' \cap T'}$, $(S \cap T \cap \Theta) \subseteq (S' \cap T' \cap \Theta)$ iff $\Theta \cap \overline{S' \cap T'} \subseteq \Theta \cap \overline{S \cap T}$.   □

An agent is expected to take a voluntary action in addition to his/her individual responsibility. To declare his/her action to another agent, an agent creates (social) commitment [14].

Definition 3.10. (commitment) A *commitment* $C(P_1, P_2, Q)$ represents a pledge of an agent P_1 to another agent P_2 to realize Q.

Commitments could be canceled, so that $C(P_1, P_2, Q)$ represents a promise of P_1 to P_2 for realizing Q, but it does not necessarily guarantee the outcome of Q.

Proposition 3.9. *$S \in AS(P_1)$ and $T \in AS(P_2)$ achieve norms for Θ only if commitments $C(P_1, P_2, U)$ and $C(P_2, P_1, V)$ are made such that $U \subseteq S$, $V \subseteq T$, and $\Theta \subseteq U \cup V$.*

Proof. $(S \cup T) \cap \Theta = \Theta$ implies the existence of U and V satisfying $U \subseteq S$ and $V \subseteq T$, and $\Theta \subseteq U \cup V$.   □

Example 3.7. In order for $S_1 = \{wine, water\}$ and $T_1 = \{juice, water\}$ to achieve norms for $\Theta = \{wine, juice, water\}$, it is requested to make commitments $C(P_1, P_2, \{wine\})$ and $C(P_2, P_1, \{juice, water\})$, for instance.

3.4 Subjection

Subjection represents a situation that the behavior of one agent is dominated by that of another agent. We model the situation by considering that certain facts included in an answer set of one program are included in an answer set of another program.

Definition 3.11. (subjection) Let P_1 and P_2 be two programs and $\Lambda \subseteq Lit$. An answer set $S \in AS(P_1)$ is *subject* to an answer set $T \in AS(P_2)$ wrt Λ if

$$T \cap \Lambda \subseteq S \cap \Lambda. \tag{5}$$

In this case, we also say that S and T are in a *subjection* relation wrt Λ.

Condition (5) represents that any element from Λ which is included in an answer set $T \in AS(P_2)$ must be included in an answer set $S \in AS(P_1)$. In other words, S is dominated by T for the selection of elements in Λ. This type of interaction is useful to specify priority or power relations in a society.

Example 3.8. Bob and John are two kids in a family, and they have limited access to the Internet. Since Bob is older than John, any site which is limited to access by Bob is also limited to John, but not vice versa. Now two sites $site_1$ and $site_2$ are considered. Programs representing accessibility to each site by John (P_1) and Bob (P_2) are:

$$P_1 : acc\_site_1 \; ; \; \neg acc\_site_1 \leftarrow usr\_John, \quad P_2 : acc\_site_1 \; ; \; \neg acc\_site_1 \leftarrow usr\_Bob,$$
$$acc\_site_2 \; ; \; \neg acc\_site_2 \leftarrow usr\_John, \qquad acc\_site_2 \; ; \; \neg acc\_site_2 \leftarrow usr\_Bob,$$
$$usr\_John \leftarrow . \qquad\qquad\qquad usr\_Bob \leftarrow .$$

Each program has four answer sets representing accessible sites. Suppose first that the $site_1$ is a site for limited access. Putting $\Lambda_1 = \{ \neg acc\_site_1 \}$, 12 pairs of answer sets, out of 16 combinations of answer sets of P_1 and P_2, are in subjection relation wrt Λ_1. For instance, the following pairs are two solutions: $S_1 = \{ \neg acc\_site_1, \neg acc\_site_2, usr\_John \}$ is subject to $T_1 = \{ acc\_site_1, acc\_site_2, usr\_Bob \}$ wrt Λ_1; and $S_2 = \{ \neg acc\_site_1, acc\_site_2, usr\_John \}$ is subject to $T_2 = \{ \neg acc\_site_1, \neg acc\_site_2, usr\_Bob \}$ wrt Λ_1.

Next, suppose that $site_2$ is added as a site for limited access. Then, Λ_1 is changed to $\Lambda_2 = \{ \neg acc\_site_1, \neg acc\_site_2 \}$. In this case, there are 9 combinations of answer sets which are in subjection relation wrt Λ_2. For instance, S_1 and T_1 are still in a subjection relation wrt Λ_2, but S_2 and T_2 are not anymore.

Proposition 3.10. *(monotonicity) If S is subject to T wrt Λ, the subjection relation holds for any Λ' such that $\Lambda' \subseteq \Lambda$.*

Proposition 3.11. *If $S \supseteq T$, S is subject to T wrt any Λ.*

If any information in $T \in AS(P_2)$ should be included in $S \in AS(P_1)$, it is achieved by putting $\Lambda = T$.

Proposition 3.12. *If S is subject to T wrt T, $S \supseteq T$.*

Proof. $T \subseteq S \cap T$ implies $S \supseteq T$. □

Note that it is always the case that S is subject to T wrt S as $S \cap T \subseteq S$. By Definitions 3.1 and 3.6, we have the following relations.

Proposition 3.13. *For any Λ,*

1. *S and T cooperate on Λ iff S is subject to T wrt Λ and T is subject to S wrt Λ.*
2. *If S and T are competitive for Λ and S is subject to T wrt Λ, then S has precedence over T wrt Λ.*

Thus, precedence is considered a special case of a subjection relation.

4   Extensions

4.1   Coordination and Priority

In Section 3 four different types of answer set interactions are introduced. These interactions are combined into a single framework in this section.

Definition 4.1. (coordination) For two programs P_1 and P_2, a tuple of sets of literals $\Omega = (\Phi, \Psi, \Theta, \Lambda)$ is called a *coordination* over P_1 and P_2. Each component X of Ω will be denoted by Ω_X hereafter and is called a *coordination condition* in Ω.

Two answer sets $S \in AS(P_1)$ and $T \in AS(T_2)$ are said to satisfy Ω_Φ (resp. Ω_Ψ, Ω_Θ, and Ω_Λ) if they satisfy the conditions in Definition 3.1 wrt Φ (resp. Definition 3.4 wrt Ψ, 3.7 wrt Θ and 3.11 wrt Λ). S and T *satisfy* $C \subseteq \{\Omega_\Phi, \Omega_\Psi, \Omega_\Theta, \Omega_\Lambda\}$, if they satisfy each $X \in C$.

Definition 4.2. (compatible) Let P_1 and P_2 be two programs and Ω a coordination over P_1 and P_2. Two answer sets $S \in AS(P_1)$ and $T \in AS(P_2)$ are *compatible* (or a *solution*) wrt Ω if S and T satisfy Ω_Φ, Ω_Ψ, Ω_Θ, and Ω_Λ.

Since answer set interactions are monotonic with respect to coordination conditions, the compatibility of answer sets is also monotonic, i.e., if S and T are compatible wrt Ω, they are also compatible wrt any $\Omega' = (\Phi', \Psi', \Theta', \Lambda')$ such that $X' \subseteq X$ for $X \in \{\Phi, \Psi, \Theta, \Lambda\}$. This coincides with the intuition that fewer requirements would open the possibility of successful coordination. On the other hand, a tuple Ω specifies different types of social interactions and there may exist conflict among their requirements.

Example 4.1. A company opens positions for a system administrator and a programmer. A system administrator can get a salary higher than a programmer. There are two applicants, P_1 and P_2, who have talents as both an administrator and a programmer. Both P_1 and P_2 share the following knowledge:

$$high\_salary \leftarrow admin,$$
$$low\_salary \leftarrow programmer,$$
$$admin \,;\, programmer \leftarrow .$$

Suppose that two applicants have the same desire to get a higher salary as a system administrator. The common goal is specified by a coordination condition $\Phi = \{high\_salary\}$. However, the company has only one position for an administrator, so the situation is specified by a coordination condition $\Psi = \{admin, programmer\}$. Both P_1 and P_2 have two answer sets: $AS(P_1) = \{S_1, S_2\}$ and $AS(P_2) = \{T_1, T_2\}$ such that $S_1 = T_1 = \{admin, high\_salary\}$ and $S_2 = T_2 = \{programmer, low\_salary\}$. S_1 and T_1 cooperate on Φ, but they are not competitive for Ψ. As a result, no two answer sets of $S \in AS(P_1)$ and $T \in AS(P_2)$ are compatible wrt $\Omega = (\Phi, \Psi, \emptyset, \emptyset)$.

Instead of returning no solution in such cases, we introduce a mechanism of *priorities* over interactions as a method of building a compromised solution. To this end, we assume a preorder relation $\succeq$, called a *priority* relation, over $\{\Omega_\Phi, \Omega_\Psi, \Omega_\Theta, \Omega_\Lambda\}$. Intuitively, $\Omega_x \succeq \Omega_y$ states that satisfying x is more important than satisfying y. A set $C \subseteq \{\Omega_\Phi, \Omega_\Psi, \Omega_\Theta, \Omega_\Lambda\}$ is a *maximal element* wrt $\succeq$ if it satisfies the two conditions: (i) if $x \succeq y$ and $y \in C$ then $x \in C$; and (ii) there exists no $C' \subseteq \{\Omega_\Phi, \Omega_\Psi, \Omega_\Theta, \Omega_\Lambda\}$ such that $C \subset C'$ and C' satisfies (i).

Definition 4.3. (compatible under priority) Let $\succeq$ be a preorder relation defined over $\{\Omega_\Phi, \Omega_\Psi, \Omega_\Theta, \Omega_\Lambda\}$. Two answer sets $S \in AS(P_1)$ and $T \in AS(P_2)$ are *compatible under priority* wrt $(\Omega, \succeq)$ if there exists some maximal element $C \subseteq \{\Omega_\Phi, \Omega_\Psi, \Omega_\Theta, \Omega_\Lambda\}$ wrt $\succeq$ and S and T satisfy C.

In Example 4.1, no pair of answer sets $S \in AS(P_1)$ and $T \in AS(P_2)$ is compatible wrt Ω, but S_1 and T_2 (or S_2 and T_1) are compatible under priority wrt $(\Omega, \{\Omega_\Psi \succeq \Omega_\Phi\})$.

4.2 Dynamic Interactions

In Section 3, Φ, Ψ, Θ, and Λ are given as sets of literals. By specifying them as sets of rules, we can specify interactions that may change depending on different contexts.

Definition 4.4. (dynamic cooperation) Let P_1 and P_2 be two programs and Π a set of rules. Two answer sets $S \in AS(P_1)$ and $T \in AS(P_2)$ make a *weak* (resp. *strong*) *dynamic cooperation* on Π if

$$S \cap X = T \cap X \qquad (6)$$

for some (resp. any) answer set X of Π.

Example 4.2. (modified from Example 3.1) John and Mary have two options for dinner, while at lunch John takes hamburger and Mary takes sandwich. The situation is encoded as the program for John (P_1) and the program for Mary (P_2) such that

P_1 : $preferred \leftarrow french$,
  $french\,;\,italian \leftarrow dinner$,
  $hamburger \leftarrow lunch$,
  $dinner \leftarrow$, $lunch \leftarrow$.

P_2 : $preferred \leftarrow italian$,
  $french\,;\,italian \leftarrow dinner$,
  $sandwich \leftarrow lunch$,
  $dinner \leftarrow$, $lunch \leftarrow$.

Suppose that Π is given as the set of five rules:

$$french \leftarrow dinner,$$
$$italian \leftarrow dinner,$$
$$hamburger \leftarrow lunch,$$
$$sandwich \leftarrow lunch,$$
$$lunch\,;\,dinner \leftarrow.$$

Π specifies that French and Italian are subject to cooperation for dinner, while hamburger and sandwich are for lunch. Now Π has two answer sets: $\{dinner, french, italian\}$ and $\{lunch, hamburger, sandwich\}$. In this situation, the answer set $\{dinner, french, preferred, lunch, hamburger\}$ of P_1 and the answer set $\{dinner, french,$

lunch, sandwich} of P_2 make a weak dynamic cooperation on Π. There is another combination of answer sets which make a weak dynamic cooperation on Π (having Italian for dinner), but there is no combination which makes a strong dynamic cooperation on Π.

In the above example, Π specifies cooperations for lunch and dinner, while P_1 and P_2 can cooperate only on dinner. The situation is explained by the existence of a weak dynamic cooperation and the lack of a strong one. Note that if two programs do not contain the fact *lunch* $\leftarrow$, a strong dynamic cooperation is also possible. Thus, Π specifies cooperations that may change depending on the context of P_1 and P_2. Similar extensions are possible for competition, norms and subjection.

4.3   Interactions among n-Agents

Answer set interactions can be generalized to systems with more than two agents.

Definition 4.5. (AS-interactions among n-agents) Let $P_1, \ldots, P_n$ be programs and $S_1 \in AS(P_1), \ldots, S_n \in AS(P_n)$ their answer sets. For any collection of k answer sets such that $\{S_{i_1}, \ldots, S_{i_k}\} \subseteq \{S_1, \ldots, S_n\}$ and $2 \leq k \leq n$,

1. $S_{i_1}, \ldots, S_{i_k}$ make a *k-cooperation* on $\Phi \subseteq Lit$ if

$$S_{i_1} \cap \Phi = \cdots = S_{i_k} \cap \Phi. \tag{7}$$

2. $S_{i_1}, \ldots, S_{i_k}$ are in a *k-competition* for $\Psi \subseteq Lit$ if

$$S_{i_1} \cap \cdots \cap S_{i_k} \cap \Psi = \emptyset. \tag{8}$$

3. $S_{i_1}, \ldots, S_{i_k}$ achieve *k-norms* for $\Theta \subseteq Lit$ if

$$(S_{i_1} \cup \cdots \cup S_{i_k}) \cap \Theta = \Theta. \tag{9}$$

4. $S_{i_1}, \ldots, S_{i_k}$ are in *k-subjection* relations wrt $\Lambda \subseteq Lit$ if

$$S_{i_k} \cap \Lambda \subseteq \cdots \subseteq S_{i_1} \cap \Lambda. \tag{10}$$

We say that $S_1, \ldots, S_n$ are *n-compatible* wrt a *coordination* $\Omega = (\Phi, \Psi, \Theta, \Lambda)$ if they satisfy the above four conditions.

Observe that Definition 4.5 reduces to the case of two agents when $n = 2$. It is worth noting that Definition 4.5 has several variants. For instance, we can define a 2-competition for Ψ for the collection of k answer sets as: S_i and S_j $(i \neq j)$ are competitive for Ψ for any pair of answer sets from $\{S_{i_1}, \ldots, S_{i_k}\}$. The notion of subjection is extended to the combination of answer sets as: $S_i \cup S_j$ is subject to S_k wrt Λ. Such variants would be also useful, but we do not pursue variants of interactions further here.

4.4   Interactions between Programs

A program generally has more than one answer sets. Then, we can apply the notion of interactions between answer sets to interactions between programs.

Definition 4.6. (interactions between programs) Let P_1 and P_2 be two programs.

1. P_1 and P_2 make a *strong cooperation* (resp. *weak cooperation*) on $\Phi \subseteq Lit$ if

$$S \cap \Phi = T \cap \Phi$$

   holds for any (resp. some) pair of answer sets $S \in AS(P_1)$ and $T \in AS(P_2)$.
2. P_1 and P_2 are in a *strong competition* (resp. *weak competition*) for $\Psi \subseteq Lit$ if

$$S \cap T \cap \Psi = \emptyset$$

   holds for any (resp. some) pair of answer sets $S \in AS(P_1)$ and $T \in AS(P_2)$.
3. P_1 and P_2 achieve *strong norms* (resp. *weak norms*) for $\Theta \subseteq Lit$ if

$$(S \cup T) \cap \Theta = \Theta$$

   holds for any (resp. some) pair of answer sets $S \in AS(P_1)$ and $T \in AS(P_2)$.
4. P_1 and P_2 are in a *strong subjection* (resp. *weak subjection*) relation wrt $\Lambda \subseteq Lit$ if

$$T \cap \Lambda \subseteq S \cap \Lambda$$

   holds for any (resp. some) pair of answer sets $S \in AS(P_1)$ and $T \in AS(P_2)$.

No interactions are defined for programs having no answer set.

Strong interactions coincide with weak interactions for two programs each of which has exactly one answer set. For two programs having multiple answer sets, however, strong interactions are very strong conditions and hard to satisfy in general. In fact, examples shown in previous sections are mostly weak interactions. We thus consider that weak interactions would be more useful than strong ones in practice. The above interactions are combined into one as Definition 4.2 and are extended to n-programs as Definition 4.5.

5   Computing Answer Set Interactions

In this section, we provide a method of computing answer set interactions between two programs in ASP.

Definition 5.1. (annotated program) Given a program P_i, its *annotated program* P^i is obtained from P_i by replacing every literal ℓ or NAF-literal $not\ \ell$ appearing in P_i with a new literal ℓ^i or $not\ \ell^i$, respectively.

Example 5.1. Given the program P_1:

$$p \,;\, \neg q \leftarrow not\ r,$$
$$r \leftarrow,$$

its annotated program P^1 becomes

$$p^1 \,;\, \neg q^1 \leftarrow not\ r^1,$$
$$r^1 \leftarrow .$$

Annotations are introduced to distinguish beliefs between different agents. Let us define

$$S^i = \{\, \ell^i \mid \ell \in S \text{ and } S \in AS(P_i)\,\}.$$

The following properties hold.

Proposition 5.1. *Let P_i be a program. S is an answer set of P_i iff S^i is an answer set of P^i.*

Proposition 5.2. *Let P_1 and P_2 be two programs. Then, U is an answer set of $P^1 \cup P^2$ iff $U = S^1 \cup T^2$ for some $S^1 \in AS(P^1)$ and some $T^2 \in AS(P^2)$.*

Proof. As P^1 and P^2 have no literal in common, the result holds by the *splitting set theorem* of [9]. □

Next we provide specification of social interactions in a program.

Definition 5.2. (social constraints) Let P_1 and P_2 be two programs and $\Omega=(\Phi, \Psi, \Theta, \Lambda)$ a coordination over P_1 and P_2. Social interactions (2), (3), (4), and (5) between P_1 and P_2 are specified as a set SC of *social constraints* as follows.

1. For each $\ell \in \Phi$, SC contains a pair of constraints:

$$\leftarrow \ell^1,\ not\ \ell^2, \tag{11}$$
$$\leftarrow \ell^2,\ not\ \ell^1. \tag{12}$$

2. For each $\ell \in \Psi$, SC contains a constraint:

$$\leftarrow \ell^1, \ell^2 . \tag{13}$$

3. For each $\ell \in \Theta$, SC contains a constraint:

$$\leftarrow not\ \ell^1,\ not\ \ell^2 . \tag{14}$$

4. For each $\ell \in \Lambda$, SC contains a constraint:

$$\leftarrow \ell^2,\ not\ \ell^1 . \tag{15}$$

The program $P^1 \cup P^2 \cup SC$ is called a *joint program*.

Constraints (11) and (12) represent that the presence of any literal $\ell \in \Phi$ in an answer set of P_1 forces the presence of the same literal in an answer set of P_2, and the other way round. The constraint (13) indicates that any literal $\ell \in \Psi$ cannot belong to an answer set of P_1 and an answer set of P_2 at the same time. By contrast, the constraint (14) expresses that every literal $\ell \in \Theta$ must belong to either an answer set of P_1 or an answer set of P_2. Finally, the constraint (15) says that every literal $\ell \in \Lambda$ in an answer set of P_2 must belong to an answer of P_1.

With this setting, the next theorem holds.

Theorem 5.3. *Let P_1 and P_2 be two programs and $\Omega = (\Phi, \Psi, \Theta, \Lambda)$ a coordination over P_1 and P_2. Two answer sets $S \in AS(P_1)$ and $T \in AS(P_2)$ are compatible wrt Ω iff $S^1 \cup T^2$ is an answer set of the joint program $P^1 \cup P^2 \cup SC$.*

Proof. By Proposition 5.2, U is an answer set of $P^1 \cup P^2$ iff $U = S^1 \cup T^2$ for some $S^1 \in AS(P^1)$ and some $T^2 \in AS(P^2)$. Then, U is an answer set of $P^1 \cup P^2 \cup SC$ iff $\ell^1 \in S^1$ and $\ell^2 \in T^2$ satisfy the constraints SC for any ℓ in each coordination condition in Ω. In this case, S and T are compatible wrt Ω. Hence, the result holds.   □

Theorem 5.4. *Let P_1 and P_2 be two programs and $\Omega = (\Phi, \Psi, \Theta, \Lambda)$ a coordination over P_1 and P_2. Deciding whether there are two answer sets $S \in AS(P_1)$ and $T \in AS(P_2)$ that are compatible wrt Ω is Σ_2^P-complete.*

Proof. Deciding the existence of an answer set of an EDP is Σ_2^P-complete [5], hence the result holds by Theorem 5.3.   □

The notion of joint programs is extended to n-agents in a straightforward manner, and compatible answer sets among n-agents are computed accordingly.

6 Discussion

6.1 Answer Set Interactions = Answer Sets + Control

In this paper, interactions among answer sets are specified *outside* of individual programs. One may wonder that such an extra mechanism is really needed to encode the specification. In Example 3.1, for instance, the set Φ could be specified inside of each program as

$$P_1' : \quad preferred\_by\_john \leftarrow john\_go\_french,$$
$$john\_go\_french \leftarrow mary\_go\_french,$$
$$john\_go\_italian \leftarrow mary\_go\_italian,$$
$$john\_go\_french \,; john\_go\_italian \leftarrow,$$

and

$$P_2' : \quad preferred\_by\_mary \leftarrow mary\_go\_italian,$$
$$mary\_go\_french \leftarrow john\_go\_french,$$
$$mary\_go\_italian \leftarrow john\_go\_italian,$$
$$mary\_go\_french \,; mary\_go\_italian \leftarrow .$$

In this case, $P_1' \cup P_2'$ has two answer sets $\{\, john\_go\_french,\ mary\_go\_french,$ $preferred\_by\_john\,\}$ and $\{\, john\_go\_italian,\ mary\_go\_italian,\ preferred\_by\_$ $mary\,\}$. These two answer sets correspond to two possible results of cooperation.

There are mainly two reasons why we do not take this solution in this paper. First, programs P_1 and P_2 represent beliefs of individual agents, while a coordination $\Omega = (\Phi, \Psi, \Theta, \Lambda)$ represents social requirements over them. Such a separation has an advantage of not only reducing codes of individual programs but specifying interactions independent of individual programs. For instance, social requirements may change in time as in Example 3.8. If social interactions are encoded in programs, programs are to be updated whenever situation changes. Thanks to the separation of Ω from individual programs, any change in Ω does not affect the content of programs. The separation of two components also accords to the principle of "*Algorithm = Logic + Control*" by Kowalski [8]. In fact, Ω represents control over answer sets. In this sense, answer set interactions are considered answer sets of different programs plus control over them.

Second, as remarked in [13], simply merging nonmonotonic logic programs does not always produce acceptable conclusions for individual agents. Consider the following situation [7]. A brave driver crosses railway tracks in the absence of information on an approaching train:

$$P_1 : \quad cross \leftarrow not\ train.$$

On the other hand, a careful driver crosses railway tracks in the presence of information on no approaching train:

$$P_2 : \quad cross \leftarrow \neg train.$$

Simply merging these two programs $P_1 \cup P_2$ produces the single answer set $\{cross\}$, which is a "brave" solution and would be unacceptable for the careful driver. The example shows that merging nonmonotonic theories does not always produce an agreement among agents, even though they do not contradict one another. Note that a joint program in Definition 5.2 also merges two programs, but the problem does not happen as P^1 and P^2 contain different annotated literals. Also it should be noted that a joint program is introduced not for merging beliefs of agents but for computing interactions among agents. Given individual programs and a coordination Ω over them, they are compiled into a single joint program to compute solutions of the coordination.

We provide different forms of interactions and various social attitudes of agents, but one may not fully agree with definitions given in this paper. In fact, "there is no universally accepted definition of agency or of intelligence" [15]. Our intention is not to provide universally accepted definitions of agent interactions, but to turn ill-defined agents problems to a well-defined semantic problem in computational logic. Answer set interactions have clear semantics, which are simple yet useful for answer set based agent programming. Moreover, interactions are defined as set theoretic relations, so that similar notions are defined for any model theoretic semantics of computational logics or logic programs.

6.2   Related Work

There are several studies which provide logics for social interactions among agents. Meyer et al. [10] introduce a logical framework for negotiating agents. They introduce two different modes of negotiation: *concession* and *adaptation*. Concession weakens an initial demand of an agent, while adaptation expands an initial demand to accommodate a demand of another agent. In [10], concession and adaptation change original theories of two agents only when they contradict each other. Those definitions are thus different from ours of Definitions 3.2 and 3.3. They provide rational postulates to characterize negotiated outcomes between two agents, and describe methods for constructing outcomes. In their framework each agent is represented by classical propositional theories, so that those postulates are not generally applied to nonmonotonic theories.

In the context of logic programming, Buccafurri and Gottlob [2] introduce a framework of *compromise logic programs*. Given a collection of programs $T=\{Q_1, \ldots, Q_n\}$, the *joint fixpoint semantics* of T is defined as the set of minimal elements in $JFP(T) = FP(Q_1) \cap \cdots \cap FP(Q_n)$ where $FP(Q_i)$ is the set of all fixpoints of Q_i. The goal of their study is providing common conclusions among different programs. Ciampolini et al. [4] propose *abductive logic agents* (ALIAS) in which two different types of coordination, *collaboration* and *competition*, are realized. A query specifies behaviors of agents to achieve goals, and ALIAS solve the goal by communicating agents. In ALIAS, coordination is operationally given using inference rules, which is different from our declarative specifications in this paper. Buccafurri and Caminiti [3] introduce a *social logic program* (SOLP) which has rules of the form: $head \leftarrow [selection\_condition]\{body\}$, where $selection\_condition$ specifies social conditions concerning either the cardinality of communities or particular individuals satisfying the body. Agent interactions are thus encoded in individual programs in SOLP, which is in contrast to our approach of separating beliefs of agents and social interactions among them. Foo et al. [6] introduce a theory of multiagent negotiation in answer set programming. Starting from the initial agreement set $S \cap T$ for an answer set S of an agent and an answer set T of another agent, each agent extends this set to reflect its own demand while keeping consistency with demand of the other agent. Their algorithm returns new programs having answer sets which are consistent with each other and keep the agreement set. Sakama and Inoue [11] propose a method of combining answer sets of different logic programs. Given two programs P_1 and P_2, they build a program Q satisfying $AS(Q) = min(\{S \cup T \mid S \in AS(P_1) \text{ and } T \in AS(P_2)\})$, which they call a *composition* of P_1 and P_2. Sakama and Inoue [12] also build a *minimal consensus* program Q satisfying $AS(Q) = min(\{S \cap T \mid S \in AS(P_1) \text{ and } T \in AS(P_2)\})$, and a *maximal consensus* program R satisfying $AS(R) = max(\{S \cap T \mid S \in AS(P_1) \text{ and } T \in AS(P_2)\})$. Composition extends one's beliefs by combining answer sets of two programs, while consensus extracts common beliefs from answer sets of two programs. Different from our approach, studies [6,11,12] *change* answer sets of the original programs for coordination results. Sakama and Inoue [13] introduce two notions of coordination between programs. A *generous coordination* constructs a program Q which has the set of answer sets such that $AS(Q) = AS(P_1) \cup AS(P_2)$, while a *rigorous coordination* constructs a program R which has the set of answer sets such that $AS(R) = AS(P_1) \cap AS(P_2)$. These two coordination methods just take the union or intersection of the collections of answer sets of two programs, and do not take extra coordination conditions into account as we do in this paper.

7   Conclusion

In this paper, we introduced the notion of answer set interactions and used it to characterize different types of interactions between agents represented as logic programs. Among other things, we considered cooperation, competition, norms, and subjection between agents. Each of these interactions can be viewed as a constraint on the collection of answer sets of the involving agents. The main advantage of this approach to specifying interactions between agents lies in its flexibility, i.e., interactions between agents are specified outside of individual agents' programs. We also discussed a possible way for computing coordinated solutions using answer set programming.

Several issues remain for further research. One such issue is the extension of answer set interactions to consider other forms of interactions between agents (e.g., resource constraints). We would also like to investigate possible ways to integrate this notion into multiagent planning. Another issue is realizing agent interactions that may evolve, such as negotiation, by incorporating belief update that may arise during interaction. For the implementation of our approach, the method of computing interactions proposed in this paper supposes situations where centralized control over all agents is possible. Typical centralized control is found in the master-slave architecture of MAS. On the other hand, it is also important to develop a framework for specifying and computing answer set interactions in a distributed setting. The issue is left for future work.

Acknowledgment. The second author is partially supported by the NSF grants IIS-0812267 and CREST-0420407.

References

1. Baral, C.: Knowledge Representation, Reasoning, and Declarative Problem Solving. Cambridge University Press, Cambridge (2003)
2. Buccafurri, F., Gottlob, G.: Multiagent compromises, joint fixpoints, and stable models. In: Kakas, A.C., Sadri, F. (eds.) Computational Logic: Logic Programming and Beyond. LNCS (LNAI), vol. 2407, pp. 561–585. Springer, Heidelberg (2002)
3. Buccafurri, F., Caminiti, G.: A social semantics for multi-agent systems. In: Baral, C., Greco, G., Leone, N., Terracina, G. (eds.) LPNMR 2005. LNCS (LNAI), vol. 3662, pp. 317–329. Springer, Heidelberg (2005)
4. Ciampolini, A., Lamma, E., Mello, P., Toni, F., Torroni, P.: Cooperation and competition in ALIAS: a logic framework for agents that negotiate. Annals of Mathematics and Artificial Intelligence 37, 65–91 (2003)
5. Eiter, T., Gottlob, G.: Complexity results for disjunctive logic programming and application to nonmonotonic logics. In: Miller, D. (ed.) Proceedings of the 1993 International Symposium on Logic Programming, pp. 266–278. MIT Press, Cambridge (1993)
6. Foo, N., Meyer, T., Zhang, Y., Zhang, D.: Negotiating logic programs. In: Proceedings of the 6th Workshop on Nonmonotonic Reasoning, Action and Change (2005)
7. Gelfond, M., Lifschitz, V.: Classical negation in logic programs and disjunctive databases. New Generation Computing 9, 365–385 (1991).
8. Kowalski, R.A.: Algorithm = Logic + Control. Communications of the ACM 22, 424–436 (1979)

9. Lifschitz, V., Turner, H.: Splitting a logic program. In: Hentenryck, P.V. (ed.) Proceedings of the 11th International Conference on Logic Programming, pp. 23–37. MIT Press, Cambridge (1994)

10. Meyer, T., Foo, N., Kwok, R., Zhang, D.: Logical foundation of negotiation: outcome, concession and adaptation. In: Proceedings of the 19th National Conference on Artificial Intelligence, pp. 293–298. MIT Press, Cambridge (2004)

11. Sakama, C., Inoue, K.: Combining answer sets of nonmonotonic logic programs. In: Toni, F., Torroni, P. (eds.) CLIMA 2005. LNCS (LNAI), vol. 3900, pp. 320–339. Springer, Heidelberg (2006)

12. Sakama, C., Inoue, K.: Constructing consensus logic programs. In: Puebla, G. (ed.) LOPSTR 2006. LNCS, vol. 4407, pp. 26–42. Springer, Heidelberg (2007)

13. Sakama, C., Inoue, K.: Coordination in answer set programming. ACM Transactions on Computational Logic 9, Article No.9 (2008); Shorter version: Coordination between logical agents. In: Leite, J., Torroni, P. (eds.) CLIMA 2004. LNCS (LNAI), vol. 3487, pp. 161–177. Springer, Heidelberg (2005)

14. Singh, M.P.: An ontology for commitments in multiagent systems: toward a unification of normative concepts. Artificial Intelligence and Law 7, 97–113 (1999)

15. Weiss, G. (ed.): Multiagent Systems: A Modern Approach to Distributed Artificial Intelligence. MIT Press, Cambridge (1999)

Argumentation-Based Preference Modelling
with Incomplete Information

Wietske Visser, Koen V. Hindriks, and Catholijn M. Jonker

Man Machine Interaction Group, Delft University of Technology
Mekelweg 4, 2628 CD Delft, The Netherlands
{Wietske.Visser,K.V.Hindriks,C.M.Jonker}@tudelft.nl

Abstract. No intelligent decision support system functions even remotely without knowing the preferences of the user. A major problem is that the way average users think about and formulate their preferences does not match the utility-based quantitative frameworks currently used in decision support systems. For the average user qualitative models are a better fit. This paper presents an argumentation-based framework for the modelling of, and automated reasoning about multi-issue preferences of a qualitative nature. The framework presents preferences according to the lexicographic ordering that is well-understood by humans. The main contribution of the paper is that it shows how to reason about preferences when only incomplete information is available. An adequate strategy is proposed that allows reasoning with incomplete information and it is shown how to incorporate this strategy into the argumentation-based framework for modelling preferences.

Keywords: Qualitative Preferences, Argumentation, Incomplete Information.

1   Introduction

In this paper we introduce an argumentation-based framework for modelling qualitative multi-attribute preferences under incomplete information. This is motivated by our interest in developing a negotiation support system, as part of a larger project. In this context, we are faced with the need to express a user's preferences. A necessary (but not sufficient) condition for an offer to become an agreement is that both parties feel that it satisfies their preferences well enough. Unfortunately, eliciting and representing a user's preferences is not unproblematic. Existing negotiation support systems are based on quantitative models of preferences. These kinds of models are based on utilities; a utility function determines for each outcome a numerical value of utility. However, it is difficult to elicit such models from users, since humans generally express their preferences in a more qualitative way. We say we like something more than something else, but it seems strange to express liking something exactly twice as much as an alternative. In this respect, qualitative preference models will have a higher cognitive plausibility as they provide a better correspondence with representations used by humans. We also think that qualitative models will allow a human user to interact more naturally with an agent negotiating on his behalf or supporting him in his negotiations, and will investigate this in future. There are, however, several challenges that need to

J. Dix, M. Fisher, and P. Novák (Eds.): CLIMA X, LNAI 6214, pp. 141–157, 2010.

be met before qualitative models can be usefully applied. Doyle and Thomason [8] provide an overview including among others the challenge to deal with partial information (information-limited rationality) and, more generally, the challenge to formalize various reasoning-related tasks (knowledge representation, reasons, and preference revision).

For any real-life application it is important to be able to handle multi-issue preferences. It is a natural approach to derive object preferences from general preferences over properties or attributes. For example, it is quite natural to say that you prefer one house over another because it is bigger and generally you prefer larger houses over smaller ones. This might still be so if the first house is more expensive and you generally prefer cheaper options. So there is an interplay between attributes and the preferences a user holds over them in determining object preferences. This means that object preferences can be quite complex. One approach to obtain preferences about objects is to start with a set of properties of these objects and derive preferences from a ranking of these properties that indicates the relative importance or priority of each of these properties. This approach to obtain preferences is typical in multi-attribute decision theory [12], a quantitative theory that derives object preferences from utility values assigned to outcomes which are derived from numeric weights associated with properties or attributes of objects. Several qualitative approaches have also been proposed [3,5,6,7,13].

A user's preferences and knowledge about the world may also be incomplete, inconsistent or changing. For example, a user may lack some information regarding the objects he has to choose between, or he might have contradictory information from different sources. Preferences may change for various reasons, e.g. new information becoming available, experience, changing goals, or interaction with persuasive others. For now, we focus on the situation in which information about objects is not complete, but will address other types of incompleteness, inconsistency and change in future.

The approach we take is based on argumentation. In recent years, argumentation has evolved to be a core study within artificial intelligence and has been applied in a range of different topics [2]. We incorporate some of the ideas introduced in existing qualitative approaches but also go beyond these approaches by introducing a framework that is able to reason about preferences also when only incomplete information is available. Because of its non-monotonic nature, argumentation is useful for handling inconsistent and incomplete information. Although a lot of work has been done on argumentation-based negotiation (for a comprehensive review, see [16]), most of this work considers only the bidding phase in which offers are exchanged. For preparation, the preferences of a user have to be made clear (both to the user himself and to the agent supporting him), hence we need to express and reason with them. We focus here on the modelling of a single user's preferences by means of an argumentation process. The idea is that a user weighs his preferences, which gives him better insight into his own preferences, and so this weighing is part of the preference elicitation process. The weighing of arguments maps nicely onto argumentation. For example, 'I like to travel by car because it is faster than going by bike' is countered by 'But cycling is healthier than driving the car and that is more important to me, so I prefer to take the bike'. This possibility to construct arguments that are attacked by counterarguments is another advantage of argumentation, since it is a very natural way of reasoning for humans and fits in with a user's own reasoning processes. This is a general feature of argumentation and we will make extensive use of it: arguments like those above form the basis of our system. We believe that this way of reasoning will also be very useful in the preference elicitation process since the user's insight into his preferences grows piece by piece as he is expressing them. The introduction of an argumentation-based framework for reasoning about preferences even when only incomplete information is available seems particularly suitable for such a step-by-step process. It allows the user to extend and refine the system representation of his preferences gradually and as the user sees fit. Another motivation to use argumentation is the link with multi-agent dialogues [1], which will be very interesting in our further work on negotiation.

In this paper we present an argumentation-based framework for reasoning with qualitative multi-attribute preferences. In Section 2, we introduce qualitative multi-attribute preferences, in particular the lexicographic preference ordering. In Section 3 we start by modelling this ordering for reasoning with complete information in an argumentation framework. Then we proceed and extend this framework in such a way that it can also handle incomplete information. Our main contribution, in Section 4, is a strategy (based on the lexicographic ordering) with some desired properties to derive object preferences in the case of incomplete information. In Section 5 this strategy is subsequently incorporated into the argumentation framework. Section 6 concludes the paper.

2   Qualitative Multi-attribute Preferences

Qualitative multi-attribute preferences over objects are based on a set of relevant attributes or goals, which are ranked according to their importance or priority. Without loss of generality, we only consider binary (Boolean) attributes (cf. [5]). Moreover, it is assumed that the presence of an attribute is preferred over its absence. For example, given that *garden* is an attribute, a house that has a garden is preferred over one that does not have one. The importance ranking of attributes is defined by a total preorder (a total, reflexive and transitive relation), which we will denote by $\succeq$. This relation is not required to be antisymmetric, so two or more attributes can have the same importance. The relation $\succeq$ yields a stratification of the set of attributes into importance levels. Each importance level consists of attributes that are deemed equally important. Together with factual information about which objects have which attributes, the attribute ranking forms the basis on which various object preference orderings can be defined. One of the most well-known preference orderings is the lexicographic ordering, which we will use here. [5] and [7] define more multi-attribute preference orderings, such as the discrimin and best-out orderings. In this paper we focus on the lexicographic ordering because it seems natural, it defines a total preference relation (contrary to the discrimin ordering) and it is more discriminating than the best-out ordering. Since the other orderings are structurally similar to the lexicographic ordering, a similar argumentation framework could be defined for them if desired. We introduce the lexicographic preference ordering by means of an example.

Example 1. Paul wants to buy a house. According to him, the most important attributes are *large* (minimally 100m²), *garden* and *closeToWork*, which among themselves are equally important. The next most important attributes are *nearShops* and *quiet*. Being *detached* is the least important. Paul can choose between three options: a *villa*, an

Table 1. An example of objects and attributes

	large	garden	closeToWork	nearShops	quiet	detached
villa	✓	✓				✓
apartment	✓		✓	✓		
cottage		✓		✓	✓	✓

apartment and a *cottage*. The attributes of these objects are displayed in Table 1. In this table, the attributes are ordered in decreasing importance from left to right. A dashed line between attributes indicates equal importance, a solid line a transistion to a lower importance level. A checkmark indicates that an object has the attribute, an empty box means that the attribute is absent. Which house should Paul choose? He first considers the highest importance level, which in this case comprises *large*, *garden* and *close-ToWork*. The *villa* and the *apartment* both have two of these attributes, while the *cottage* only has one. So at this moment Paul concludes that both the *villa* and the *apartment* are preferred to the *cottage*. For the preference between the *villa* and the *apartment* he has to look further. At the next importance level, the *apartment* has one attribute and the *apartment* has none. So the *apartment* is preferred over the *villa*. Note that although the *cottage* has the most attributes in total, it is still the least preferred option because of its bad score at the more important attributes.

Definition 1. (Lexicographic preference ordering) *Let $\mathcal{P}$ be a set of attributes or goals, and $\succeq$ a total preorder on $\mathcal{P}$. We write $P \succ Q$ for $P \succeq Q$ and $Q \not\succeq P$, and $P \approx Q$ for $P \succeq Q$ and $Q \succeq P$. We use $|\cdot|$ to denote the cardinality of a set. Object a is strictly preferred over object b according to the lexicographic ordering if there exists an attribute P such that $|\{P' \mid a \text{ has } P' \text{ and } P \approx P'\}| > |\{P' \mid b \text{ has } P' \text{ and } P \approx P'\}|$ and for all $Q \succ P$: $|\{Q' \mid a \text{ has } Q' \text{ and } Q \approx Q'\}| = |\{Q' \mid b \text{ has } Q' \text{ and } Q \approx Q'\}|$. Object a is equally preferred as object b according to the lexicographic ordering if for all P: $|\{P' \mid a \text{ has } P' \text{ and } P \approx P'\}| = |\{P' \mid b \text{ has } P' \text{ and } P \approx P'\}|$.*

3   Argumentation Framework for Complete Information

In order to formally model and reason with preferences we define an argumentation framework (AF). We use as our starting point the well-known argumentation theory of Dung [10]. An abstract AF in the sense of Dung consists of a set of arguments and a defeat relation (informally, a counterargument relation) among those arguments. An AF is abstract in the sense that both the set of arguments and the defeat relation are assumed to be given, and the construction and internal structure of arguments is not taken into account. If we want to reason with argumentation, we have to instantiate an abstract AF by specifying the structure of arguments and the defeat relation. Section 3.1 presents the logical *language* that we will use. Arguments are built from this language by chaining inferences. *Inferences* are instantiations of general inference schemes, such as modus ponens. The inference schemes of our AF are presented in Section 3.2. Section 3.3 defines the *defeat* relation, which is based on certain relations between the elements of arguments. Together with a knowledge base, the inference schemes and defeat relation provide a specific AF for arguing about multi-attribute preferences. Which arguments are justified is determined by the semantics used (Section 3.4). Section 3.5 shows that the presented AF indeed models lexicographic preference.

3.1 Language

The language has to allow us to express everything we want to talk about when reasoning about preferences. To start, we need to be able to state the facts about objects: which attributes they do and do not have. We also have to express the importance ranking of attributes, so we need to be able to say that one attribute is more important than another, or that two attributes are equally important. Of course, we want to say that one object is preferred over another, and that two objects are equally preferred. Finally, we need to be able to express how many attributes of equal importance a certain object has, since the lexicographic preference ordering is based on counting these. To this end, we introduce a special predicate $has(a, [P], n)$ which expresses that object a has n attributes of the importance level of attribute P. Since we have no names for importance levels, we denote them by any attribute of that level, placed between square brackets. It is not necessary that the attribute used is among the attributes that the object has; in our example, $has(apartment, [quiet], 1)$ is true even though the *apartment* is not *quiet*. All of the things described can be expressed in the following language.

Definition 2. (Language) *Let $\mathcal{P}$ be a set of attribute names with typical elements P, Q, and $\mathcal{O}$ a set of object names with typical elements a, b, and let n be a non-negative integer. The input language $\mathcal{L}_{KB}$ and full language $\mathcal{L}$ are defined as follows.*

$$\varphi \in \mathcal{L}_{KB} ::= P(a) \mid \neg P(a) \mid P \succ Q \mid P \approx Q$$

$$\psi \in \mathcal{L} ::= \varphi \in \mathcal{L}_{KB} \mid pref(a,b) \mid eqpref(a,b) \mid has(a,[P],n)$$

Formulas of this language have the following informal meaning:

$P(a)$	object a has attribute P
$\neg P(a)$	object a does not have attribute P
$P \succ Q$	attribute P is more important than attribute Q
$P \approx Q$	attribute P is equally important as attribute Q
$pref(a,b)$	object a is strictly preferred over object b
$eqpref(a,b)$	object a is equally preferred as object b
$has(a,[P],n)$	object a has n attributes equally important as attribute P (not necessarily including P itself)

The idea is that preferences over objects are derived from facts about which objects have which attributes, and the importance order among attributes. These facts are contained in a *knowledge base*, which is a set of formulas from $\mathcal{L}_{KB}$. A knowledge base is complete if, given a set of objects to compare and a set of attributes to compare them on, it contains for every object a and for every attribute P, either $P(a)$ or $\neg P(a)$, and for all attributes P, Q, either $P \succ Q$, $Q \succ P$ or $P \approx Q$.

Example 2. The information from Example 1 can be expressed in the form of the following knowledge base that is based on the language $\mathcal{L}_{KB}$.

$large \approx garden \approx closeToWork \succ nearShops \approx quiet \succ detached$

$large(villa)$	$large(apartment)$	$\neg large(cottage)$
$garden(villa)$	$\neg garden(apartment)$	$garden(cottage)$
$\neg closeToWork(villa)$	$closeToWork(apartment)$	$\neg closeToWork(cottage)$
$\neg nearShops(villa)$	$nearShops(apartment)$	$nearShops(cottage)$
$\neg quiet(villa)$	$\neg quiet(apartment)$	$quiet(cottage)$
$detached(villa)$	$\neg detached(apartment)$	$detached(cottage)$

3.2 Inferences

An argument is a derivation of a conclusion from a set of premises. Such a derivation is built from multiple steps called inferences. Every inference step consists of premises and a conclusion, and has a label. Inferences can be chained by using the conclusion of one inference step as a premise in the following step. Thus a tree of chained inferences is created, which we use as the formal definition of an argument.

Definition 3. (Argument) *An argument is a tree, where the nodes are inferences, and an inference can be connected to a parent node if its conclusion is a premise of that node. Leaf nodes only have a conclusion (a formula from the knowledge base), and no premises. A subtree of an argument is also called a* subargument. *We define* inf *to be a function that returns the last inference of an argument (the root node), and* conc *to be a function that returns the conclusion of an argument, which is the same as the conclusion of the last inference.*

The inferences that can be made are defined by inference schemes. The inference schemes of our framework are listed in Table 2. The first and second inference schemes are used to count the number of attributes of equal importance as some attribute P that object a has. This type of inference is inspired by *accrual* [14], which combines multiple arguments with the same conclusion into one accrued argument for the same conclusion. Although our application is different, we use a similar mechanism. We want all attributes that are present to be counted. Otherwise we would conclude incorrect preferences (e.g. if the *large* attribute of the *apartment* were not counted, we would incorrectly derive that the *villa* were preferred over the *apartment*). Inference scheme 1, which counts 0, can always be applied since it has no premises. Inference scheme 2 can be applied on any subset of the set of attributes of some importance level that an object a has. This means that it is possible to construct an argument that does not count all attributes that are present (a so-called non-maximal count). To ensure that only maximal counts are used, we provide an inference scheme to make arguments that defeat non-maximal counts (inference scheme 3). An argument of this type says that any count which is not maximal is not applicable. This type of defeat is called undercut (see below). Inference scheme 4 says that an object a is preferred over an object b if the number of attributes of a certain importance level that a has is higher than the number of attributes on that same level that b has. For the lexicographic ordering, it is also required that a and b have the same number of attributes on any level higher than that of P. We model this by defining an inference scheme 5 that undercuts scheme 4 if there is a more important level than that of P on which a and b do not have the same number of attributes. Finally, inference schemes 6 and 7 do the same as 4 and 5, but for

Table 2. Inference schemes

$$1 \quad \overline{has(a,[P],0)} \ \ count(a,[P],\varnothing)$$

$$2 \quad \frac{P_1(a) \quad \ldots \quad P_n(a) \quad P_1 \approx \ldots \approx P_n}{has(a,[P_1],n)} \ \ count(a,[P_1],\{P_1,\ldots,P_n\})$$

$$3 \quad \frac{P_1(a) \quad \ldots \quad P_n(a) \quad P_1 \approx \ldots \approx P_n \approx P}{count(a,[P],S \subset \{P_1,\ldots,P_n\}) \text{ is inapplicable}} \ \ count(a,[P],S)uc$$

$$4 \quad \frac{has(a,[P],n) \quad has(b,[P'],m) \quad P \approx P' \quad n > m}{pref(a,b)} \ \ prefinf(a,b,[P])$$

$$5 \quad \frac{has(a,[Q],n) \quad has(b,[Q'],m) \quad Q \approx Q' \succ P \quad n \neq m}{prefinf(a,b,[P]) \text{ is inapplicable}} \ \ prefinf(a,b,[P])uc$$

$$6 \quad \frac{has(a,[P],n) \quad has(b,[P'],m) \quad P \approx P' \quad n = m}{eqpref(a,b)} \ \ eqprefinf(a,b,[P])$$

$$7 \quad \frac{has(a,[Q],n) \quad has(b,[Q'],m) \quad Q \approx Q' \not\approx P \quad n \neq m}{eqprefinf(a,b,[P]) \text{ is inapplicable}} \ \ eqprefinf(a,b,[P])uc$$

equal preference. We need these because equal preference cannot be expressed in terms of strict preference.

Example 3. We now illustrate the inference schemes with some arguments that can be made from the knowledge base in Example 2. The example arguments are listed in Table 3 (for space reasons, the inference labels are left out). Argument A illustrates the general working; a preference for the apartment over the cottage is derived, based on the facts that the apartment has two attributes of some level and the cottage only one. Argument B illustrates a zero count. Here a preference for the apartment over the villa is derived, based on the facts that the apartment has one attribute of some level and the villa zero. In argument C a non-maximal count is used (stating that the apartment has zero attributes of the level of *nearShops*), which leads to another conclusion, namely that the villa and the apartment are equally preferred. However, there are undercutters to attack such arguments (argument D).

Note that the lexicographic ordering results in a complete transitive order of weak preference on objects (an object is weakly preferred over another if it is either more preferred than, or equally preferred as the other object). This means that it is not necessary to define inference rules for the property of transitivity, because any preference that follows from transitivity can also be derived directly from the definition of lexicographic ordering. For example, if $pref(a,b)$ and $eqpref(b,c)$ hold, then $pref(a,c)$ also holds, but this can be derived using the inference schemes of Table 2. The same holds for the asymmetry of strict preference (if $pref(a,b)$ holds, then $pref(b,a)$ does not hold) and the symmetry of equal preference (if $eqpref(a,b)$ holds, then $eqpref(b,a)$ also holds).

Table 3. Example arguments

$$\cfrac{\cfrac{large(apartment) \quad closeToWork(apartment) \quad large \approx closeToWork}{has(apartment,[large],2)} \qquad \cfrac{garden(cottage)}{has(cottage,[garden],1)} \quad large \approx garden \quad 2 > 1}{pref(apartment,cottage)}$$

A:

$$\cfrac{\cfrac{nearShops(apartment)}{has(apartment,[nearShops],1)} \qquad has(villa,[nearShops],0) \quad nearShops \approx nearShops \quad 1 > 0}{pref(apartment,villa)}$$

B:

$$\cfrac{has(villa,[nearShops],0) \qquad has(apartment,[nearShops],0)^* \quad nearShops \approx nearShops \quad 0 = 0}{eqpref(villa,apartment)}$$

C:

$$\cfrac{nearShops(apartment)}{*}$$ is inapplicable

D:

3.3 Defeat

With the language and the inference rules defined in the previous sections we can construct arguments. To complete our argumentation framework, we also need to specify a defeat relation. This section provides the formal definition of defeat that we will use. The most common type of defeat is rebuttal. An argument rebuts another argument if its conclusion is the negation of the conclusion of the other argument. Rebuttal is always mutual. Another type of defeat is undercut. An undercutter is an argument for the inapplicability of an inference used in another argument (for the specific undercutters used in our framework, see the previous section). Undercut works only one way. Defeat is defined recursively, which means that rebuttal can attack an argument on all its premises and (intermediate) conclusions, and undercut can attack ist on all its inferences.

Definition 4. (Defeat) *An argument A* defeats *an argument B if*

- $conc(A) = \varphi$ *and* $conc(B) = \neg\varphi$ *(rebuttal), or*
- $conc(A) =$ '$\mathtt{inf}(B)$ *is inapplicable' (*undercut*), or*
- *A defeats a subargument of B.*

3.4 Semantics

By specifying the inference schemes and the definition of defeat, together with a knowledge base, we have instantiated an argumentation framework consisting of a set of arguments and a defeat relation among them. Now we define which arguments are justified. For this we use Dung's [10] grounded semantics.[1] Grounded semantics is defined as follows.

---

[1] For the argumentation system defined in this paper (including the extended version of Section 5), the choice of semantics is not relevant; we could also have used other semantics such as preferred or stable semantics (also from [10]). There would be a difference when we allow the use of an inconsistent knowledge base, in which case another semantics may be more suitable. This is something for further investigation.

Definition 5.   – *An argument A is* acceptable *with respect to a set S of arguments iff each argument defeating A is defeated by an argument in S.*
  - *The* characteristic function, *denoted by F_{AF}, of an argumentation framework AF is defined as follows: $F_{AF}(S) = \{A \mid A$ is acceptable with respect to $S\}$.*
  - *The* grounded extension *of AF is defined as the least fixed point of F_{AF}.*
  - *An argument is* justified *with respect to grounded semantics iff it is a member of the grounded extension.*

3.5   Validity

The argumentation framework defined in previous sections indeed models lexicographic preference, assuming a complete and consistent knowledge base.

Proposition 1. *Let $\mathcal{A}(KB)$ denote all arguments that can be built from a knowledge base KB. Then there is an argument $A \in \mathcal{A}(KB)$ such that the conclusion of A is $pref(a,b)$ and A is justified under grounded semantics iff a is preferred over b according to the lexicographic preference ordering (Definition 1) given KB.*

Proof. Suppose a is preferred over b. This means that there exists an attribute P such that $|\{P' \mid a$ has P' and $P \approx P'\}| > |\{P' \mid b$ has P' and $P \approx P'\}|$ and for all $Q \succ P$: $|\{Q' \mid a$ has Q' and $Q \approx Q'\}| = |\{Q' \mid b$ has Q' and $Q \approx Q'\}|$. Let $P_1 \ldots P_n$ denote all attributes of equal importance as P such that a has P_i and let $P'_1 \ldots P'_m$ denote all attributes of equal importance as P such that b has P_i. Note that $n > m$. Then the knowledge base is as follows: $P_1 \approx \ldots \approx P_n \approx P'_1 \approx \ldots P'_m$ and $P_1(a) \ldots P_n(a)$ and $P'_1(b) \ldots P'_m(b)$. The following argument (A) can be built (note that this argument can also be built if m is equal to 0, by using the empty set count):

$$\frac{\dfrac{P_1(a) \quad \ldots \quad P_n(a) \quad P_1 \approx \ldots \approx P_n}{has(a,[P_1],n)} \qquad \dfrac{P'_1(b) \quad \ldots \quad P'_m(b) \quad P'_1 \approx \ldots \approx P'_m}{has(b,[P'_1],m)} \qquad P_1 \approx P'_1 \quad n > m}{pref(a,b)}$$

We will now play devil's advocate and try to defeat this argument. We can try rebuttal and undercut of the argument and its subarguments. Rebuttal of premises is not applicable, since the knowledge base is consistent. Rebuttal of (intermediate) conclusions is not possible either, since there is no way to derive a negation. Then there are three inferences we can try to undercut (the last inference of the argument and the last inferences of two subarguments). For the left-hand count, this can only be done if there is another P_j such that $P_j \approx P$ and $P_j \notin \{P_1, \ldots, P_n\}$ and $P_j(a)$ is the case. However, $P_1 \ldots P_n$ encompass all such attributes, so count undercut is not possible. The same argument holds for the other count. At this point it is useful to note that these two counts are the only ones that are undefeated. Any lesser count will be undercut by the count undercutter that takes all of $P_1 \ldots P_n$ (resp. $P'_1 \ldots P'_m$) into account. Such an undercutter has no defeaters, so any non-maximal count is not justified. The final thing that is left to try is undercut of $prefinf(a,b,[P_1])$. The undercutter of $prefinf(a,b,[P_1])$ is based on two counts. We have seen that any non-maximal count will be undercut. If the maximal counts are used, we have $n = m$, since we have for all $Q \succ P$: $|\{Q' \mid a$ has Q' and $Q \approx Q'\}| = |\{Q' \mid b$ has Q' and $Q \approx Q'\}|$. So the undercutter inference rule cannot be applied since $n \neq m$ is not true. This means that for every possible type of defeat, either the defeat is inapplicable or the defeater of A is itself defeated by undefeated arguments. This means that A is in the grounded extension and hence justified according to grounded semantics.

Suppose a is not preferred over b. This means that for all attributes P, either $|\{P' \mid a$ has P' and $P \approx P'\}| \leq |\{P' \mid b$ has P' and $P \approx P'\}|$ or there exists an attribute $Q \succ P$ such that $|\{Q' \mid a$ has Q' and $Q \approx Q'\}| \neq |\{Q' \mid b$ has Q' and $Q \approx Q'\}|$. This means that any argument with conclusion $pref(a,b)$ (which has to be of the form above) is either under-cut by $count(b,[P]S)uc$ because it uses a non-maximal count, or by $prefinf(a,b,[P])uc$ because there is a more important level where a preference can be derived. This means that any such argument will not be justified under grounded semantics.

The same line of argument can be followed for $eqpref$.   □

4 Strategies for Handling Incomplete Information

So far, we have defined an argumentation system that can reason about preferences according to the lexicographic preference ordering. Above, we have assumed that the information about the objects that are compared is complete. But, as stated in the in-troduction, this is often not the case. In this section we will investigate how incomplete information can best be handled when reasoning about preferences.

Suppose it is not known whether an object has a specific attribute, e.g. we know that $P(a)$ but we do not know whether $P(b)$ or $\neg P(b)$. This might not be a problem. If the preference between a and b can be decided based on attributes that are more important than P, the knowledge whether $P(b)$ or $\neg P(b)$ is the case is irrelevant. But often this information will be needed to decide a lexicographic preference. In that case, different approaches or strategies for drawing conclusions are possible. However, not all strategies give desired results. In the following, we will discuss some naive strategies and their shortcomings, from which we will derive some desired properties of strategies, and define and model a strategy that gives intuitive results.

4.1 Naive Strategies

Optimistic, resp. Pessimistic, Strategy. This strategy always assumes that an object has, resp. does not have, the attribute that is not known. This strategy can always derive some preference between two objects, since it completes the knowledge by making certain assumptions, and can then derive a complete preference ordering over objects. But there is no guarantee that the inferences made are correct. In fact, any inferred preference can only be correct if all the assumptions it is based on are either correct or irrelevant. Since we do not know whether assumptions are correct and the strategy does not check for relevance, the inference can only be correct by chance. For example, suppose it is not known whether the *villa* has a *garden* and whether it is *closeToWork*. The optimistic strategy would assume that it has both attributes, in which case an incorrect preference of the *villa* over the *apartment* would be derived. The pessimistic strategy on the other hand would assume the *villa* has neither of the attributes, and would derive an incorrect preference of the *cottage* over the *villa*.

Note that using the framework defined above without adaptation would boil down to using a pessimistic strategy: if it is not known whether an object has a certain attribute,

Table 4. Example of intransitive preference with the Disregard Attribute Strategy

	P	Q	R
a	✓	?	
b		✓	?
c	?		✓

the attribute is (implicitly) assumed to be absent. This is due to the fact that only attributes for which it is known that an object has them are counted. Attributes that an object does not have and attributes for which this information is unavailable are treated the same way (i.e. not taken into account when counting).

Disregard Attribute Strategy. This strategy does not take into account the attributes for which information about the objects to be compared is incomplete. This strategy can always derive some preference between two objects, since the information regarding the remaining attributes is complete, so a complete preference ordering over objects can be derived. But the inference might not be correct, since the attributes that are disregarded might be relevant in defining a preference order. For example, suppose it is not known whether the *cottage* is *large*. In that case, the attribute *large* will not be taken into account when comparing the *cottage* to another object. This leaves only the attributes *garden* and *closeToWork* on the highest importance level, of which all attributes have exactly one. Since the *cottage* has the most attributes on the next importance level, a preference of the *cottage* over the *villa* as well as the *apartment* will be derived, even though in the original example the *cottage* was the least preferred object.

This strategy has another unwanted effect. Consider the situation in Table 4. When comparing *a* and *b*, this strategy only takes attribute *P* into account, and concludes a preference of *a* over *b*. Similarly, preferences of *b* over *c*, and of *c* over *a* can be derived. So with this strategy, intransitive preferences can be derived, which is unwanted.

Cautious Strategy. In order to prevent the derivation of preferences that are only correct by chance, a natural alternative is to use a cautious strategy that prevents such inferences. This strategy infers nothing unless all information about the objects under comparison is available. It never makes incorrect preference inferences, but it lacks in decisiveness. Even if the unknown information is irrelevant to make an inference, nothing is inferred.

4.2   Desired Properties for Strategies

Given the limitations of the strategies discussed above, it is clear that we need a more balanced strategy that takes two main concerns into account, which we call decisiveness and safety.

Decisiveness. We call a strategy *decisive* if it does not infer too little. As mentioned above, an unknown attribute might be irrelevant for deciding a preference. This is the case if the preference is already determined by more important attributes. For example, suppose that we do not know whether the *apartment* has attribute *nearShops*. Then we can still conclude that the *apartment* is preferred over the *cottage*, based on the attributes *large*, *garden*, and *closeToWork*. It is not required that a preference is derived in every case, since the missing information might be essential, but all preferences that are certain (for which no essential information is missing) should be derived. The cautious strategy is not decisive.

Safety. We call a strategy *safe* if it does not infer too much. Suppose again that we do not know whether the *apartment* has attribute *nearShops*. Whereas this is irrelevant for deciding a preference between *apartment* and *cottage*, we do need this information for deciding the preference between the *villa* and the *apartment*. A strategy that makes assumptions about the missing information, or that disregards the attribute in question, will make unfounded inferences, and hence be unsafe. The optimistic, pessimistic and disregard attribute strategies are not safe.

4.3 A Decisive and Safe Strategy

We have seen above what may go wrong when a naive strategy is used to deal with incomplete information. In this section we define an alternative strategy that does satisfy the properties of decisiveness and safety identified above. A preference inference should never be based on an unfounded assumption for a strategy to be safe. But to be decisive, a strategy needs to be able to distinguish relevant from irrelevant information. Our approach is based on the following intuition. When comparing two objects under incomplete information, multiple situations are possible. That is, whenever it is not known whether an object has an attribute, there is a possibility that it does and a possibility that it does not. If a preference can be inferred in every possible situation, then apparently the missing information is not relevant, and it is safe to infer that preference. It is not necessary to check every possible situation, but it suffices to look at extreme cases. For every object, we can construct a best- and worst-case scenario, or best and worst possible situation. A possible situation is a *completion* of an object in the sense that all missing information is filled in.

Definition 6. (Completion) *A completion of an object a is an extension of the knowledge base with (previously missing) facts about a such that for every attribute P, either $P(a)$ or $\neg P(a)$ is in the extended knowledge base. So if a has n unspecified attributes, there are 2^n possible completions of a.*

Since we assumed that presence of an attribute is preferred over absence, the most preferred completion assumes presence of all unknown attributes, and the least preferred completion assumes absence. If even the least preferred completion of a is preferred over the most preferred completion of b, then a must always be preferred over b, since a could not be worse and b could not be better. For example, consider the objects and attributes in Table 5a. In the worst case for a, a does not have attribute R. In the best case for b, b has attribute P. But even in this situation, a will be preferred over b, based on attribute Q. There is no way that this situation can improve for b or deteriorate for a, so it is safe to infer a preference for a over b. The strategy's power to make such inferences makes it decisive.

Table 5. Examples of objects and attributes with incomplete information

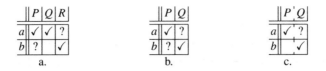

         a.   b.   c.

The next example illustrates that this approach does not infer a preference when the missing information is relevant. Consider Table 5b. In the situation that is worst for a and best for b, b will be preferred because it has both attributes, while a only has P. But in the other extreme situation, that is best for a and worst for b, a is preferred. This means that in reality, anything is possible, and it is not safe to infer a preference.

We have seen when a preference for a over b can be inferred, and in which case no preference can be inferred. There are, however, two more possibilities. One is the case in which a preference of the most preferred completion of a over the least preferred completion of b can be derived, but only equal preference between the least preferred completion of a and the most preferred completion of b. This is illustrated in Table 5c. In this case, we would like to derive at least a weak preference of a over b. This is important, because in many cases a weak preference is strong enough to base a decision on, even if a strict preference cannot be derived. When having to decide between a and b, choosing a cannot be wrong when a is weakly preferred over b. Failing to derive a weak preference makes a strategy less decisive.

The last possibility is equal preference. We only want to derive an equal preference between two objects a and b if all possible completions of a are equally preferred as all possible completions of b. This also means that the most and least preferred completions of a and b have to be equally preferred. This can only be the case if all information about a and b is known, for as soon as some information is missing, there will be multiple possible completions which are not equally preferred.

5   Argumentation Framework for Incomplete Information

This section presents how our framework is extended to incorporate the decisive and safe strategy for incomplete information as presented in Section 4.3. We first present the changes to the language and then the changes to the inference rules. The defeat definition does not have to change.

5.1   Language

To distinguish between the different completions of an object, we introduce a completion label. We use the object name without label to denote the object in general, that is, the object with any completion. The superscript $^+$ is used for the most preferred completion of an object, $^-$ for the least preferred completion. For example, consider object a in Table 5a. The most preferred completion of a has attribute R, and is denoted a^+. The least preferred completion of a does not have attribute R, and is denoted a^-.

Table 6. Inference schemes for incomplete information

1
$$\frac{}{has(a^x,[P],0)}\ count(a^x,[P],\varnothing)$$

2a
$$\frac{\sim\neg P_1(a)\quad\ldots\quad\sim\neg P_n(a)\quad P_1\approx\ldots\approx P_n}{has(a^+,[P_1],n)}\ count(a^+,[P_1],\{P_1,\ldots P_n\})$$

2b
$$\frac{P_1(a)\quad\ldots\quad P_n(a)\quad P_1\approx\ldots\approx P_n}{has(a^-,[P_1],n)}\ count(a^-,[P_1],\{P_1,\ldots P_n\})$$

3a
$$\frac{\sim\neg P_1(a)\quad\ldots\quad\sim\neg P_n(a)\quad P_1\approx\ldots\approx P_n}{count(a^+,[P_1],S\subset\{P_1,\ldots,P_n\})\ \text{is inapplicable}}\ count(a^+,[P_1],\{P_1,\ldots,P_n\})uc$$

3b
$$\frac{P_1(a)\quad\ldots\quad P_n(a)\quad P_1\approx\ldots\approx P_n}{count(a^-,[P_1],S\subset\{P_1,\ldots,P_n\})\ \text{is inapplicable}}\ count(a^-,[P_1],\{P_1,\ldots,P_n\})uc$$

4
$$\frac{has(a^x,[P],n)\quad has(b^y,[P'],m)\quad P\approx P'\quad n>m}{pref(a^x,b^y)}\ prefinf(a^x,b^y,[P])$$

5
$$\frac{has(a^x,[Q],n)\quad has(b^y,[Q'],m)\quad Q\approx Q'\succ P\quad n\neq m}{prefinf(a^x,b^y,[P])\ \text{is inapplicable}}\ prefinf(a^x,b^y,[P])uc$$

6
$$\frac{has(a^x,[P],n)\quad has(b^y,[P'],m)\quad P\approx P'\quad n=m}{eqpref(a^x,b^y)}\ eqprefinf(a^x,b^y,[P])$$

7
$$\frac{has(a^x,[Q],n)\quad has(b^y,[Q'],m)\quad Q\approx Q'\not\succ P\quad n\neq m}{eqprefinf(a^x,b^y,[P])\ \text{is inapplicable}}\ eqprefinf(a^x,b^y,[P])uc$$

8
$$\frac{}{\sim\varphi}\ asm(\sim\varphi)$$

9
$$\frac{\varphi}{asm(\sim\varphi)\ \text{is inapplicable}}\ asm(\sim\varphi)uc$$

10
$$\frac{pref(a^-,b^+)}{pref(a,b)}$$

11
$$\frac{eqpref(a^-,b^+)\quad pref(a^+,b^-)}{wpref(a,b)}$$

12
$$\frac{eqpref(a^+,b^-)\quad eqpref(a^-,b^+)}{eqpref(a,b)}$$

Reasoning with completions as discussed above can be viewed as a kind of assumption-based reasoning. To be able to support such reasoning, we extend the language and introduce weak negation, denoted by $\sim$, which is also used in [15]. This is used to formalize a kind of assumption-based reasoning. A formula $\sim\varphi$ can always be assumed, but is defeated by φ (see the next section for the details). So the statement $\sim\varphi$ should be interpreted as 'φ cannot be derived'.

Finally, we add formulas of the type $wpref(a,b)$ which express weak preference, just as $pref(a,b)$ and $eqpref(a,b)$ express strict and equal preference, respectively. We use

Table 7. Example arguments

$$A:\quad \cfrac{\cfrac{\dfrac{Q(a)}{has(a^-,[Q],1)}\quad \overline{has(b^+,[Q],0)}\quad Q\approx Q\quad 1>0}{pref(a^-,b^+)}}{pref(a,b)}$$

$$B:\quad \cfrac{\cfrac{\dfrac{P(a)}{has(a^-,[P],1)}\ \dfrac{\sim\neg Q(b)}{has(b^+,[Q],1)}\ P\approx Q\ 1=1}{eqpref(a^-,b^+)}\qquad \cfrac{\sim\neg P(a)\ \dfrac{\sim\neg Q(a)}{has(a^+,[P],2)}\ P\approx Q\ \dfrac{Q(b)}{has(b^-,[Q],1)}\ P\approx Q\ 2>1}{pref(a^+,b^-)}}{wpref(a,b)}$$

weak preference in the sense that an object a is weakly preferred over an object b if any completion of a is either preferred over or equally preferred as any completion of b, but no strict or equal preference can be derived with certainty.

This leads to the following redefinition of the language.

Definition 7. (Language) *Let $\mathcal{P}$ be a set of attribute names with typical elements P,Q, and $\mathcal{O}$ a set of object names with typical elements a,b, and let n be a non-negative integer, and $x,y \in \{+,-,\{\}\}$ a label for objects (where $\{\}$ means no label). The input language $\mathcal{L}_{KB}$ and full language $\mathcal{L}$ are defined as follows.*

$$\varphi \in \mathcal{L}_{KB} ::= P(a) \mid \neg P(a) \mid P \succ Q \mid P \approx Q$$

$$\psi \in \mathcal{L} ::= \varphi \in \mathcal{L}_{KB} \mid pref(a^x,b^y) \mid eqpref(a^x,b^y) \mid wpref(a^x,b^b) \mid has(a^x,[P],n) \mid \sim \psi$$

5.2 Inferences

The inference rules of the extended framework are listed in Table 6. Two inference rules are added that define the meaning of the weak negation $\sim$. According to inference rule 8, a formula $\sim \varphi$ can always be inferred, but such an argument will be defeated by an undercutter built with inference rule 9 if φ is the case.

P is supposed to be among the attributes of the least preferred completion of a (a^-) only if it is known that a has P. This is modelled by inference rule 2b in Table 6. For the most preferred completion of a, it is only required that it is not known that a does not have P; if this is not known, a^+ will be assumed to have P. This is modeled by using premises of the form $\sim \neg P(a)$ instead of $P(a)$. This can be seen in inference rule 2a. Inference rules 4 through 7 remain unchanged, except that completion labels are added.

To infer overall preferences from the preferences over certain completions, three more inference rules are defined. Inference rule 10 states that if (even) a^- is preferred over b^+, then a must be preferred over b, as we saw above. When a^+ is preferred over b^-, but a^- is only equally preferred as b^+, this not strong enough to infer a strict preference of a over b, but we can infer a weak preference of a over b using inference rule 11. Rule 12 states that in order to infer equal preference between a and b, both the most preferred completion of a and the least preferred completion of b, and the least preferred completion of a and the most preferred completion of b must be equally preferred.

Example 4. In the case of Table 5a, argument A in Table 7 can be built. Argument B shows that a weak preference can be inferred in the situation of Table 5c.

6   Conclusion

In this paper we have made the following contributions. Approaches based on argumentation can be used to model qualitative multi-attribute preferences such as the lexicographic ordering. The advantage of argumentation over other approaches emerges most clearly in the case of incomplete information. Our approach allows to reason about preferences from best- and worst-case perspectives (called completions here), and the consequences for overall preferences.

In our current approach it is still often the case that no preference can be inferred. What should we do in such a case? One approach is to ask the user for the missing information. But the user might not have this information, and might not have the time or resources to look it up. In some situations it might be fruitful to relax the notion of safety, which we have used in a very strict sense here; a conclusion is only called safe if it can be drawn in every possible situation. But we might want to draw a conclusion if it follows in the most likely situation. Of course, to model this we need information about the likelihood of situations. This could for example be modelled by a normality ranking [3] or a possibility ranking [9]. Also, although general default assumptions are often not safe, some domain-specific default assumptions may be safe enough. For example, if nothing to the contrary is known, one may safely assume that a house has electricity. Some default assumptions may be conditional, for example, a detached house usually has a garden. One interesting extension therefore is to add such default reasoning and more general reasoning about the beliefs of an agent to the framework. Default rules (e.g. $detached(a) \Rightarrow garden(a)$) can be placed in the knowledge base. Next, an inference rule is needed that applies these rules and can infer $garden(a)$ from $detached(a)$ and $detached(a) \Rightarrow garden(a)$. Finally, a strength mechanism is needed, so that factual information always defeats rebutting default assumptions (e.g. if $\neg garden(a)$ is known for a fact, then this defeats the conclusion $garden(a)$ that was derived using a default rule, but not vice versa).

In our future work we would like to distinguish more explicitly between mental attitudes such as beliefs, goals, desires and preferences. This will also allow us to reason about these attitudes, for example that a certain preference we have is based on some specific beliefs. We hope to gain insight from modal preference languages with belief operators such as the one presented in [13]. Other interesting areas for future work include the representation of dependent preferences (e.g. 'I only want a balcony if the house does not have a garden, otherwise I do not care'), and the relation with e.g. CP-nets [4] and value-based argumentation [11].

Finally, we believe that the argumentation-based framework for preferences presented here can be usefully applied in the preference elicitation process. It allows the user to extend and refine the system representation of his preferences gradually and as the user sees fit. To facilitate this elicitation process more research is needed on how our framework can support a user e.g. by indicating which information is still missing.

Acknowledgements

This research is supported by the Dutch Technology Foundation STW, applied science division of NWO and the Technology Program of the Ministry of Economic Affairs. It is part of the Pocket Negotiator project with grant number VICI-project 08075.

References

1. Amgoud, L., Maudet, N., Parsons, S.: Modelling dialogues using argumentation. In: Proc. ICMAS (2000)
2. Bench-Capon, T.J.M., Dunne, P.E.: Argumentation in artificial intelligence. Artificial Intelligence 171, 619–641 (2007)
3. Boutilier, C.: Toward a logic for qualitative decision theory. In: Proc. KR, pp. 75–86 (1994)
4. Boutilier, C., Brafman, R.I., Domshlak, C., Hoos, H.H., Poole, D.: CP-nets: A tool for representing and reasoning with conditional ceteris paribus preference statements. Journal of Artificial Intelligence Research 21, 135–191 (2004)
5. Brewka, G.: A rank based description language for qualitative preferences. In: Proc. ECAI (2004)
6. Brewka, G., Benferhat, S., Le Berre, D.: Qualitative choice logic. Artificial Intelligence 157(1-2), 203–237 (2004)
7. Coste-Marquis, S., Lang, J., Liberatore, P., Marquis, P.: Expressive power and succinctness of propositional languages for preference representation. In: Proc. KR, pp. 203–212 (2004)
8. Doyle, J., Thomason, R.H.: Background to qualitative decision theory. AI Magazine 20(2), 55–68 (1999)
9. Dubois, D., Prade, H.: Possibility theory as a basis for qualitative decision theory. In: Proc. IJCAI (1995)
10. Dung, P.M.: On the acceptability of arguments and its fundamental role in nonmonotonic reasoning, logic programming and n-person games. Artificial Intelligence 77, 321–357 (1995)
11. Kaci, S., van der Torre, L.: Preference-based argumentation: Arguments supporting multiple values. Int. J. of Approximate Reasoning 48, 730–751 (2008)
12. Keeney, R.L., Raiffa, H.: Decisions with multiple objectives: preferences and value trade-offs. Cambridge University Press, Cambridge (1993)
13. Liu, F.: Changing for the Better: Preference Dynamics and Agent Diversity. PhD thesis, Universiteit van Amsterdam (2008)
14. Prakken, H.: A study of accrual of arguments, with applications to evidential reasoning. In: Proc. ICAIL, pp. 85–94 (2005)
15. Prakken, H., Sartor, G.: Argument-based extended logic programming with defeasible priorities. Journal of Applied Non-Classical Logics 7, 25–75 (1997)
16. Rahwan, I., Ramchurn, S.D., Jennings, N.R., McBurney, P., Parsons, S., Sonenberg, L.: Argumentation-based negotiation. Knowledge Engineering Review 18(4), 343–375 (2004)

A Characterization of Mixed-Strategy Nash Equilibria in PCTL Augmented with a Cost Quantifier

Pedro Arturo Góngora and David A. Rosenblueth

Instituto de Investigaciones en Matemáticas Aplicadas y en Sistemas
Universidad Nacional Autónoma de México
A.P. 20-726, C.P. 01000, México D.F., México
pedro.gongora@gmail.com, drosenbl@servidor.unam.mx

Abstract. The game-theoretic approach to multi-agent systems has been incorporated into the model-checking agenda by using temporal and dynamic logic to characterize notions such as Nash equilibria. Recent efforts concentrate on pure-strategy games, where intelligent agents act deterministically guided by utility functions. We build upon this tradition by incorporating stochastic actions. First, we present an extension of the Probabilistic Computation-Tree Logic (PCTL) to quantify and compare expected costs. Next, we give a discrete-time Markov chain codification for mixed-strategy games. Finally, we characterize mixed-strategy Nash equilibria.

1 Introduction

As a decision theory for multi-agent settings, game theory is undoubtedly in the interest of Computer Science and Artificial Intelligence. Recent works have incorporated this interest into the model-checking agenda, characterizing various game-theoretic notions in temporal and dynamic logic (cf. [3,5,9]). These works concentrate on pure-strategy games, where intelligent agents act deterministically guided by utility functions. The focus has been on characterizing notions such as Nash equilibria, Pareto optimality, and dominating/dominated strategies. In this paper, we build upon this tradition by incorporating stochastic actions, focusing on the characterization of mixed-strategy Nash equilibria for finite strategic games.

Previous works include, but are not limited to, characterizations of Nash equilibria. In [3] the author gives a characterization of backward induction predictions (i.e., Nash equilibria for extensive-form games) using a branching-time logic. In [5] the authors proceed in a similar vein, but using Propositional Dynamic Logic (PDL). Another similar approach is in [9], where the authors introduce Alternating-Time Temporal Logic (ATL) augmented with a counterfactual operator. This extension to ATL allows us to express properties such as *"if player 1 committed to strategy a, then φ would follow"*. Counterfactual reasoning is then used to characterize Nash equilibria for strategic-form games. Further works emphasize other game-theoretic notions, such as automated mechanism-design (cf.

J. Dix, M. Fisher, and P. Novák (Eds.): CLIMA X, LNAI 6214, pp. 158–177, 2010.

[8,10]). None of these previous works handle mixed strategies. In [2], the authors make a quantitative analysis of a bargaining game, but do not provide a characterization of Nash equilibria. In [6], the author provides a characterization of Nash equilibria using a multi-valued temporal logic.

We start from Probabilistic Computation-Tree Logic (PCTL, [4]) augmented with costs as our underlying framework and proceed as follows. First, we present an extension of PCTL for quantifying the values in the expected-cost formulas (e.g., in $\mathcal{E}_{\bowtie x}[\varphi]$, x might be existentially or universally quantified). Next, we give a discrete-time Markov chain codification of a finite strategic game. The codification consists in unfolding the outcomes of a game, under a mixed-strategy profile, into a treelike structure that models the possibilities of action for each agent. Finally, we give a simple formula of the extended logic characterizing Nash equilibria under our codification.

The rest of the paper is organized as follows. Section 2 is devoted to presenting all the definitions used from game theory. In Sect. 3 we introduce discrete-time Markov chains and PCTL with costs. In Sect. 4 we present the cost-quantifier extension to PCTL and discuss its model checking. In Sect. 5 we present the game codification on Markov chains, a characterization of a Nash equilibrium, and prove its correctness. We finish with some final thoughts and a discussion of future and related work.

2   Strategic Games

Game theory studies the interaction between rational agents. Here, rationality is directly related to the maximization of utility. A game is just a formal description of that interaction. We will deal with games in which the sets of possible actions are those of individual players, sometimes called non-cooperative. For brevity, we will refer to non-cooperative games simply as games.

Of the two formalizations for games, strategic and extensive games, we will use the former. There exist several concepts of solution for games of which, arguably, the most widely known is that of Nash equilibrium. Broadly speaking, a Nash equilibrium is characterized by the decisions made by all players of a game, such that no player can increase her/his payoff by taking another action, assuming that every other player will stick to her/his decision.

This section is based on the first chapters of [7], to where we refer the reader for a more thorough discussion.

Definition 1 (Finite Strategic Game). *A finite strategic game is a structure:*

$$G = \langle N, \{A_i\}_{i \in N}, \{u_i\}_{i \in N} \rangle$$

where $N = \{1, \ldots, n\}$ is a finite set of n agents, A_i is a finite set of the pure strategies of agent i, $u_i : A \to \mathbb{R}$ is the payoff or utility function of agent i, and $A = \times_{i \in N} A_i$ is the set of all pure-strategy profiles of G.

Example 1 (Bach or Stravinsky). Consider the game known as *Bach or Stravinsky* (BoS) for players 1 and 2. The players wish to decide which concert to go to,

Bach or Stravinsky. Player 1 prefers twice as much Bach, while player 2 prefers twice as much Stravinsky. Both players prefer to go to either concert over disagreement. Each player makes her/his choice independently of the other but accounting that preferences are common knowledge among them. Two-player finite strategic games can be described using payoff matrices. The matrix shown in Fig. 1 defines the utility functions for BoS, e.g., $u_1(B_1, B_2) = 2$, $u_2(B_1, B_2) = 1$.

	B_2	S_2
B_1	$2, 1$	$0, 0$
S_1	$0, 0$	$1, 2$

Fig. 1. Payoff matrix for the strategic game BoS

We use the following notational conventions. We use Latin letters a and a' to range over the set A of strategy profiles. If a is a strategy profile, we use a_i to refer to the strategy of agent i specified in a. Also, as a notational abuse, we denote with a_{-i} the strategy profile which specifies the strategies of every agent but i, such that if $a_i \in A_i$, then $(a_{-i}, a_i) \in A$. We also assume that A_i sets are pairwise disjoint and, when it is clear, we will identify a strategy profile $a \in A$ with another n-tuple a' iff they contain exactly the same elements regardless of the order.

Definition 2 (Best-Response Strategy and Nash Equilibrium). *Given a finite strategic game $G = \langle N, \{A_i\}_{i \in N}, \{u_i\}_{i \in N}\rangle$, we say that a strategy a_i is a best-response to strategy profile a iff $u_i(a_{-i}, a_i) \geq u_i(a_{-i}, a'_i)$ for each $a'_i \in A_i$. We say that a strategy profile a is a Nash Equilibrium of G iff every strategy a_i such that $a = (a_{-i}, a_i)$ is a best-response to a itself.*

Consider the previous definition and the matrix in Fig. 1. We can easily verify that both strategy profiles (B_1, B_2) and (S_1, S_2), are Nash equilibria of BoS (Example 1).

Definition 3 (Mixed Extension of a Game). *Let $\Delta(B)$ be the set of all probability distributions over the finite set B. For any finite strategic game:*

$$G = \langle N, \{A_i\}_{i \in N}, \{u_i\}_{i \in N}\rangle$$

we define its mixed extension as the structure:

$$\widehat{G} = \langle N, \{\Delta(A_i)\}_{i \in N}, \{U_i\}_{i \in N}\rangle$$

where $\Delta(A_i)$ is the set of all the mixed-strategies of player i, $U_i : \widehat{A} \to \mathbb{R}$ is the mathematical expectation of utility with respect to the probability measure induced by a mixed-strategy profile, and $\widehat{A} = \times_{i \in N} \Delta(A_i)$ is the set of all mixed-strategy profiles of $\widehat{G}$.

We use Greek letters α and α' to range over $\widehat{A}$. All other notational conventions for pure-strategy games are used as well for their mixed extensions. As α_i is a probability distribution over A_i, we use $\alpha_i(a_i)$ to denote the probability assigned by α_i to the event that pure strategy a_i is selected. For a mixed strategy α_i, the set of elements of A_i to which α_i assigns probability greater than 0 is called the *support* of α_i. We denote by $supp(\alpha_i)$ the subset of A_i whose elements are in the support of mixed strategy α_i. We say that *a mixed strategy α_i degenerates to a pure strategy a_i* iff it assigns probability 1 to the event a_i (i.e., $\alpha_i(a_i) = 1$). Finally, we say that mixed-strategy profile α is a Nash equilibrium of a game G if it is a Nash equilibrium of its mixed extension $\widehat{G}$.

The expected utility under some mixed-strategy profile is the mean value of such a utility. For some mixed-strategy profile α and player i the utility function is determined by:

$$U_i(\alpha) = \sum_{a \in A} p_\alpha(a) u_i(a)$$

$$p_\alpha(a) = \prod_{j \in N} \alpha_j(a_j)$$

The following theorem provides a useful characterization of Nash equilibria. See Lemma 33.2 in [7, p. 33] for a similar characterization and a proof for the *if* direction.

Theorem 1. *Given any finite strategic game $G = \langle N, \{A_i\}_{i \in N}, \{u_i\}_{i \in N} \rangle$, a mixed-strategy profile $\alpha \in \widehat{A}$ is a Nash equilibrium of G iff the following two conditions hold for each player $i \in N$:*

1. *The equality $U_i(\alpha_{-i}, a_i) = U_i(\alpha_{-i}, a_i')$ holds for each (degenerate strategy) a_i and a_i' in $supp(\alpha_i)$.*
2. *The inequality $U_i(\alpha) \geq U_i(\alpha_{-i}, a_i)$ holds for each (degenerate strategy) a_i in $A_i - supp(\alpha_i)$.*

Consider again the matrix in Fig. 1. We can use Theorem 1 to verify that the mixed-strategy profile $\alpha = \left(\left(\frac{2}{3}, \frac{1}{3} \right), \left(\frac{1}{3}, \frac{2}{3} \right) \right)$ is a Nash equilibrium for BoS. For example, for player 1, we replace α_1 with one of the degenerate mixed-strategies that assigns probability 1 to B_1 or S_1, and compare the expected utility in both cases. For $B_1 = (1, 0)$ and $S_1 = (0, 1)$ we have: $U_1 \left(B_1, \left(\frac{1}{3}, \frac{2}{3} \right) \right) = U_1 \left(S_1, \left(\frac{1}{3}, \frac{2}{3} \right) \right) = \frac{2}{3}$. We can follow the same procedure for player 2 to conclude that α is a Nash equilibrium for BoS.

3   Markov Chains and PCTL

PCTL formulas describe qualitative and quantitative properties of probabilistic systems, sometimes modeled as Markov chains. These formulas address properties such as *"the probability of getting p satisfied is at least one half"*, or *"the expected cost (or reward) of getting p satisfied is at most 10"*. This section has the purpose of introducing Markov chains and PCTL. We first introduce Markov chains, that will serve as the semantic model for PCTL formulas. Next, we introduce PCTL syntax and satisfaction. For details on the material presented in this section, we refer the reader to the original paper [4], and also to the book [1].

Definition 4 (Discrete-Time Markov Chain). *A Discrete-Time Markov Chain (DTMC) is a structure:*

$$M = \langle S, s_{init}, \mathbf{P}, \mathbf{C}, AtProp, \ell \rangle$$

where S is a finite set whose elements are called states, s_{init} is a distinguished element of S which is called the initial state, $\mathbf{P} : S \times S \to [0, 1]$ is a transition probability function, such that for any state $s \in S$, $\sum_{s' \in S} \mathbf{P}(s, s') = 1$, $\mathbf{C} : S \to [0, \infty)$ is a cost function, AtProp is a set of countably many atomic propositions, and $\ell : S \to 2^{AtProp}$ is a labelling function that marks each state in S with a subset of AtProp.

$Post_M(s) = \{s' \mid \mathbf{P}(s, s') > 0\}$ is the set of states which are possible to visit from s in one step. A *path* of a DTMC M is a possibly infinite sequence of states $\pi = s_0 s_1 \cdots$ such that for any s_i and s_{i+1}, $\mathbf{P}(s_i, s_{i+1}) > 0$. A path is finite if the sequence is finite. We denote by $Paths_M$ the set of all infinite paths of M, and by $Paths_M^{\text{fin}}$ the set of all finite paths of M. Given a path $\pi = s_0 s_1 \cdots s_i \cdots$, we use $\pi[i] = s_i$ to refer to the ith element of π, and $\pi[0, i]$ to refer to the finite prefix $s_0 \cdots s_i$ of π. The set $Paths_M(s) = \{\pi \mid \pi \in Paths_M \text{ and } \pi[0] = s\}$ denotes the set of all infinite paths of M beginning with s. Similarly, the set $Paths_M^{\text{fin}}(s) = \{\pi \mid \pi \in Paths_M^{\text{fin}} \text{ and } \pi[0] = s\}$ denotes the set of all finite paths of M beginning with s.

For any finite path π, the *cylinder set* of π is the set $Cyl(\pi) = \{\pi' \in Paths_M \mid \pi' \text{ has the prefix } \pi\}$. The *probability measure* Pr_s associated with a DTMC M and state s is that of the smallest σ-algebra Σ_s that contains all the cylinder sets $Cyl(\pi)$, for $\pi \in Paths_M^{\text{fin}}(s)$. For finite paths $\pi = s_0 \cdots s_n$, the probability of π is defined as $\mathbf{P}(\pi) = \prod_{i<n} \mathbf{P}(s_i, s_{i+1})$. The probability of $Cyl(\pi)$ under Pr_s is determined by $Pr_s(Cyl(\pi)) = \mathbf{P}(\pi)$. Let $\{C_i\}_{i \in I}$ be a collection of pairwise disjoint cylinder sets for some countable index I. The probability of the countable union $\bigcup_{i \in I} C_i$ is determined by $Pr_s\left(\bigcup_{i \in I} C_i\right) = \sum_{i \in I} Pr_s(C_i)$.

The application $\mathbf{C}(s)$ for some s in DTMC M denotes the cost (or reward, depending on the model in consideration) gained at *leaving* state s. Then, for any finite $\pi = s_0 \cdots s_n$ in $Paths_M^{\text{fin}}$ the *cumulative cost of π* is defined by $Cost_M(\pi) = \sum_{0 \leq i < n} \mathbf{C}(s_i)$. Note that the cost of leaving the last state of a path is not in the sum, and that for paths consisting of a single state s, $Cost_M(s) = 0$.

For an infinite path $\pi \in Paths_M(s)$ and $A \subseteq S$, we define the *cumulative cost of reaching a state in A* as:

$$Cost_M(\pi, A) = \begin{cases} Cost_M(\pi[0, n]) & \text{if } \exists n \geq 0 : \pi[n] \in A \wedge \forall 0 \leq i < n : \pi[i] \notin A \\ \infty & \text{otherwise} \end{cases}$$

For some state s and $A \subseteq S$, we define the set $\{s \models \mathcal{F}A\}$ of all finite paths $\pi = s_0 \cdots s_n$, such that $s_0 = s$, $s_n \in A$ and $\forall 0 \leq i < n : s_i \notin A$. Note that the set $\{s \models \mathcal{F}A\}$ is measurable, therefore $Pr_s(\{s \models \mathcal{F}A\})$ is the *probability of reaching a state in A from s*. We now define the *expected cumulative cost of reaching a state in A from s* as:

$$ExpCost_M(s, A) = \begin{cases} \sum_{\pi \in \{s \models \mathcal{F}A\}} \mathbf{P}(\pi) Cost_M(\pi) & \text{if } Pr_s(\{s \models \mathcal{F}A\}) = 1 \\ \infty & \text{otherwise} \end{cases}$$

Definition 5 (PCTL Well-formed Formulas). *The set of well-formed formulas φ of PCTL for some countable set of atomic propositions AtProp is defined as the set generated by the following BNF grammar:*

$$\varphi ::= \top \mid p \mid \neg\varphi \mid (\varphi \wedge \varphi) \mid \mathcal{P}_{\bowtie a}[\tau] \mid \mathcal{E}_{\bowtie c}[\varphi]$$
$$\tau ::= \mathcal{X}\varphi \mid \varphi \, \mathcal{U} \, \varphi$$

where $p \in AtProp$, $a \in [0, 1]$, $c \in [0, \infty)$ and $\bowtie \in \{<, >, \leq, \geq\}$.

PCTL formulas describe properties of the infinite computations of a probabilistic system. We can study two classes of formulas: path or temporal formulas and state formulas. Path formulas inherit their meaning from LTL. $\mathcal{X}\varphi$ is satisfied by paths in which the next state satisfies φ. $\varphi \, \mathcal{U} \, \psi$ is satisfied by paths where there exists a future or present state that satisfies ψ, while all the previous states satisfy φ. State formulas inherit their meanings from CTL. The formula $\top$ is satisfied by every DTMC at every state. The formulas $\neg\varphi$, for negation, and $(\varphi \wedge \psi)$, for conjunction, have their usual meanings. The CTL path quantifiers are replaced with the operator $\mathcal{P}$. A formula $\mathcal{P}_{\bowtie a}[\tau]$ means that the probability of the temporal formula τ being satisfied is $\bowtie a$. $\mathcal{E}_{\bowtie c}[\varphi]$ is satisfied at states where the expected cost of reaching another state where φ is satisfied is $\bowtie c$.

The other connectives from the propositional logic are defined as usual:

$$\bot = \neg\top$$
$$(\varphi \vee \psi) = \neg(\neg\varphi \wedge \neg\psi)$$
$$(\varphi \rightarrow \psi) = (\neg\varphi \vee \psi)$$
$$(\varphi \leftrightarrow \psi) = ((\varphi \rightarrow \psi) \wedge (\psi \rightarrow \varphi))$$

where $\bot$ is not satisfied by any DTMC at any state, $(\varphi \vee \psi)$ is a disjunction, $(\varphi \rightarrow \psi)$ is a material implication and $(\varphi \leftrightarrow \psi)$ is a biconditional.

We also define the following derived formulas:

$$\mathcal{P}_{\bowtie a}[\mathcal{F}\varphi] = \mathcal{P}_{\bowtie a}[\top \, \mathcal{U} \, \varphi]$$
$$\mathcal{P}_{\bowtie a}[\mathcal{G}\varphi] = \mathcal{P}_{\overline{\bowtie} 1-a}[\mathcal{F}\neg\varphi]$$
$$\mathcal{P}_{=a}[\tau] = (\mathcal{P}_{\geq a}[\tau] \wedge \mathcal{P}_{\leq a}[\tau])$$
$$\mathcal{E}_{=a}[\varphi] = (\mathcal{E}_{\geq a}[\varphi] \wedge \mathcal{E}_{\leq a}[\varphi])$$

where $\overline{<} = >, \overline{>} = <, \overline{\leq} = \geq$ and $\overline{\geq} = \leq$. The derived path formulas also inherit their meanings from LTL. $\mathcal{F}\varphi$ is satisfied by paths where there exists a future or present state that satisfies φ. $\mathcal{G}\varphi$ is satisfied by paths where φ is satisfied at every state of the path.

Definition 6 (PCTL Satisfaction). *Let $M = \langle S, s_{init}, \mathbf{P}, \mathbf{C}, AtProp, \ell \rangle$ be a DTMC. The satisfaction relation $\models$ between pairs (M, s) with $s \in S$ and well-formed formulas with atomic propositions in AtProp is defined as the smallest relation such that:*

$$(M, s) \models \top$$
$$(M, s) \models p \qquad \Leftrightarrow p \in \ell(s) \ (p \in AtProp)$$
$$(M, s) \models \neg\varphi \quad \Leftrightarrow (M, s) \not\models \varphi$$
$$(M, s) \models (\varphi \wedge \psi) \Leftrightarrow (M, s) \models \varphi \text{ and } (M, s) \models \psi$$
$$(M, s) \models \mathcal{P}_{\bowtie a}[\tau] \Leftrightarrow p_s(\tau) \bowtie a$$
$$(M, s) \models \mathcal{E}_{\bowtie c}[\varphi] \Leftrightarrow e_s(\varphi) \bowtie c$$

where the functions $p_s(\tau)$ and $e_s(\varphi)$ are the following:

$$p_s(\tau) = Pr_s(\{\pi \in Paths_M(s) \mid \pi \models \tau\})$$
$$e_s(\varphi) = ExpCost_M(s, \{s' \mid (M, s') \models \varphi\})$$

Pr_s is the probability measure described before and the relation $\models$ between paths in $Paths_M$ and temporal formulas is defined as:

$$\pi \models \mathcal{X}\varphi \quad \Leftrightarrow \pi[1] \models \varphi$$
$$\pi \models \varphi \, \mathcal{U} \, \psi \Leftrightarrow \exists n \geq 0 : \forall i < n : \pi[i] \models \varphi \wedge \pi[n] \models \psi$$

If there is some φ such that $(M, s_{init}) \models \varphi$, then we say that φ is initially satisfied, and write $M \models \varphi$.

Note that the set $\{\pi \in Paths_M(s) \mid \pi \models \tau\}$ is a measurable set. The case $\tau = \mathcal{X}\varphi$ is straightforward. When $\tau = \varphi \, \mathcal{U} \, \psi$, the set coincides with the countable union of cylinder sets $Cyl(\pi')$, for finite prefix π' of π such that only its last state s_n satisfies ψ, and all its previous states s_i satisfy φ.

Example 2 (Simple protocol). Let M be the DTMC depicted in Fig. 2. This example models a simple protocol for sending a message through an unreliable channel [1]. After sending the message, a failure may occur with probability 0.1. In such a case, the protocol only dictates to try again. Consider the following:

- There are infinitely many possible paths from the initial state s_0 to the state s_3 (representing that the message is delivered). For example:

$$\pi_0 = s_0 s_1 s_3$$
$$\pi_1 = s_0 s_1 s_2 s_0 s_1 s_3$$
$$\pi_2 = s_0 s_1 s_2 s_0 s_1 s_2 s_0 s_1 s_3$$

- Each prefix spans a cylinder set. Therefore, it is possible to measure its probability. For example:

$$Pr_{s_0}(Cyl(\pi_0)) = 0.9$$
$$Pr_{s_0}(Cyl(\pi_1)) = 0.1 \cdot 0.9$$
$$Pr_{s_0}(Cyl(\pi_2)) = (0.1)^2 \cdot 0.9$$

- The probability of delivering the message, $p_{s_0}(\mathcal{F}\,delivered)$, is the (infinite) sum of the probabilities of each cylinder:

$$p_{s_0}(\mathcal{F}\,delivered) = 0.9 + (0.1)^1 \cdot 0.9 + (0.1)^2 \cdot 0.9 + \cdots = 1$$

This fact is expressed in PCTL as follows:

$$(M, s_0) \models \mathcal{P}_{=1}[\mathcal{F}\,delivered]$$

- For this model, the cumulative cost of a path where the message is eventually delivered (i.e., the path reaches s_3) counts the number of tries. For example:

$$Cost_M(\pi_0) = 1$$
$$Cost_M(\pi_1) = 2$$
$$Cost_M(\pi_2) = 3$$

- The expected cost of reaching s_3 is calculated by the following sum:

$$e_{s_0}(delivered) = 1 \cdot 0.9 + 2 \cdot (0.1)^1 \cdot 0.9 + 3 \cdot (0.1)^2 \cdot 0.9 + \cdots = 1\frac{1}{9}$$

This value represents the average number of tries for the message to be delivered. Also, this fact is expressed in PCTL as follows:

$$(M, s_0) \models \mathcal{E}_{=1\frac{1}{9}}[delivered]$$

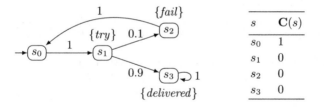

s	$\mathbf{C}(s)$
s_0	1
s_1	0
s_2	0
s_3	0

Fig. 2. Sending a message through an unreliable channel

If a DTMC is reduced to a Kripke structure, the PCTL formula $\mathcal{P}_{>0}[\tau]$ is equivalent to the CTL formula $\exists\tau$. On the contrary, the PCTL formula $\mathcal{P}_{=1}[\tau]$ *is not equivalent* to the CTL formula $\forall\tau$. See the example above: there is an infinite path never reaching a *delivered*-state, although $\mathcal{P}_{=1}[\mathcal{F}\,delivered]$ holds.

Given a DTMC M, a state s of M and a PCTL formula φ, the problem of deciding whether $(M, s) \models \varphi$ is called the *PCTL model-checking problem*. The basic algorithm for solving the model-checking problem consists in recursively computing the set $Sat(\varphi) = \{s \in S \mid (M, s) \models \varphi\}$. The computation of Sat for atomic formulas is given by the labelling function ℓ. Only basic set operations are needed for computing Sat for formulas with basic logical connectives. The computation of *Sat* for formulas $\mathcal{P}_{\bowtie}[\tau]$ and $\mathcal{E}_{\bowtie}[\varphi]$ involves the calculation of reachability probabilities and expected costs for every state. These tasks can be reduced to the problem of finding a solution to a system of linear equations. We cannot give a detailed explanation of these algorithms here; for the details we refer the reader to [4,1].

4   A Cost Quantifier for PCTL

In this section, we present the language of Cost-Quantified PCTL (CQ-PCTL). CQ-PCTL extends its ancestor by adding the possibility to quantify the values of the expected cost operator. The model-checking algorithm, however, is limited to formulas satisfying a syntactic constraint: *the occurrence of quantified variables cannot be nested.* We first define the syntax of the modified language, followed by the algorithm for model checking.

The syntax of CQ-PCTL is almost the same as that of PCTL. We modify the definition of expected cost formulas and add an extra clause to the grammar defining the syntax of PCTL formulas.

Definition 7 (CQ-PCTL Well-formed Formulas). *For some countable set of atomic propositions AtProp and some set Var of countably many variable names, the set of the well-formed formulas φ of CQ-PCTL is defined as the set generated by the following BNF grammar:*

$$\varphi ::= \top \mid p \mid \neg\varphi \mid (\varphi \wedge \varphi) \mid \mathcal{P}_{\bowtie a}[\tau] \mid \mathcal{E}_{\bowtie c}[\varphi] \mid \exists x.\varphi$$
$$\tau ::= \mathcal{X}\varphi \mid \varphi \, \mathcal{U} \, \varphi$$

where $p \in AtProp$, $a \in [0,1]$, $c \in ([0,\infty) \cup Var)$, $x \in Var$ and $\bowtie \in \{<,>,\leq,\geq\}$.

From the basic syntax we can derive the universal quantifier:

$$\forall x.\varphi = \neg\exists x.\neg\varphi$$

Also, we say that *a variable x occurs free in φ* if x does not occur under the scope of an existential or universal quantifier; otherwise we say that x is *bound*. For a formula φ, we say that it has no *nested variables* if for any subformula $\mathcal{E}_{\bowtie x}[\psi]$ of φ: (i) the set of free variables of ψ contains at most x and (ii) the set of bound variables of ψ is empty. A formula with no free variables is called a *sentence*.

Remark 1. In the rest of this paper we will assume that formulas are sentences without nested variables.

We now define the satisfaction relation for CQ-PCTL. Because of remark 1, it is sufficient to incorporate a new clause to the PCTL satisfaction definition for treatment of the new existential formulas.

Definition 8 (CQ-PCTL Satisfaction). *The satisfaction relation is defined as follows for the new formulas:*

$$(M, s) \models \exists x.\varphi \Leftrightarrow there\ exists\ c \in [0, \infty)\ such\ that\ (M, s) \models \varphi[x := c]$$

where $\varphi[x := c]$ is the syntactic substitution replacing all the free occurrences of the variable x in φ by the non-negative real c. The satisfaction for the rest of the formulas is defined as for PCTL.

Before presenting the model-checking algorithm for CQ-PCTL, it is necessary to introduce a transformation for the subformulas of $\exists x.\varphi$ so as to eliminate negative formulas. This is done by transforming φ into its *Positive Normal Form* (PNF) [1].

Definition 9 (Positive Normal Form). *A formula φ is non-negative iff $\varphi \neq \neg\varphi'$ for some φ'. Also, we say that φ is in Positive Normal Form if φ, and all of its subformulas, excepting atomic propositions and the constants $\top$ and $\bot$, are non-negative.*

Note that it is possible to transform every formula into another equivalent formula in PNF. This can be done by (i) introducing the constant $\bot$, the disjunction, and the universal quantifier into the base syntax; (ii) applying De Morgan's and double negation Laws; and (iii) applying the following additional equivalences:

$$\neg\mathcal{P}_{\bowtie a}[\tau] \Leftrightarrow \mathcal{P}_{\neg\bowtie a}[\tau] \tag{1}$$

$$\neg\mathcal{E}_{\bowtie c}[\varphi] \Leftrightarrow \mathcal{E}_{\neg\bowtie c}[\varphi] \tag{2}$$

where $\neg< \,=\, \geq$, $\neg> \,=\, \leq$, $\neg\leq \,=\, >$ and $\neg\geq \,=\, <$.[1] Also, we will use $PNF(\varphi)$ to denote a PNF formula equivalent to φ.

The readers familiar with CTL may notice that the release operator $\mathcal{R}$ (dual of $\mathcal{U}$) is not included in the basic language. The $\mathcal{R}$ operator is necessary for defining PNF for CTL, but not for (CQ-)PCTL. The reason is that in (1) the negation is absorbed by the predicate $\bowtie a$. Leaving out the $\mathcal{R}$ operator does not alter the expressiveness of (CQ-)PCTL in PNF. Despite this fact, the CQ-PCTL model-checking algorithm must take into account these implicit negations.

For their shared formulas, the model-checking algorithm for CQ-PCTL is essentially the same as for PCTL. In the rest of this section we will only present the method for calculating the set $Sat(\exists x.\varphi)$ for the new quantified formulas.

The algorithm for computing $Sat(\exists x.\varphi)$ consists of two steps. The first step computes a set $I(\exists x.\varphi)$ of intervals. These intervals are constraints that a value c assigned to x must satisfy for $\varphi[x := c]$ being satisfied at some state in S. The second step consists of several attempts to compute $Sat(\varphi[x := c])$, each attempt using a value for c taken from an interval obtained beforehand.

---

[1] Note that $\neg\bowtie$ negates $\bowtie$, while the $\bowtie$ notation from Sect. 3 indicates inverting the direction of $\bowtie$.

The application $I(\exists x.\varphi) = i(x, \varphi)$ of Def. 10 below builds a set containing intervals of real numbers. The values c in these intervals may cause $\varphi[x := c]$ to be satisfied. Moreover, this set is constructed in such a way that if there is a satisfying c (i.e., $\varphi[x := c]$ is satisfiable at some state), then there is an interval A such that $c \in A \in i(x, \varphi)$. In such a case, it is also important that the interval contains only satisfying values (Theorem 2), for we have to choose just one of the possibly infinitely many values in the interval.

Definition 10 (Set $I(\exists x.\varphi)$). *Given a DTMC $M = \langle S, S_{init}, \mathbf{P}, \mathbf{C}, AtProp, \ell \rangle$ and a CQ-PCTL existential formula in PNF $\exists x.\varphi$, the set $I(\exists x.\varphi) = i(x, \varphi)$ of intervals of non-negative reals is inductively constructed by the following definition:*

$$
\begin{aligned}
i(x, l) &= \{[0, \infty)\} &&(\text{where } l \in AtProp \cup \{\top, \bot\}) \\
i(x, \neg p) &= \{[0, \infty)\} &&(\text{where } p \in AtProp) \\
i(x, (\psi \vee \psi')) &= i(x, \psi) \cup i(x, \psi') \\
i(x, (\psi \wedge \psi')) &= \{A \cap B \mid A \in i(x, \psi), B \in i(x, \psi')\} \\
i(x, \mathcal{E}_{\bowtie x}[\psi]) &= \{i(s, x, \mathcal{E}_{\bowtie x}[\psi]) \mid s \in S\} \\
i(x, \mathcal{E}_{\bowtie a}[\psi]) &= \|(i(x, \psi)) \cup \|(i(x, PNF(\neg\psi))) \\
i(x, \mathcal{P}_{\bowtie a}[\mathcal{X}\psi]) &= \|(i(x, \psi)) \cup \|(i(x, PNF(\neg\psi))) \\
i(x, \mathcal{P}_{\bowtie a}[\psi \, \mathcal{U} \, \psi']) &= \{A \cap B \mid A \in \|(i(x, \psi)), B \in \|(i(x, \psi')\}) \\
&\quad \cup \{A \cap B \mid A \in \|(i(x, PNF(\neg\psi))), B \in \|(i(x, PNF(\neg\psi')))\})
\end{aligned}
$$

where $i(s, x, \mathcal{E}_{\bowtie x}[\psi]) = \{r \in [0, \infty) \mid e_s(\psi) \bowtie r\}$ and $\|(\mathcal{I}) = \{\bigcap X \mid X \in 2^{\mathcal{I}}\}$ for $\mathcal{I}$ a set of intervals and $\bigcap \emptyset = [0, \infty)$.

The set $i(x, \varphi)$ is constructed inductively. At the basis of the induction there are the atoms and the formulas $\mathcal{E}_{\bowtie x}\psi$. The atoms do not pose any constraints on the values assignable to x. For $\mathcal{E}_{\bowtie x}\psi$, the computation of the bounds for the required intervals is straightforward using the PCTL model-checking algorithm. For disjunctions, the set interval may be in the union of the sets calculated for both disjuncts. The case of conjunction is more complicated: if there is a satisfying c, then c must be at the same time in one interval calculated for each one of the conjuncts. For the formulas $\mathcal{E}_{\bowtie a}[\psi]$ (resp. $\mathcal{P}_{\bowtie a}[\tau]$), a similar reasoning to that for the conjunctions is made. If there is a c such that $\psi[x := c]$ (resp. $\tau[x := c]$) satisfies the given predicate at each state of some subset of S, then c may need to be contained in several of the intervals calculated for the immediate subformulas of ψ (resp. τ).

Note that, because (1) and (2), the formulas $\mathcal{E}_{\bowtie a}[\psi]$ and $\mathcal{P}_{\bowtie a}[\tau]$ may represent an implicit negation contained in their predicate $\bowtie a$. For this reason, the algorithm must search for values that may satisfy the complementary paths when the immediate subformulas are negated.

Also, observe that the intersection $\bigcap \emptyset$ in Def. 10 is not the same as $\emptyset \cap \emptyset$. On the one hand, $\bigcap \emptyset$ represent a constraint posed by the empty set of states. On the other hand, $\emptyset \cap \emptyset$ is the intersection of the empty set with itself.

Example 3 (Interval computation). Let M be the DTMC depicted in the left panel of Fig. 3. Using the PCTL model-checking algorithm it is possible to compute the expected costs of reaching s_3 and s_4 (characterized by atoms p and q, resp.). These values are shown in the table in the right panel of the same figure. Consider the following examples:

- Given the values in the table we can compute the following sets:

$$i(x, \mathcal{E}_{\geq x}[p]) = \{[0, 10], [0, 5], [0, 0], [0, \infty)\}$$
$$i(x, \mathcal{E}_{\leq x}[q]) = \{[20, \infty), [15, \infty), [10, \infty), [0, \infty)\}$$

  The intervals in these sets give a direct solution to the question of whether $(M, s) \models \exists x.\mathcal{E}_{\geq x}[p]$ or $(M, s) \models \exists x.\mathcal{E}_{\leq x}[q]$ hold for some s.
- Let $\varphi = \mathcal{P}_{=0.2}[\mathcal{E}_{\geq x}[p] \, \mathcal{U} \, \mathcal{E}_{\leq x}[q]]$ (for simplicity, assume that $\mathcal{P}_{=a}[\tau]$ is primitive in the basic language). The only assignable value to x making $(M, s_0) \models \exists x.\varphi$ to hold is 10. This value makes the path $\pi = s_0 s_2 s_3 \ldots$ satisfy the until subformula. The first two states of π satisfy the left part of the until, whereas the third state of π satisfies the right part. The satisfying value is computed as the intersection $[10, 10] = [0, 10] \cap [10, \infty)$ where:

$$[0, 10] \in \|(i(x, \mathcal{E}_{\geq x}[p]))\| \quad \text{(because of } s_0 \text{ and } s_2)$$
$$[10, \infty) \in \|(i(x, \mathcal{E}_{\leq x}[q]))\| \quad \text{(because of } s_3)$$

- Consider the problem of whether $(M, s_0) \models \exists x.\neg\varphi$ holds. Transforming to PNF we have: $PNF(\neg\varphi) = \mathcal{P}_{\neq 0.2}[\mathcal{E}_{\geq x}[p] \, \mathcal{U} \, \mathcal{E}_{\leq x}[q]]$. The previous solution makes the probability of the satisfying path equal to 0.2, but the problem ask for other complementary values of x. Following this reasoning, the algorithm tries to calculate intervals for complementary paths satisfying $\mathcal{E}_{< x}[p] \, \mathcal{U} \, \mathcal{E}_{> x}[q]$. One solution is the interval $(20, \infty) = [0, \infty) \cap (20, \infty)$ such that:

$$[0, \infty) \in \|(i(x, \mathcal{E}_{< x}[p]))\| \quad \text{(because of the empty set)}$$
$$(20, \infty) \in \|(i(x, \mathcal{E}_{> x}[q]))\| \quad \text{(because of } s_0)$$

  A value c from this interval never satisfies the original until, thus $p_{s_0}(\mathcal{E}_{\geq c}[p] \, \mathcal{U} \, \mathcal{E}_{\leq c}[q]) = 0 \neq 0.2$, satisfying the predicate.

The following theorem states the property necessary for using the set $I(\exists x.\varphi)$ in the model-checking algorithm.

Theorem 2. *Let M be a DTMC, s a state of M, and $\exists x.\varphi$ a CQ-PCTL formula in PNF. Then, for all $c \in [0, \infty)$ the following two conditions hold:*

1. *If $(M, s) \models \varphi[x := c]$, then there exists $A \in i(x, \varphi)$ such that $c \in A$ and for all $c' \in A$, $(M, s) \models \varphi[x := c']$*
2. *If $(M, s) \not\models \varphi[x := c]$, then there exists $A \in i(x, PNF(\neg\varphi))$ such that $c \in A$ and for all $c' \in A$, $(M, s) \models PNF(\neg\varphi)[x := c']$.*

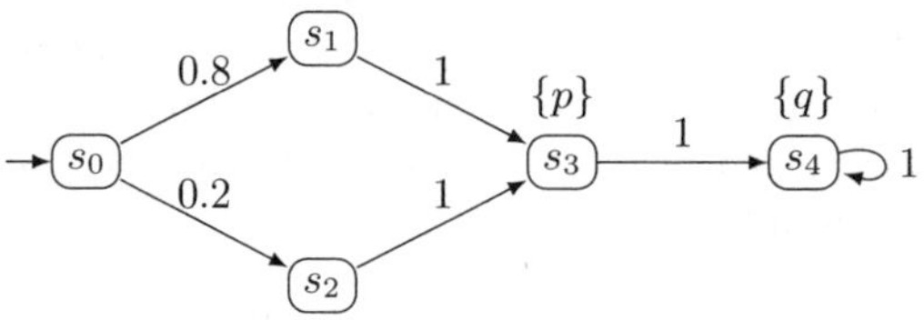

s	$\mathbf{C}(s)$	$e_s(p)$	$e_s(q)$
s_0	4	10	20
s_1	5	5	15
s_2	10	10	20
s_3	11	0	10
s_4	0	∞	0

Fig. 3. DTMC model for Example 3 and some expected costs

Theorem 2 suggests the last step of the algorithm. Given a CQ-PCTL formula in PNF $\exists x.\varphi$, we build the set $Sat(\exists x.\varphi)$ as follows:

$$Sat(\exists x.\varphi) = \bigcup_{A \in I(\exists x.\varphi)} \{Sat(\varphi[x := c]) \mid c \in A\}$$

Note that Theorem 2 also implies that it suffices to choose a single c from each interval A.

The basic algorithm presented here can be easily extended to the case where the values of $\mathcal{P}_{\bowtie a}$ formulas are also quantified. Also, it is possible to extend the results of this section to the general case of formulas, not only sentences, by enriching the models with variable-interpretation functions. For clarity, however, we restrict ourselves to sentences.

Some nesting constraints (remark 1) can be weakened, as long as there are no circular dependencies between the quantified variables. Nonetheless, the restriction for arbitrary nesting cannot be lifted. For example, consider the following simple sentence:

$$\exists x. (\varphi[x] \wedge \exists y.(\psi[x, y]))$$

where $\varphi[x]$ is a formula with free occurrences of x and $\psi[x, y]$ is a formula with free occurrences of both x and y. In this example, the problems of finding suitable values for x and y may be mutually dependent. For arbitrary nesting levels the problem may be even more complicated.

5   Model-Checking Games for Nash Equilibria

In this section, we show how to construct a DTMC $M_{G,\alpha}$ for a finite strategic game G and its mixed-strategy α. Although the construction is for strategic-form games, it is based on extensive forms.

Extensive-form games differ from strategic-form ones in that the sequentiality of the actions is important. An extensive game can be described by a tree structure. In a game tree each node represents the turn of only one player, and for each possible action, such a tree has one arc to another player's turn. In a strategic game it is assumed that each agent executes her/his action independently from and without knowing the other players' actions. To model this in an extensive game, states are grouped in such a manner that they represent the next player's uncertainty about previous actions (see Fig. 4 for an extensive form of BoS; dotted lines group player 1 moves as a single state, as player 2 does not know which action has been taken).

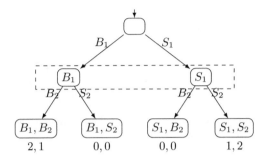

Fig. 4. An extensive form of BoS; utilities are shown under the leaf nodes

Given the game and the mixed-strategy profile, in our codification we build a structure similar to an extensive-form tree. In the built structure each arc, except the arcs leaving the root, is labelled with the probability that the mixed-strategy profile assigns to that particular action. As we cannot group states in a DTMC, we build one subtree for each player and each pure strategy. Each one of these subtrees models the situation where player i chooses some strategy a_i, but the other players follow the mixed-strategy.

By proceeding in this manner, each leaf node corresponds to one strategy profile of the strategic-form game. Consequently, each leaf node is associated with its utility via the cost function **C**. As the cost function models the cost of *leaving* the state, we need to add a fictitious absorbing node below the leafs, representing the ending of the game.

Figure 5 illustrates one of the subtrees described above. Note that there is exactly one path from $s_{(i,a_i)}$ to the ending state, and going through each strategy profile. The arcs of such a path are the probabilities assigned by the mixed-strategy profile to that action. Hence, the expected cost coincides with the expected utility. We can therefore use a cost-quantified formula to compare expected costs and verify if Theorem 1 is applicable.

Definition 11 (DTMC Game Model). *For any game:*

$$G = \langle N, \{A_i\}_{i \in N}, \{u_i\}_{i \in N} \rangle$$

and a mixed-strategy profile α of its mixed extension $\widehat{G}$, we define the DTMC $M_{G,\alpha}$ as the structure:

$$M_{G,\alpha} = \langle S, s_{init}, \mathbf{P}, \mathbf{C}, AtProp, \ell \rangle$$

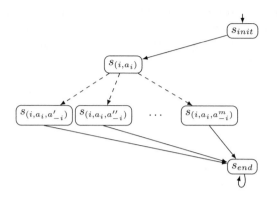

Fig. 5. After player i chooses strategy a_i other players make their own decisions, thus creating various strategy profiles

where the set of states is:

$$S = \{s_{init}\} \cup \{s_{end}\} \cup \{s_x\}_{x \in Idx}$$

Idx is the following index set:

$$Idx = \bigcup_{\substack{i \in N \\ a_i \in A_i}} \{(i, a_i), (i, a_i, a_{j_1}), \dots, (i, a_i, a_{j_1}, \dots, a_{j_m})$$

$$| \; j_k \in N - \{i\}, j_k < j_{k+1}, \text{ and } (a_i, a_{j_1}, \dots, a_{j_m}) \in A\}$$

The probability transition function is defined by cases:

$$\mathbf{P}(s_{init}, s_{(i,a_i)}) = 1/n \qquad \text{for } i \in N, a_i \in A_i, n = |\bigcup_{j \in N} A_j|$$

$$\mathbf{P}(s_{(x)}, s_{(x,a_j)}) = \alpha_j(a_j) \qquad \text{for } j \in N, x \in Idx$$

$$\mathbf{P}(s_{(i,a)}, s_{end}) = 1 \qquad \text{for } i \in N, a \in A$$

$$\mathbf{P}(s_{end}, s_{end}) = 1$$

$$\mathbf{P}(s, s') = 0 \qquad \text{otherwise}$$

The cost function is defined as follows:

$$\mathbf{C}(s_{(i,a)}) = u_i(a) \qquad \text{for } a \in A$$

$$\mathbf{C}(s) = 0 \qquad \text{otherwise}$$

Finally, the set of atomic propositions and the labelling function are the following:

$$AtProp = \{end\} \cup \bigcup_{i \in N} A_i$$

$$\ell(s_{end}) = \{end\}$$
$$\ell(s_{(i,a_i)}) = \{a_i\} \qquad\qquad for\ i \in N, a_i \in A_i$$
$$\ell(s) = \emptyset \qquad\qquad otherwise$$

Remark 2. The cost function of a DTMC requires non-negative values. We thus assume that games' utility functions also assign non-negative values only. If this is not the case, it is possible to add a constant sufficiently large to every value returned by the u_i functions, in order to make them non-negative. The addition of such a constant does no affect any result, as we only compare the mean values of utilities.

Example 4. (Model for BoS) The DTMC model M constructed for the game BoS and the mixed-strategy profile $\alpha = \left(\left(\frac{2}{3}, \frac{1}{3}\right), \left(\frac{1}{3}, \frac{2}{3}\right)\right)$ is depicted in Fig. 6. We can verify the following facts:

$$(M, s_{(1,B_1)}) \models B_1 \wedge \mathcal{E}_{=\frac{2}{3}} end \qquad\qquad (M, s_{(2,B_2)}) \models B_2 \wedge \mathcal{E}_{=\frac{2}{3}} end$$
$$(M, s_{(1,S_1)}) \models S_1 \wedge \mathcal{E}_{=\frac{2}{3}} end \qquad\qquad (M, s_{(2,S_2)}) \models S_2 \wedge \mathcal{E}_{=\frac{2}{3}} end$$

For every player, all the pure strategies in the support of α yield the same payoff. Then, by Theorem 1 α is a Nash equilibrium. We can characterize this fact with a formula of CQ-PCTL:

$$(M, s_{init}) \models \exists x. (\mathcal{P}_{>0}[\mathcal{X}(B_1 \wedge \mathcal{E}_{=x} end)] \wedge \mathcal{P}_{>0}[\mathcal{X}(S_1 \wedge \mathcal{E}_{=x} end)])$$
$$\wedge \exists x. (\mathcal{P}_{>0}[\mathcal{X}(B_2 \wedge \mathcal{E}_{=x} end)] \wedge \mathcal{P}_{>0}[\mathcal{X}(S_2 \wedge \mathcal{E}_{=x} end)])$$

The previous example shows how it is possible to characterize a mixed-strategy Nash equilibrium of a game with CQ-PCTL. Although it is not the case in BoS, by Theorem 1 we must verify that the expected cost is effectively a best response. This is achieved by verifying that the expected cost of deviating from the profile does not exceed that of the strategies in the support. The following definition captures this constraint.

Definition 12 (Mixed-strategy Nash Equilibria Characterization). *For a DTMC game model $M_{G,\alpha}$, the CQ-PCTL characterization of a mixed-strategy Nash equilibrium is the formula $NE_{G,\alpha}$ defined as follows:*

$$NE_{G,\alpha} = \bigwedge_{i \in N} \exists x. \left(f_{supp(\alpha_i)} \wedge f_{\overline{supp}(\alpha_i)}\right)$$

$$f_{supp(\alpha_i)} = \bigwedge_{a_i \in supp(\alpha_i)} \mathcal{P}_{>0}[\mathcal{X}(a_i \wedge \mathcal{E}_{=x} end)]$$

$$f_{\overline{supp}(\alpha_i)} = \bigwedge_{a_i \in \overline{supp}(\alpha_i)} \mathcal{P}_{>0}[\mathcal{X}(a_i \wedge \mathcal{E}_{\leq x} end)]$$

where $\overline{supp}(\alpha_i)$ denotes the complement of $supp(\alpha_i)$.

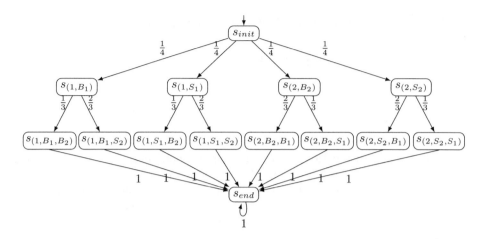

Fig. 6. DTMC for the game BoS and its mixed-strategy Nash equilibrium

Finally, we end this section stating a theorem asserting the correctness of the whole construction.

Theorem 3. *Let $M_{G,\alpha}$ be a DTMC game model. The mixed-strategy profile α is a Nash equilibrium of G if and only if $M_{G,\alpha} \models NE_{G,\alpha}$ holds.*

6   Conclusions

In this paper, we have addressed the problem of characterizing a mixed-strategy Nash equilibrium using PCTL enriched with an expected-cost quantifier: CQ-PCTL. Previous works include [3,5,9], where the authors give a characterization of pure-strategy Nash equilibria and other game-theoretic notions using temporal and dynamic logic. Our work also differs from [3,5] in that their characterization is validity-based, whereas our characterization is satisfaction-based, making our approach directly suitable for model-checking. In [2], the authors incorporate stochastic actions. They provide a model for a bargaining game (Rubinstein's alternating offers negotiation protocol, see [7]). With this model, the authors use PCTL formulas for making a quantitative analysis for several mixed strategies of the game. They, however, do not provide characterizations for Nash equilibria.

There are two general routes for future research: one dealing with CQ-PCTL and the other with its game-theoretic concepts.

As for the first route, recall that in Sect. 4 we presented an algorithm for model-checking a fragment of CQ-PCTL. The whole language includes formulas with nested variables. The nested variables introduce circular dependencies that our current algorithm cannot deal with. We do not know whether such an algorithm exists. As for the complexity of our algorithm, we do know that in the worst case it is exponential in the size of the formula. It is important to improve on this bound, if possible.

It would also be desirable, in the spirit of this work, to address other game solution concepts, such as evolutionary and correlated equilibria (cf. [7]). Beyond finite strategic games, it would be interesting to deal with other classes of games, like Bayesian and iterated games. Finally, further investigation would be necessary to determine if model-checking tools can be used to calculate solutions, besides characterizing them.

There is an implementation of the CQ-PCTL model checker and DTMC game construction of this paper written in the programming language Haskell. This implementation can be obtained by request to the authors.

Acknowledgments. We thank IIMAS and UNAM for their facilities. Pedro Arturo Góngora is sponsored by CONACyT. Finally, we also thank the anonymous referees for their comments.

References

1. Baier, C., Katoen, J.-P.: Principles of Model Checking. The MIT Press, Cambridge (2008)
2. Ballarini, P., Fisher, M., Wooldridge, M.: Automated game analysis via probabilistic model checking: a case study. In: Proceedings of the Third Workshop on Model Checking and Artificial Intelligence, pp. 125–137 (2006)
3. Bonanno, G.: Branching time, perfect information games, and backward induction. Games and Economic Behavior 36, 57–73 (2001)
4. Hansson, H., Jonsson, B.: A logic for reasoning about time and reliability. Formal Aspects of Computing 6, 102–111 (1994)
5. Harrenstein, P., van der Hoek, W., Meyer, J.-J., Witteveen, C.: On modal logic interpretations of games. In: Proceedings of the Fifteenth European Conference on Artificial Intelligence, pp. 28–32 (2002)
6. Jamroga, W.: A temporal logic for multi-agent mdp's. In: Proceedings of the AAMAS Workshop on Formal Models for Multi-Robot Systems, pp. 29–34 (2008)
7. Osborne, M.J., Rubinstein, A.: A Course in Game Theory. The MIT Press, Cambridge, Massachusetts (1994)
8. Pauly, M., Wooldridge, M.: Logic for mechanism design — a manifesto. In: In Proceedings of the 2003 Workshop on Game Theory and Decision Theory in Agent Systems, GTDT 2003 (2003)
9. van der Hoek, W., Jamroga, W., Wooldridge, M.: A logic for strategic reasoning. In: AAMAS 2005: Proceedings of the Fourth International Joint Conference on Autonomous Agents and Multiagent Systems, pp. 157–164. ACM, New York (2005)
10. van der Hoek, W., Roberts, M., Wooldridge, M.: Social laws in alternating time: Effectiveness, feasibility, and synthesis. Synthese 156(1), 1–19 (2007)

A   Proofs

Proof (Theorem 1). For the first part suppose that the equation $U_i(\alpha_{-i}, a_i) = U_i(\alpha_{-i}, a_i')$ does not hold for some i. Then either side must be greater than the other, but that contradicts the hypothesis of α being a Nash equilibrium, as i could increase his/her expected utility by assigning more probability to the pure strategy that increases his/her utility. The second part follows from the definition of Nash equilibria. The converse is direct: if both parts hold for each i, then it is impossible to increase some agent's utility by increasing the probability for some strategy (both parts show the worst-case probability of 1 for each strategy and agent), hence the profile is a best-response to itself.   □

Proof (Theorem 2). We will show only the case when x occurs in φ. The proof is by induction on φ.

- Case $\varphi = \psi \vee \psi'$. Condition (1): the required interval A is in $i(x, \psi) \cup i(x, \psi')$. Condition (2): by the induction hypothesis we have corresponding intervals $A \in i(x, PNF(\neg\psi))$ and $B \in i(x, PNF(\neg\psi'))$. Therefore the required interval $A \cap B$ is in $i(x, PNF(\neg\psi) \wedge PNF(\neg\psi'))$.
- Case $\psi \wedge \psi'$. Condition (1): by the induction hypothesis we have corresponding intervals $A \in i(x, \psi)$ and $B \in i(x, \psi')$. Therefore the required interval $A \cap B$ is in $i(x, (\psi \wedge \psi'))$. Condition (2): by the induction hypothesis we have the corresponding intervals $A \in i(x, PNF(\neg\psi))$ and $B \in i(x, PNF(\neg\psi'))$. Therefore the required interval is in $i(x, PNF(\neg\psi)) \cup i(x, PNF(\neg\psi'))$.
- Case $\mathcal{E}_{\bowtie x}[\psi]$. Condition (1): direct by definition. Condition (2): also by definition and the equivalence $\neg\mathcal{E}_{\bowtie x} \Leftrightarrow \mathcal{E}_{\neg\bowtie x}$.
- Case $\mathcal{E}_{\bowtie a}[\psi]$ $(a \neq x)$. Condition (1): there are two subcases: (a) $e_s(\psi) \in [0, \infty)$ and (b) $e_s(\psi) = \infty$. (a) There is a path from s to a state in the nonempty set $Sat(\psi[x := c])$. By the induction hypothesis, for each state s_j in $Sat(\psi[x := c])$ there is a corresponding interval A_j. Then the required interval for $\mathcal{E}_{\bowtie a}[\psi]$ must be the intersection of some A_j intervals (contained in $\|(i(x, \psi))\|$). (b) The set $Sat(\neg\psi[x := c])$ is nonempty. Again by the induction hypothesis, for each $s_j \in Sat(\neg\psi[x := c])$ there is a corresponding interval A_j (contained in $\|(i(x, PNF(\neg\psi)))\|$). Condition (2): holds by the equivalence $\neg\mathcal{E}_{\bowtie a} \Leftrightarrow \mathcal{E}_{\neg\bowtie a}$.
- Case $\mathcal{P}_{\bowtie a}[\mathcal{X}\psi]$. Condition (1): there are two possibilities: (a) $p_s(\mathcal{X}\psi[x := c]) \bowtie a$ holds when $\psi[x := c]$ is satisfiable at some states reachable from s in one step, and (b) $p_s(\mathcal{X}\psi) \bowtie a$ holds when $\psi[x := c]$ is not satisfiable at some states reachable from s in one step. For (a) the required interval is in $\|(i(x, \psi))\|$. For (b) the required interval is in $\|(i(x, PNF(\neg\psi)))\|$. Condition (2): holds by the equivalence $\neg\mathcal{P}_{\bowtie a} \Leftrightarrow \mathcal{P}_{\neg\bowtie a}$.
- Case $\mathcal{P}_{\bowtie a}[\psi \; \mathcal{U} \; \psi']$. Condition (1): once again, $p_s(\psi \; \mathcal{U} \; \psi') \bowtie a$ may hold when either the subformulas are satisfiable or not. The first possibility is included in $\{A \cap B \mid A \in \|(i(x, \psi)), B \in \|(i(x, \psi')\}$. The second and complementary possibility is included in $\{A \cap B \mid A \in \|(i(x, PNF(\neg\psi))), B \in \|(i(x, PNF(\neg\psi'))\}$. Condition (2): holds by the equivalence $\neg\mathcal{P}_{\bowtie a} \Leftrightarrow \mathcal{P}_{\neg\bowtie a}$.   □

Lemma 1. *Let $M_{G,\alpha}$ be a DTMC game model. For any player $i \in N$ and any strategy $a_i \in A_i$, the equation $U_i(a_i, \alpha_{-i}) = ExpCost_{M_{G,\alpha}}(s_{(i,a_i)}, s_{end})$ holds.*

Proof. Let $a = (a_i, a_{j_1}, \ldots, a_{j_m}) \in A$ be a profile such that its components follow the constraints of the index Idx. From the definitions of S and $\mathbf{P}$ we have that there is a unique path $\pi = s_{(i,a_i)}s_{(i,a_i,a_{j_1})} \cdots s_{(i,a_i,a_{j_1},\ldots,a_{j_m})}s_{\{end\}}$. For such a path, we have that:

$$Pr_{s_{(i,a_i)}}(\pi) = \mathbf{P}(\pi)$$
$$= \mathbf{P}(s_{(i,a_i)}, s_{(i,a_i,a_{j_1})}) \cdots \mathbf{P}(s_{(i,a_i,a_{j_1},\ldots,a_{j_m})}, s_{end})$$
$$= \prod_{j \in N} \alpha_j(a_j)$$
$$= p_\alpha(a)$$
$$Cost_{M_{G,\alpha}}(\pi) = \mathbf{C}(s_{(i,a_i)}) + \cdots + \mathbf{C}(s_{(i,a)})$$
$$= u_i(a)$$

Moreover, the set of all such paths is equal to $P_{(i,a_i)} = \{s_{(i,a_i)} \models \mathcal{F}\{s_{end}\}\}$. Therefore:

$$ExpCost_{M_{G,\alpha}}(s_{(i,a_i)}, \{s_{end}\}) = \sum_{\pi \in P_{(i,a_i)}} \mathbf{P}(\pi) Cost_{M_{G,\alpha}}(\pi)$$
$$= \sum_{a \in A} p_\alpha(a) u_i(a)$$
$$= U_i(\alpha)$$

$\square$

Proof (Theorem 3). We show the implication only in one direction (*if*); the proof for the converse is similar. Suppose as a contradiction that the consequent does not hold. Therefore, there must be some player $i \in N$ for which $\exists x. \left(f_{supp(\alpha_i)} \wedge f_{\overline{supp}(\alpha_i)} \right)$ is not initially satisfied. It follows by Lemma 1 that for any $a_i \in A_i$, if $u = U_i(a_i, \alpha_{-i})$, then $(M_{G,\alpha}, s_{(i,a_i)}) \models a_i \wedge \mathcal{E}_{=u}end$ holds (the first conjunct by def. of ℓ and the second conjunct by Lemma 1). Let $c = U_i(a_i, \alpha_{-i})$ for some $a_i \in supp(\alpha_i)$. Then, by the previous fact and Theorem 1, the formulas $f_{supp(\alpha_i)}[x := c]$ and $f_{\overline{supp}(\alpha_i)}[x := c]$ are both initially satisfied. A contradiction. $\square$

On the Implementation of Speculative Constraint Processing

Jiefei Ma[1], Alessandra Russo[1], Krysia Broda[1]
Hiroshi Hosobe[2], and Ken Satoh[2]

[1] Imperial College London, United Kingdom
{jm103,ar3,kb}@doc.ic.ac.uk
[2] National Institute of Informatics, Japan
{hosobe,ksatoh}@nii.ac.jp

Abstract. Speculative computation has been proposed for reasoning with incomplete information in multi-agent systems. This paper presents the first multi-threaded implementation for speculative constraint processing with iterative revision for disjunctive answers in master-slave multi-agent systems.

1 Introduction

In the context of distributed problem solving with multi-agent systems, communication among agents plays a very important role, as it enables coordination and cooperation between agents. However, in practice communication is not always guaranteed. For example, the physical channel may delay/lose messages, or agents may break down or take unexpectedly long time to compute answers. Moreover, agents are often unable to distinguish between the above situations. All such problems/uncertainties can seriously affect the system performance, especially for result-sharing applications. For example, in a multi-agent scheduling problem, if some agents cannot respond to the queries of their local resources in time, then the computation of the overall resource assignment will be impossible or delayed.

Speculative computation has been proposed in [1,2,3,4,5] as a solution to the problem. In the proposal, a *master* agent prepares default answers to the questions that it can ask to the *slaves*. When communication is delayed or failed, the master can use the default answers to continue the computation. If later a real answer is returned (e.g. the communication channel or the slave agent is recovered), the computation already done by the master, which is using the default answers, will be revised. One of the main advantages of speculative computation relies then on the fact that the computation process of an agent is never halted when waiting for other agent's responses. Examples of real life situations where speculative computation is useful can be found in [1,2,3,4,5].

Within the last few years, speculative computation has gone through various stages of development and extensions. In [1] an abductive-based algorithm has been proposed for speculative computation with yes/no answers for master-slave systems. In [2], the algorithm has been generalised for hierarchical multi-agent systems where agents are assumed to be organised into a hierarchy of

J. Dix, M. Fisher, and P. Novák (Eds.): CLIMA X, LNAI 6214, pp. 178–195, 2010.

master/slaves. The method proposed in [2] also considers only yes/no type of answers. This approach has been extended in [3] to allow more general queries, whereby an agent can ask *possible values* or *constraints* of given queries, but within the context of master-slave systems. This speculative constraint processing takes into account the possibility that the agent's response may neither entail nor contradict the default answer assumed during the computation. In this case the two alternative computations – the one that uses the default and the one that uses the agent's response – are maintained active. The approach described in [3] assumes, however, that only the master agent can perform speculative computation, and that the answer of a slave agent is therefore final and cannot be changed during the entire computation. This limitation has been further addressed in [4], where asked agents may provide disjunctive answers to a query at different times, and may also change the answers they have sent previously. In this context, a dynamic iterative belief revision mechanism has been deployed to handle chain reactions of belief revisions among agents involved in a computational process.

Among the operational models proposed for speculative computation [1,2,3,4,6], the one in [4] is the most complex but also the most powerful. A practical implementation for it is very much desired, not only for proof-of-context testing and benchmark investigation, but also for discovering further improvements and/or extensions of the model. The contribution of this paper is to provide the first multi-threaded implementation of a multi-agent system for speculative disjunctive constraint processing. The system allows the master agent to performs speculative computation locally (using multi-threading or-parallelism), and to ask constraint queries to the slave agents. The speculative master agent is associated with one manager thread (MT) and a set of worker threads (WT). The description of the implementation given in the paper re-organises the operational model proposed in [4] to distinguish the tasks of the MT and WTs. A concurrency control mechanism has been introduced to maximise the concurrent execution of the MT and WTs. This implementation design is shown to be good enough to allow for future extensions of the speculative framework to, for instance, hierarchical multi-agent systems.

The paper is organised as follows. Section 2 briefly reviews the operational model of speculative constraint processing presented in [4]. Section 3 describes the multi-threaded implementation in details, as well as the solutions to several concurrent computation issues. Section 4 compares the implementation to the pseudo-parallel approach, and suggests a hybrid-implementation for situations where computational resources (for multi-threading) are limited. Finally, conclusion and future work are given in Section 5.

2   Speculative Disjunctive Constraint Processing

In this section we review the framework of speculative constraint processing and its operational model that has been proposed in [4].

2.1 Speculative Constraint Processing Framework

Definition 1. *Let Σ be a finite set of constants. We call an element in Σ a slave agent identifier. An* atom *is of the form either $p(t_1, ..., t_n)$ or $p(t_1, ..., t_n)@S$, where p is a predicate, $t_i (1 \leq i \leq n)$ is a term, and S is in Σ.*

We call an atom with an agent identifier an "*askable atom*", and an atom without an identifier a "*non-askable atom*".

Definition 2. *A* framework for speculative constraint computation, *in a master-slave system, is a triple $\langle \Sigma, \Delta, \mathcal{P} \rangle$, where:*

- *Σ is a finite set of constants;*
- *Δ is a set of rules of the following form, called* default rules *w.r.t. $Q@S$:*

$$Q@S \leftarrow C\|,$$

  where $Q@S$ is an askable atom, each of whose arguments is a variable, and C is a set of constraints, called default constraints *for $Q@S$;*
- *$\mathcal{P}$ is a constraint logic program, that is, a set of rules R of the form:*

$$H \leftarrow C\|B_1, B_2, ..., B_n,$$

  where:
  - *H is a non-askable atom; we refer to H as the* head *of R, denoted as $head(R)$;*
  - *C is a set of constraints, called the* constraints *of R, and denoted as $const(R)$;*
  - *each B_i of $B_1, ..., B_n$ is either an askable atom or a non-askable atom, and we refer to $B_1, ..., B_n$ as the* body *of R denoted as $body(R)$.*

For the semantics of the above framework, we index the semantics of a constraint logic program by a *reply set*, which specifies a reply for an askable atom.

Definition 3. *A* reply set *is a set of rules in the form:*

$$Q@S \leftarrow C\|,$$

where $Q@S$ is an askable atom, each of whose arguments is a variable, and C is a constraint over these variables.

Let $\langle \Sigma, \Delta, \mathcal{P} \rangle$ be a framework for speculative constraint computation, and $\mathcal{R}$ be a reply set. A belief state *w.r.t. $\mathcal{R}$ and Δ is a reply set defined as:*

$$\mathcal{R} \cup \{ \text{``}Q@S \leftarrow C\|\text{''} \in \Delta \mid \neg \exists\, C' \text{ s.t. ``}Q@S \leftarrow C'\|\text{''} \in \mathcal{R} \}$$

and denoted as $BEL(\mathcal{R}, \Delta)$.

We introduce the above belief state since, if the answer is not returned, we use a default rule for an unreplied askable atom.

Definition 4. *A goal is of the form* $\leftarrow C\|B_1, ..., B_n$, *where* C *is a set of constraints and the* B_i*'s are atoms. We call* C *the* constraint *of the goal and* $B_1, ..., B_n$ *the* body *of the goal.*

Definition 5. *A* reduction *of a goal* $\leftarrow C\|B_1, ..., B_n$ *w.r.t. a constraint logic program* $\mathcal{P}$, *a reply set* $\mathcal{R}$, *and an atom* B_i, *is a goal* $\leftarrow C'\|B'$ *such that:*

- *there is a rule* R *in* $\mathcal{P} \cup \mathcal{R}$ *s.t.* $C \wedge (B_i = head(R)) \wedge const(R)$ *is consistent*[1].
- $C' = C \wedge (B_i = head(R)) \wedge const(R)$
- $B' = \{B_1, ...B_{i-1}, B_{i+1}, ..., B_n\} \cup body(R)$

Definition 6. *A* derivation *of a goal* $G =\leftarrow C\|Bs$ *w.r.t. a framework for speculative constraint computation* $\mathcal{F} = \langle \Sigma, \Delta, \mathcal{P} \rangle$ *and a reply set* $\mathcal{R}$ *is a sequence of reductions "*$\leftarrow C\|Bs$*",...,"*$\leftarrow C'\|\emptyset$*"*[2] *w.r.t.* $\mathcal{P}$ *and* $BEL(\mathcal{R}, \Delta)$, *where in each reduction step, an atom in the body of the goal in each step is selected.* C' *is called an* answer constraint *w.r.t.* G, $\mathcal{F}$, *and* $\mathcal{R}$. *We call a set of all answer constraints w.r.t.* G, $\mathcal{F}$, *and* $\mathcal{R}$ *the* semantics *of* G *w.r.t.* $\mathcal{F}$ *and* $\mathcal{R}$.

We refer the readers to [4] for a hotel room reservation example.

2.2   The Operational Model

We briefly describe the execution of the speculative framework. The detailed description can be found in [4]. The execution is based on two phases: a *process reduction phase* and a *fact arrival phase*. The process reduction phase is a normal execution of a program in a master agent, and the fact arrival phase is an interruption phase when an answer arrives from a slave agent.

Figures 1–4 intuitively explain how processes are updated according to askable atoms. In the tree, each node represents a process, but we only show constraints associated with the process. The top node represents a constraint for the original process, and the other nodes represent added constraints for the reduced processes. Let us note that we specify *true* for non-top nodes without added constraints, since the addition of the *true* constraint does not influence the solutions of existing constraints. The leaves of the process tree represent the current processes. Processes that are not in the leaves are deleted processes.

Figure 1 shows a situation of the processes represented as a tree when an askable atom, whose reply has not yet arrived, is executed in the process reduction phase. In this case, the current process, represented by the processed constraints C, is split into two different kinds of processes: the first one is a process using default information, C_d, and is called *default process* [3]; and the other one is the current process C itself, called *original process*, suspended at this point.

When, after some reduction of the default processes (represented in Fig. 2 by dashed lines), the first answer comes from a slave agent, expressing constraint

---

[1] A notation $B_i = head(R)$ represents a conjunction of constraints equating the arguments of atoms B_i and $head(R)$.

[2] $\emptyset$ denotes an empty goal.

[3] In this figure, we assume that there is only one default for brevity.

Fig. 1. When $Q@S$ is processed in process reduction phase

C_f for this askable literal, we update the default processes as well as the original suspended process as follows:

- Default processes are reduced to two different kinds of processes: the first kind is a process adding C_f to the problem to solve, and the other is the current process itself which is suspended at this point.
- The original process is reduced to two different kinds of processes as well: the first kind is a process adding $\neg C_d \wedge C_f$, and the other is the original process, suspended at this point.

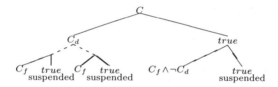

Fig. 2. When the first answer C_f for $Q@S$ arrives

Let $\leftarrow C\|Bs$ be a goal containing $Q@S$. Suppose that it is reduced into $\leftarrow C \wedge C_d\|Bs\backslash\{Q@S\}$ by a default rule "$Q@S \leftarrow C_d\|$". To retain the previous computation as much as possible, we process the query by the following execution:

1. We add C_f to the constraint of every goal derived from the default process.
2. In addition to the above computation, we also start computing a new goal:

$$\leftarrow C \wedge \neg C_d \wedge C_f\|Bs\backslash\{Q@S\}$$

to guarantee completeness.

When an alternative answer, with the constraint C_a, comes from a slave agent (Fig. 3), we need to follow the same procedure as when the first answer comes (Fig. 2), except that now the processes handling only default information are suspended. So, this is done by splitting the suspended default process(es), in order to obtain the answer constraints that are logically equivalent to the answer constraints of:

$$\leftarrow C \wedge C_d \wedge C_a\|Bs\backslash\{Q@S\},$$

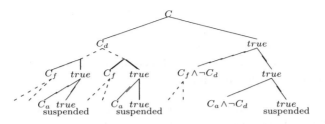

Fig. 3. When the alternative answer C_a for $Q@S$ arrives

as well as by splitting the suspended original process, in order to obtain the answer constraints that are logically equivalent to the answer constraints of $\leftarrow C \wedge \neg C_d \wedge C_a \| Bs \backslash \{Q@S\}$ (Fig. 3). By gathering these answer constraints, we can compute all answer constraints for the alternative reply.

On the other hand, when a revised answer with the constraint C_r arrives, all processes using the first (or current) answer are split, in order to obtain the answer constraints that are logically equivalent to the answer constraints of:

$$\leftarrow C \wedge C_f \wedge C_r \| Bs \backslash \{Q@S\},$$

and the suspended original process is split as well, in order to obtain the answer constraints that are logically equivalent to the answer constraints of $\leftarrow C \wedge \neg C_f \wedge C_r \| Bs \backslash \{Q@S\}$ (Fig. 4). By gathering these answer constraints, we can override the previous reply by the revised reply.

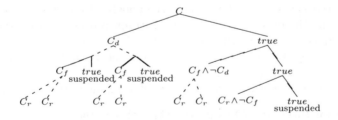

Fig. 4. When the revised answer C_r for $Q@S$ arrives

3   A Multi-threaded Implementation

In [4], the detailed operational model is described as a multi-*processing* computation. There are two types of processes – *finished processes* that represent successfully terminated computational branches, and *ordinary processes* that represent non-terminated branches. An ordinary process can be either an *original process* that is always suspended or an *active process* that searches down an open branch.

In practice the operational model can be implemented in two ways:

1. we represent each *process* as a state, and use a single process/thread to manipulate the states in a pseudo-multi-threading (serialised) fashion. This is very close to the model description;
2. we execute each process using a real thread, so that different (non-suspended) processes can execute concurrently.

The multi-threaded approach avoids overheads caused by state selection and management that the serialised approach has, and allows or-parallelism which will benefit the proof search. However, using one thread for each process may not always be necessary and may cause extra overheads such as in inter-threads communication. For example, original processes are always suspended and can never be resumed, though it may spawn new processes that are not suspended. Preferably they should be managed as states instead, for easy update when a relevant answer is returned. This is also true for finished process. In this section, we describe a practical implementation for the operational model, which considers various efficiency aspects.

3.1 Overview

The model is implemented as a *speculative computation module*, and we refer to it as a *speculative agent*. A set of agents (some of them may not be speculative agents) can be deployed to one or more host machines on a network. Agents interact with each other via messages (containing queries or answers). Since the operational model proposed in [4] is for simple master-slave systems only, in this paper we also assume that there can be only one master, i.e. the only speculative agent, in the set of deployed agents, and the rest are the slaves. The master can send queries to the slaves, but a slave cannot send queries to the master or other slaves. Hence, only the master can perform constraint processing with iterative revision for disjunctive answers. But bear in mind that our implementation is in fact designed in a way that it can be easily extended for hierarchical multi-agent systems similar to that defined in [2].

As illustrated in Fig. 5, each agent has the following internal components:

Communication Interface Module (COM): this is the only interface for inter-agent communications. It accepts queries or answers sent by the agent's master or slaves, and forwards the agent's answers or queries to the master or the appropriate slaves. The *reception list* and the *address book* are used for keeping track of the queries received and the master/slave addresses[4].
Speculative Computation Unit (SCU): this is the central processing unit of the agent that performs speculative computations for one or more queries.
Default Store (Δ) and Program ($\mathcal{P}$): they are self-explained, and form the *static knowledge* of the agent.
Answer Entry, Choice Point and Finish Point Stores (AES, CPS, FPS): AES stores the *answer entries* that are created from either Δ or the returned

---

[4] Both these features will be essential when the implementation is extended for hierarchical multi-agent systems.

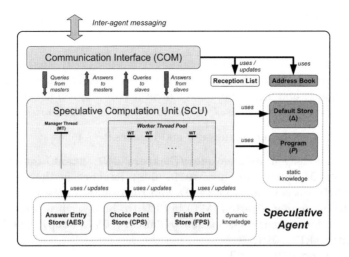

Fig. 5. Agent Internal Components

answers from the slaves (i.e. the reply set $\mathcal{R}$). CPS stores the computation choice points (CP), each of which represents the state of a (suspended) original process. FPS stores the finish points (FP), which contain the results of finished processes. The three stores are used by SCU and form the *dynamic knowledge* of the agent.

In the following sections, we describe how these components are implemented.

3.2 Implementing the Communication Interface Module (COM)

Agents communicate asynchronously via messages sent over TCP connections. Each agent on the network is uniquely identified by a *socket* of the form `IP:Port`, where `IP` is the network address of the agent's host and `Port` is the port number reserved for the agent on the host. Therefore, several agents may run simultaneously on a host.

During the design of an agent's program, the sockets for the slaves may not be known, or they may be changed during agent deployment. Therefore, each agent uses aliases to identify its slaves locally. For example, in an askable atom $Q@S$ appearing in $\mathcal{P}$ or Δ, S is the alias of a slave. The address book stores the mapping between the slave aliases and the slave sockets, and it can be generated/updated during agent (re-)deployment.

There are two types of messages for inter-agent communications:

- a *query message* of the form `query(From, Q@S, Cmd)`, where `From` is the socket of the sender, `Q` is a query, `S` is the recipient's alias used by the sender, and `Cmd` is a command of either `start` or `stop`. If the command is `start`, it indicates a request for the recipient (i.e. the slave) to start a computation for the query; otherwise if the command is `stop`, it asks the recipient to stop the computation for a query previously requested and to free the resources. The "stop" signal (in this paper) is merely used for the execution control of the agent.

– an *answer message* of the form answer(From, Q@S, ID, Ans), where From, Q and S are described as above, Ans is a set of constraints as the answer to the query, and ID is the answer identifier by the sender and is used to distinguish between a *revised answer* and an *alternative answer*.

COM waits for any incoming message and handles it as follows:

– if it is an inter-agent message query(Master, Q@S, start) from the agent's socket, COM creates an entry <RID, Q@S, Master> in the reception list, where RID is a new query entry ID, and then sends a message start(RID, Q@S) to the *manager thread* (MT) in SPU (to be described soon);
– if it is an inter-agent message query(Master, Q@S, stop), COM removes the entry <RID, Q@S, Master> from the reception list, and then sends a message stop(RID) to MT;
– if it is an inter-agent message answer(Slave, Q@S, ID, Ans), COM simply forwards it as answer(Q@S, ID, Ans) to MT;
– if it is an internal message answer(RID, Q, ID, Ans) from MT or from one of the *worker threads* (WT) in SPU, COM looks up <RID, Q@S, Master> from the reception list, and then sends the inter-agent message answer(Self, Q@S, ID, Ans) to the master, where Self is the current agent's socket;
– if it is an internal message query(Q@S) from a WT, COM looks up the slave's socket from the address book using S, and then sends the inter-agent message query(Self, Q@S, start) to the slave.

3.3   Implementing the Speculative Computation Unit (SCU)

SCU can be seen as a collection of concurrent threads. Specifically, there is a persistent *manager thread* (MT) and zero or more *worker threads* (WT). MT is responsible for updating/revising the choice points/finish points and for spawning new WT(s) when a new query or answer is received, and WTs are responsible for constraint processing.

The three stores AES, CPS and FPS are used and maintained by both MT and WTs. AES stores three types of answer entries (AE), all of which have the form <AID, Q@S, Type, Ans>, where AID is the entry ID, Q@S is the query and the slave alias, Type is the entry's type and Ans is the set of constraints associated with the entry:

– If Type is so, then this is a *speculative original answer entry*, and Ans is equal to the conjunction of the negations of all the defaults in Δ for Q@S[5] if there is any default, and is equal to true otherwise;
– if Type is nso, then this is a *non-speculative original answer entry* and Ans is true;

---

[5] i.e. $\bigwedge_{(Q@S \leftarrow C_d\|) \in \Delta} \neg C_d$.

- If `Type` is `d`, then this is a *default answer entry*, and `Ans` is equal to a corresponding default answer for `Q@S` in Δ;
- otherwise, `Type` is `r(ID)` and this is an *ordinary answer entry*, where `ID` and `Ans` are from an answer returned by the slave `S` for `Q`.

CPS stores the states of original processes (or called *choice points* (CP)), each of which has the form `<QID, PID, G, C, WA, AA>`, where `QID` is the (top level) query and its ID, `PID` is the process ID, `G` and `C` are the set of remaining sub-goals and the set of constraints collected so far respectively, `WA` and `AA` are the set of awaiting answer entries and the set of assumed answer entries respectively. `QID` is used by a process to "remember" what query its computation is for, and hence has two components $(RID\text{-}Q_{top})$, where `RID` is the reception entry ID, and Q_{top} is the initial query for the process. It is necessary to record Q_{top} so that when a process finishes successfully (i.e. `G` becomes empty), the variable bindings between the answer (i.e. set of constraints) and the initial query can be preserved. Each element in `WA` and `AA` has the form `(AID, Q@S)`, where `AID` is the ID of an answer entry that the process is awaiting or is assuming for the sub-goal `Q@S`. Note that it is also necessary to record `Q@S` here despite having already recorded `AID`, because if later an assumed answer needs to be revised, the correct variable bindings between the query sent (to the slave) and the answer returned (from the slave) can be obtained.

FPS stores the states of finished processes (or called *finish points* (FP)), each of which has the form `<QID, PID, C, AA>`, where `QID`, `PID` and `AA` are as described above, and `C` is the final set of constraints collected, i.e. the answer, already sent to the master for the query associated with `QID`.

Each WT represents an active process, and its state can be represented as `<QID, PID, G, C, AA>`. It is just like a CP except that it does not have the awaiting answer entry set (i.e. no `WA`).

It is also important to keep track of what AE is currently assumed/awaited by what WTs, CPs and FPs. Such usages of AE are recorded as *subscriptions* in a *directory* as a part of AES. Each subscription has the form `sub(AID, PID)`, where `AID` is the answer entry ID and PID is the ID of a WT, CP or FP.

3.4   The Execution of the Manager Thread and the Worker Threads

The multi-threaded operational model is based on the pseudo-parallel (serialised) operational model proposed in [4], but with improved "process management" allowing true or-parallelism during the computation:

- In the serialised model, the computation interleaves with the *process reduction phase* and the *fact arrival phase*. When it enters the process reduction phase, one active process is selected at a time for resolving a sub-goal. In the multi-threaded model, each WT can enter the process reduction phase and resolve sub-goals independently and concurrently to others. No process selection is required.
- In the serialised model, when it enters the fact arrival phase, all the relevant processes (active or suspended) are updated, and necessary new processes

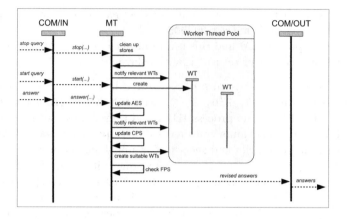

Fig. 6. Execution of MT

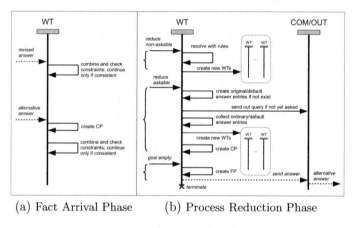

(a) Fact Arrival Phase   (b) Process Reduction Phase

Fig. 7. Execution of WT

from original processes are created at the same time. In the multi-threaded model, the fact arrival phase is splitted and is done by the MT and WTs separately. The MT is responsible for revising the answers from existing finished processes (i.e. the finish points), updating original processes (i.e. the choice points) and creating appropriate new WTs from choice points. The MT also notifies relevant WTs about the newly returned answer via messaging, but will not change the state of WTs directly. On the other hand, when a WT receives such notification from MT, it will check for consistency of the new answer independently from others, and create new choice point if needed (e.g. in the case where it is assuming a default answer and an alternative answer is received). Different WTs can update themselves concurrently.

The key execution steps for MT and WT are illustrated in Figure 6 and Figure 7. The detailed descriptions are provided in Appendix A.1 and Appendix A.2.

3.5   Resolving Concurrency Issues

Inside SPU, MT and WTs execute concurrently, and they all require read/write access to the three stores AES, CPS and FPS. Potential conflicts between MT and a WT, or between WTs may arise. Firstly, it is possible that after a WT spawns several children WTs, and just before it can make all the answer entry subscriptions for the children, MT receives an answer and notifies only some of its children (e.g. the subscription process is not yet complete). Secondly when two WTs encounter the same askable atom at the same time, and if there is no original answer entry for that atom yet, then the original answer entry may be created twice and the query may be sent twice by the two WTs. Hence, the three stores are considered as "critical regions" and need to be protected. One naïve solution is to make all the iteration steps performed by WT or MT atomic. But this will greatly reduce the chance for concurrent processing and hence remove almost all the benefits brought by the multi-threaded implementation. Therefore, "fine grained" atomicity control is needed for the executions of MT and WTs.

Let's consider the first problem. The potential conflict is between MT and WT, and is not between WTs. Although several WTs may need to update the subscriptions in the directory of AES, they only modify the ones associated with their IDs or with their new born children's IDs. As long as the children WTs do not start working until their parent WT has made all the correct subscriptions for them, there won't be any conflict. Also, WTs can only create new choice points in CPS and create new finish points in FPS according to their own states, there is no potential conflict of updating CPS and FPS either. Therefore, the execution of a MT's message handling step cannot (safely) interleave with that of the process reduction step or the fact arrival step of any WT, but the executions of WTs' steps can interleave without problems. To impose such control, we have introduced an atomic counter[6] called the "busy worker counter" (BC). Whenever a WT starts to perform a fact arrival step or reduction step, it will increment BC; and whenever it finishes one step, it will decrement BC. We also introduce an atomic flag called the "waiting/working manager flag"(WF). Whenever MT receives an answer, it will *set* WF to 1; and when MT finishes handling one returned answer, it will *clear* WF to 0. The safe exclusive execution control between MT and WTs using BC and WF are as follows[7],

WT's Execution Cycle	MT's Execution Cycle
1. (atomic step) waits for WF to be cleared and then increments BC; 2. *performs either fact arrival step or reduction step;* 3. decrements BC	1. waits for a returned answer; 2. sets WF 3. waits for BC to reach 0; 4. *handles returned answer;* 5. clears WF

---

[6] I.e. its value update is atomic.

[7] Pseudo-code in Prolog is provided in Appendix B.

Hence, whenever a WT performing a fact arrival step or process reduction step, MT is not allowed to process any received answer; whenever MT has an answer waiting to be processed or being processed, no WT can perform a new step.

Let's now consider the second problem. The potential conflict is between two WTs when they both try to collect/create answer entries for an askable goal. The solution is relatively easy: we have introduced a mutex M_{AES} and control the WT's execution as follows,

When a WT tries to collect answer entries for Q@S:

- if an original answer entry for Q@S exists in AES, *continues as normal*;
- otherwise, (1) locks M_{AES}; (2) if AES still does not contain an original answer entry for Q@S, then *creates the original and default answer entries, and then sends out the query*; (3) unlocks M_{AES}.

The operation of locking a mutex succeeds immediately if the mutex has not been locked by any other thread yet; otherwise it causes the current thread to be suspended. The suspended thread is revived only when the mutex is unlocked, and then the revived thread tries again to lock the mutex. In the above example, it is possible that while a thread is waiting to lock M_{AES}, the thread already locking M_{AES} creates the answer entries. Therefore, in Step 2 checking again whether an original answer entry exists is necessary.

4   Discussions

The described mutli-threaded implementation is implemented in YAP Prolog [7]. We chose YAP not only because it has the necessary CLP and multi-threading supports, but also because it is considered as the one of the fastest Prolog engines that is free and open source.

We have tested the implementation with meeting scheduling examples described in [4] but with increased size. During the testing, we used YAP's default maximum number of WTs of 100 and were able to compute the correct answers within the order of 1 second. For large problems, e.g. if a query would lead to more than 10 (non-askable) sub-goals, each with more than 10 rules with constraints that are always consistent, the number of WTs would exceed 100. Our implementation is able to cope with such problems by setting a higher WT number limit, e.g. 1000, at the expense of initial memory consumed by YAP[8].

In practice, to strike a balance between the number of WTs and the memory consumption, our implementation can be adapted to use a *hybrid* approach, which would implement two types of WTs: *normal workers* and *super worker*. A *normal worker* would execute as an active process as described in the multi-threaded model. A *super worker* would behave like the serialised model [4] and manage several processes in a round-robin fashion. In this way, memory consumption would be reduced whilst maintaining the effect of a high number of

---

[8] 100 maximum threads in YAP require about 2MB memory, 1000 threads require about 4MB and 9999 threads require about 109MB.

WTs. For example, let M be the maximum number of WTs that an agent's SPU can have, then there can be $M-1$ (at most) normal workers and 1 super worker. During the computation, when there are N ($N > M-1$) active processes, $M-1$ of them are handled by the normal workers, and the rest of them are handled by the super worker. When an active process terminates (either due to failure or finish), the normal worker can release it and acquire another active process state from the super worker to continue.

5   Conclusion

In this paper, we have presented a practical multi-threaded implementation for speculative constraint processing with iterative revision for disjunctive answers, and suggested a hybrid implementation for situation where multi-threading support is limited by resource constraint. Although the implementations are based on the operational model described in [4], which is for simple master-slave systems where only the master can perform speculative computation, they are designed to be extendable for hierarchical master-slave systems. As a future work, we will prove the correctness of an extended operational model for a hierarchy of master-slave agents and extend the current implementation to support this more general type of multi-agent systems. We will also perform benchmarking of the system with large examples, and apply it in real world applications, such as planning and online booking systems.

Acknowledgment

This research was partially supported by the Ministry of Education, Science, Sports and Culture, Japan, Grant-in-Aid for Scientific Research (B), 19300053, and is continuing through participation in the International Technology Alliance sponsored by the U.S. Army Research Laboratory and the U.K. Ministry of Defence.

References

1. Satoh, K., Inoue, K., Iwanuma, K., Sakama, C.: Speculative computation by abduction under incomplete communication environments. In: ICMAS, pp. 263–270 (2000)
2. Satoh, K., Yamamoto, K.: Speculative computation with multi-agent belief revision. In: AAMAS, pp. 897–904 (2002)
3. Satoh, K., Codognet, P., Hosobe, H.: Speculative constraint processing in multi-agent systems. In: Lee, J.-H., Barley, M.W. (eds.) PRIMA 2003. LNCS (LNAI), vol. 2891, pp. 133–144. Springer, Heidelberg (2003)
4. Ceberio, M., Hosobe, H., Satoh, K.: Speculative constraint processing with iterative revision for disjunctive answers. In: Toni, F., Torroni, P. (eds.) CLIMA 2005. LNCS (LNAI), vol. 3900, pp. 340–357. Springer, Heidelberg (2006)
5. Satoh, K.: Speculative computation and abduction for an autonomous agent. IEICE Transactions 88-D(9), 2031–2038 (2005)

6. Inoue, K., Kawaguchi, S., Haneda, H.: Controlling speculative computation in multi-agent environments. In: Proc. Second Int. Workshop on Computational Logic in Multiagent Systems (CLIMA 2001), pp. 9–18 (2001)
7. YAP Prolog 5.1.3 manual (June 2008),
   http://www.dcc.fc.up.pt/~vsc/Yap/index.html

A   Execution Description of MT and WT

A.1   Execution of MT (Illustrated in Fig. 6)

MT processes each message it receives from COM:

- if the message is $start(RID, Q)$, it spawns a new WT with initial state $\langle QID, PID_{new}, Q, \emptyset^9, \emptyset^{10} \rangle$, where $QID = (RID, Q)$, PID_{new} is a new process ID.
- if the message is $stop(RID)$, then
  1. it removes all the choice points in CPS and all the finish points in FPS that are associated with RID;
  2. it broadcasts a message $stop(RID)$ to all the WTs;
- if the message is $answer(Q@S, ID, C_{new})$:
  - if there exists an answer entry $\langle AID, Q@S, r(ID), C_{old} \rangle$ in AES, then **the received answer is a revised answer** (following Fig. 4):
    1. MT updates the existing answer entry to be $\langle AID, Q@S, r(ID), C_{new} \rangle$;
    2. for each WT subscribing AID, MT sends a message $rev(AID, Q@S, C_{new})$ to the WT (so that the WT can check C_{new} for consistency);
    3. for each FP of $\langle QID, PID, C_{final}, AA \rangle$ that is subscribing AID and $QID = (RID, Q_{top})$, if $C_{final} \neq C_{final} \wedge C_{new}$, then MT sends a message $answer(RID, Q_{top}, PID, C_{final} \wedge C_{new})$ to COM;
    4. for each CP of $\langle QID, PID, G, C, WA, AA \rangle$ that is subscribing AID, if $C_{all} = C \wedge C_{new}$ is consistent, then MT updates it to be $\langle QID, PID, G, C_{all}, WA, AA \rangle$; otherwise, MT removes the CP and the CP's subscriptions;
    5. let $\langle AID_o, Q@S, O, C_o \rangle$ be an original answer entry for $Q@S$, where O is either so or nso, for each choice point of $\langle QID, PID, G, C, WA, AA \rangle$ that is subscribing AID_o and $C_{all} = C \wedge \neg C_{old} \wedge C_{new}$ is consistent:
       * if WA contains only $(AID_o, Q@S)$, then MT creates a new WT with $\langle QID, PID_{new}, G, C_{all}, AA \cup \{(AID, Q@S)\} \rangle$, and subscribes all the answer entries in AA and that with AID for the new WT (i.e. for each $(AID', Q'@S') \in AA \cup \{(AID, Q@S)\}$, it adds $sub(AID', PID_{new})$ to the directory in AES);
       * otherwise, MT creates a new CP of $\langle QID, PID_{new}, G, C_{all}, WA \setminus \{(AID_o, Q@S)\}, AA \cup \{(AID, Q@S)\} \rangle$ in AES, and subscribes all the answer entries in AA and in WA for the new CP;
  - **otherwise, it is a first/alternative answer** (following Fig. 2 and Fig. 3):
    1. MT creates a new answer entry $\langle AID_{new}, Q@S, r(ID), C_{new} \rangle$ in AES;
    2. for each default answer entry $\langle AID_d, Q@S, d, C_d \rangle$ in AES:

---

[9] This is the initially empty set of constraints.
[10] This is the initially empty set of assumed answer entries.

* for each WT subscribing AID_d, MT sends a message $alt(AID_{new},$ $AID_d, Q@S, C_{new})$ to it;
* for each FP of $\langle QID, PID, C_{final}, AA \rangle$ that is subscribing AID_d and $QID = (RID, Q_{top})$, if $C_{final} \neq C_{final} \wedge C_{new}$, then MT sends a message $answer(RID, Q_{top}, PID, C_{final} \wedge C_{new})$ to COM;
* for each CP of $\langle QID, PID, G, C, WA, AA \rangle$ that is subscribing AID_d,
  (a) MT updates the CP to be $\langle QID, PID_{new}, G, C, WA \cup \{(AID_d, Q@S)\},$
    $AA \setminus \{(AID_d, Q@S)\} \rangle$;
  (b) if $C_{all} = C \wedge C_{new}$ is consistent, then
    · if WA contains only $(AID_d, Q@S)$, then MT creates a new WT with $\langle QID, PID_{new}, G, C_{all}, AA \cup \{(AID, Q@S)\} \rangle$, and sub-scribes all the answer entries in AA and that with AID for the new WT;
    · otherwise, MT creates a new CP of $\langle QID, PID_{new}, G, C_{all},$ $WA \setminus \{(AID_d, Q@S)\}, AA \cup \{(AID, Q@S)\} \setminus \{(AID_d, Q@S)\} \rangle$ in AES, and subscribes all the answer entries in $AA \cup WA \cup \{(AID, Q@S)\} \setminus \{(AID_d, Q@S)\}$ for the new CP;

3. let $\langle AID_o, Q@S, O, C_o \rangle$ be an original answer entry for $Q@S$, where O is *so* or *nso*, for each choice point of $\langle QID, PID, G, C, WA, AA \rangle$ that is subscribing AID_o and $C_{all} = C \wedge C_o \wedge C_{new}$ is consistent:
   * if WA contains only $(AID_o, Q@S)$, then MT creates a new WT with $\langle QID, PID_{new}, G, C_{all}, AA \cup \{(AID, Q@S)\} \rangle$, and subscribes all the answer entries in AA and that with AID for the new WT;
   * otherwise, MT creates a new CP of $\langle QID, PID_{new}, G, C_{all},$ $WA \setminus \{(AID_o, Q@S)\}, AA \cup \{(AID, Q@S)\} \rangle$ in AES, and subscribes all the answer entries in $AA \cup WA \cup \{(AID, Q@S)\} \setminus \{(AID_o, Q@S)\}$ for the new CP;

A.2   Execution of WT (Illustrated in Fig. 7)

The execution of a WT can be seen as a loop with the following steps performed at each iteration (let its initial state at each iteration be $\langle QID, PID, G, C, AA \rangle$):

– If there is an internal message received by the WT (i.e. from MT), it enters the **Fact Arrival Phase**:
  • if the message is $rev(AID, Q@S, C_r)$ where $(AID, Q@S) \in AA$ (see Fig. 4), let $C_{all} = C \wedge C_r$: if C_{all} is consistent, then the WT continues with $\langle QID, PID, G, C_{all}, AA \rangle$. Otherwise, the WT removes all of its subscriptions in AES and terminates;
  • if the message is $alt(AID_a, AID_d, Q@S, C_a)$ where AID_d is an ID of a default answer entry (following Fig. 2),
    1. it creates a new CP of $\langle QID, PID_{new}, G, C, \{(AID_d, Q@S)\},$ $AA \setminus \{(AID_d, Q@S)\} \rangle$ in CPS, and subscribes for all the answer entries in AA for the new CP;
    2. if $C_{all} = C \wedge C_a$ is consistent, then the WT continues with $\langle QID, PID, G, C_{all},$ $AA \cup \{(AID_a, Q@S)\} \setminus \{(AID_d, Q@S)\} \rangle$. Otherwise, it removes all of its subscriptions and terminates;

- if the message is $stop(RID)$, and RID is equal to the query ID in QID, then the WT removes all of its subscriptions and terminates;
- Otherwise, it enters the **Process Reduction Phase** and *tries to* select L from G:
  - if G is empty and thus no L can be selected, the current computation succeeds:
    1. let $QID = (RID, Q_{top})$, the current WT sends a message $answer(RID, Q_{top}, PID, C)$ to COM;
    2. it creates a FP of $\langle QID, PID, C, AA \rangle$ and then terminates. Note that it does not need to make answer entry subscriptions for the new FP or to remove its subscriptions, because the new FP "inherits" them.
  - if L is not an askable atom, for every rule R such that $C_{new} = C \wedge (L = head(R)) \wedge const(R)$ is consistent, the current WT spawns a new WT with state $\langle QID, PID_{new}, G \setminus \{L\} \cup body(R), C_{new}, AA \rangle$ and subscribes all the answer entries in AA for the new WT. Then the current WT removes all of its subscriptions and terminates[11].
  - if L is an askable atom $Q@S$ (where S must be ground): if there exists $(AID, Q'@S) \in AA$ such that Q and Q' are identical (i.e. they are not variants), then the WT continues with $\langle QID, PID, G \setminus \{L\}, C, AA \rangle$[12]. Otherwise (following Fig. 1),
    1. it collects $(AIDo, AIDS)$ from AES as follows:
       * if there exists some ordinary answer entries for $Q@S$, let $AIDo$ be the non-speculative original answer entry ID for $Q@S$, and $AIDS$ be the set of ordinary answer entry IDs, whose associated answer constraints are consistent with C;
       * otherwise,
       (a) if there exists no original answer entry for $Q@S$, then the WT
         i. creates $\langle AID_{new}^{so}, Q@S, so, C_{so} \rangle$ in AES, where C_{so} is the conjunction of the negations of all the default constraints for $Q@S$ in Δ if there is some default constraint, or is $true$ if there is none;
         ii. creates $\langle AID_{new}^{nso}, Q@S, nso, C_{nso} \rangle$ in AES, where C_{nso} is $true$;
         iii. creates a default answer entry $\langle AID_{new}^i, Q@S, d, C_d^i \rangle$ for each default constraint C_d^i for $Q@S$ in Δ;
         iv. sends a message $query(Q@S)$ to COM;
       (b) let $AIDo$ be AID_{new}^{so}, and $AIDS$ be the set of default answer entry IDs, whose associated answer constraints are consistent with C;
    2. for each answer entry $\langle AID, Q@S, Type, C_a \rangle$ such that $AID \in AIDS$, the current WT spawns a new WT with state $\langle QID, PID_{new}, G \setminus \{Q@S\}, C \wedge C_a, AA \cup \{(AID, Q@S)\} \rangle$ and subscribes all the answer entries in $AA \cup \{(AID, Q@S)\}$ for the new WT;
    3. the current WT creates a new CP of $\langle QID, PID_{new}, G \setminus \{Q@S\}, C, \{(AIDo, Q@S)\}, AA \rangle$ in CPS, and subscribes all the answer entries in AA plus that with $AIDo$ for the new CP;
    4. the current WT removes all of its subscriptions and terminates[13].

---

[11] As an optimisation, if there are $N > 0$ possible new processes (states), then only $N - 1$ new WTs are spawned, and the current WT continues as Nth process.

[12] This is an optimisation to the original operational model, which prevents unnecessary new processes (threads) to be created.

[13] Optimisation similar to footnote 11 can be applied.

B   Pseudo-Code for the Implementation of Exclusive Control between the Manager Thread and Worker Threads

YAP Prolog only provides *message queues* and *mutexes* for multi-threading support [7].

```
% "m_bc" and "m_wf" are the
    mutexes for BC and WF;
% "v_bc" is the counter for BC
% "mq_bc" is the message queue    % for MT
    for notifications about BC    mt_loop :-
                                    // wait for received answer,
% for WT                          mutex_lock(m_wf),
wt_loop :-                        wait_for_zero_bc,
  mutex_lock(m_wf),                // handle received answer
  mutex_lock(m_bc),               mutex_unlock(m_wf),
  mutex_unlock(m_wf),             mt_loop.
  increment(v_bc),
  mutex_unlock(m_bc),            wait_for_zero_bc :-
  // process reduction or fact     mutex_lock(m_bc),
        arrival step               clear_any_notification_in(mq_bc),
  mutex_lock(m_bc),               (v_bc(V), V > 0 ->
  decrement(v_bc),                  mutex_unlock(m_bc),
  (v_bc(V), V == 0 ->              wait_for_notification_in(mq_bc),
    send_notification_to(mq_bc     wait_for_zero_bc
        )                        ;
  ;                                mutex_unlock(m_bc)
    true                         ).
  ),
  mutex_unlock(m_bc),
  wt_loop.
```

Author Index

Baral, Chitta   46
Broda, Krysia   178
Bulling, Nils   22

Cliffe, Owen   102

Dastani, Mehdi   83
Dennis, Louise   64
De Vos, Marina   102

Farwer, Berndt   22

Góngora, Pedro Arturo   158

Hindriks, Koen V.   141
Hopton, Luke   102
Hosobe, Hiroshi   178

Jonker, Catholijn M.   141

Ma, Jiefei   178
Meyer, John-Jules   64

Nguyen, Ngoc-Hieu   1

Padget, Julian   102
Pontelli, Enrico   1, 46

Rosenblueth, David A.   158
Russo, Alessandra   178

Sakama, Chiaki   122
Satoh, Ken   178
Son, Tran Cao   1, 46, 122
Steunebrink, Bas R.   83

Tinnemeier, Nick   64

Visser, Wietske   141

Printing: Mercedes-Druck, Berlin
Binding: Stein+Lehmann, Berlin